East Bali
Pages 104–127

Lombok
Pages 154–167

Bali Sea

Amlapura

Lombok Strait

Senggigi

LOMBOK

Labuhan Lombok

Mataram

Kopang

Selong

Praya

Kuta

0 kilometres 15

0 miles 15

EYEWITNESS TRAVEL

BALI
& LOMBOK

EYEWITNESS TRAVEL
BALI
& LOMBOK

LONDON, NEW YORK,
MELBOURNE, MUNICH AND DELHI
www.dk.com

Produced by Editions Didier Millet, Singapore
Editorial Director Timothy Auger
Project Editor Choo Lip Sin
Art Director Tan Seok Lui
Editors Samantha Hanna Ascui, Marilyn Seow
Senior Designer Felicia Wong Yit Har
Designers Nelani Jinadasa, Norreha Sayuti, Annie Teo Ai Min

Contributors
Andy Barski, Albert Beaucourt, Bruce Carpenter, John Cooke,
Jean Couteau, Diana Darling, Sarah Dougherty,
Julia Goh, Lorca Lueras, Tim Stuart, Tony Tilford

Maps
Era-Maptech Ltd, Ireland

Photographers
John Cooke, Koes Karnadi,
Tim Stuart, Tony Tilford, Richard Watson

Illustrators
Anuar Bin Abdul Rahim, Denis Chai Kah Yune, Chang Huai-Yan,
Choong Fook San, Koon Wai Leong, Lee Yoke Ling, Poo Lee Ming,
Thomas Sui, Peggy Tan, Yeap Kok Chien

Printed in Malaysia

First published in the UK in 2001
by Dorling Kindersley Limited
80 Strand, London WC2R 0RL

15 16 17 18 10 9 8 7 6 5 4 3 2 1

Reprinted with Revisions 2005, 2007, 2009, 2011, 2013, 2016

Copyright 2001, 2016 © Dorling Kindersley Limited, London
A Penguin Random House Company

ISBN 978-0-2411-9841-4

MIX
Paper from
responsible sources
FSC™ C018179

Front cover main image: Pura Agung, Besakih temple complex, East Bali

◀ Pura Ulun Danu Bratan, a temple dedicated to the lake goddess *(see p145)*

Contents

Shop in Jalan Legian, selling traditional
Balinese crafts

Introducing Bali and Lombok

The slopes of Gunung Batur in East Bali,
seen through a line of clouds

Mayura Water Palace in Mataram, built in 1844, with Pura Meru in the background

Surfers at Kuta Beach, a location suitable for all levels of ability

Rice goddess

A Balinese house compound, home to an extended family

HOW TO USE THIS GUIDE

This guide will help you to get the most from your visit to Bali and Lombok. It provides both expert recommendations and detailed practical information. *Introducing Bali and Lombok* maps the islands and sets them in their historical and cultural context, covering a wide range of topics from festivals and music to wildlife and diving. This is followed by four chapters on Bali's regions, plus one on Lombok, all of which describe the sights of interest, using maps, photographs and illustrations throughout. Restaurant and hotel recommendations can be found in *Travellers' Needs* and the *Survival Guide* contains useful advice on everything from personal security to public transport.

Bali and Lombok Area by Area

The island of Bali is divided into four areas, each with its own chapter. A further chapter covers the island of Lombok. A map of these regions can be found inside the front cover of this book. All the sights are numbered and plotted on each chapter's *Regional Map*.

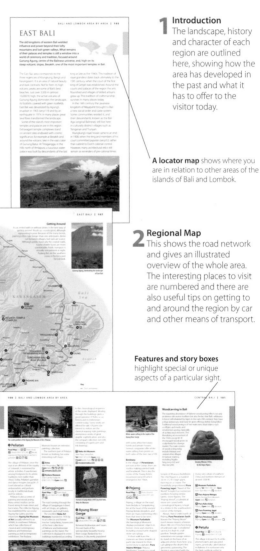

1 Introduction
The landscape, history and character of each region are outlined here, showing how the area has developed in the past and what it has to offer to the visitor today.

A locator map shows where you are in relation to other areas of the islands of Bali and Lombok.

Each area can be quickly identified by its colour coding.

2 Regional Map
This shows the road network and gives an illustrated overview of the whole area. The interesting places to visit are numbered and there are also useful tips on getting to and around the region by car and other means of transport.

Features and story boxes highlight special or unique aspects of a particular sight.

3 Detailed Information
The sights in each area are described individually following the numerical sequence on the *Regional Map*. Road map references, addresses, telephone numbers, opening hours, information on admission charges, as well as transport options, are provided where applicable.

4 Major Towns
An introduction covers the history, character and geography of the city or town. The main sights are plotted on the map and described in more detail.

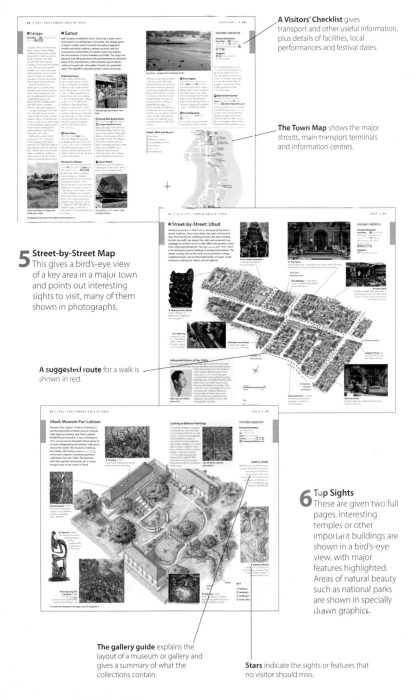

A Visitors' Checklist gives transport and other useful information, plus details of facilities, local performances and festival dates.

The Town Map shows the major streets, main transport terminals and information centres.

5 Street-by-Street Map
This gives a bird's-eye view of a key area in a major town and points out interesting sights to visit, many of them shown in photographs.

A suggested route for a walk is shown in red.

6 Top Sights
These are given two full pages. Interesting temples or other important buildings are shown in a bird's-eye view, with major features highlighted. Areas of natural beauty such as national parks are shown in specially drawn graphics.

The gallery guide explains the layout of a museum or gallery and gives a summary of what the collections contain.

Stars indicate the sights or features that no visitor should miss.

INTRODUCING BALI & LOMBOK

DISCOVERING BALI AND LOMBOK

These three itineraries to the key attractions on Bali and Lombok have been designed to help you make the most of your time in the region. South Bali is the most popular area with tourists, and most travellers spend at least a few days here. The three-day tour features some of the highlights: expansive beaches, holy temples, sophisticated bars, restaurants and boutiques. Lombok, by contrast, is far less visited than Bali, but the tourist industry here is developing fast. The seven-day tour takes you from the mainland beach resorts of Kuta and Senggigi to the

trendy Gili Isles and the dramatic national park around the Gunung Rinjani volcano. Back on Bali, the two-week tour looks beyond South Bali's major resorts and focuses on the rest of the island. It starts in the compelling cultural hub of Ubud, before taking in the Gunung Batur and Gu- nung Agung volcanoes, the relaxed island of Nusa Lembongan, diving spots such as Tulamben, and the pristine Bali Barat National Park. The itineraries may be customized, mixed and matched, and combined, depending on your personal interests and the time available.

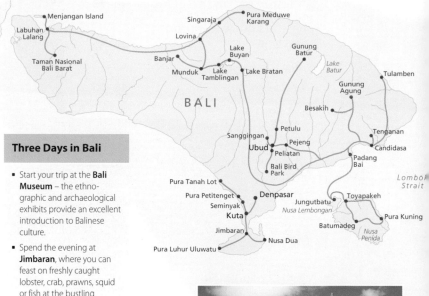

Three Days in Bali

- Start your trip at the **Bali Museum** – the ethno- graphic and archaeological exhibits provide an excellent introduction to Balinese culture.

- Spend the evening at **Jimbaran**, where you can feast on freshly caught lobster, crab, prawns, squid or fish at the bustling seafood stalls.

- One of Bali's holiest temples, **Pura Luhur Uluwatu** is perched above the churning surf on the southern edge of the island.

- Set on an isle just off the coast, the pretty little temple of **Pura Tanah Lot** is one of the best sunset spots on Bali.

- Before heading home, scour for a bargain or splash out on a treat at **Seminyak**'s myriad clothing, craft and homeware shops.

Bali Museum, Denpasar
One of the best collections of Balinese art is held at this museum, which is located in an incredible setting.

◀ Traditional Indonesian painting depicting village life

Two Weeks in Central, East, North and West Bali

- **Ubud** is the perfect place to start your trip, with its cultural shows, museums, innovative restaurants, and relaxed vibe.

- Visit the **Gunung Batur** volcano, where you can hike or cycle amid epic scenery.

- A visit to East Bali would not be complete without a stop at **Gunung Agung**, whose slopes are home to the **Besakih temple complex**.

- Keen divers should head to the **Tulamben**; the wreck of the *Liberty* lies just off its coast.

- A short boat ride southeast lies the tranquil island of **Nusa Lembongan** – perfect for whiling away an afternoon on the beach with a book.

- Back on the mainland, **Munduk** is the jumping-off point for a range of outdoor activities at **Lake Tamblingan**.

- The atmospheric **Pura Meduwe Karang** temple is just a day trip away from the popular north-coast resort of **Lovina**.

- End your trip in **Bali Barat National Park**, where the mangroves, wetlands, reefs and rainforests simply teem with wildlife.

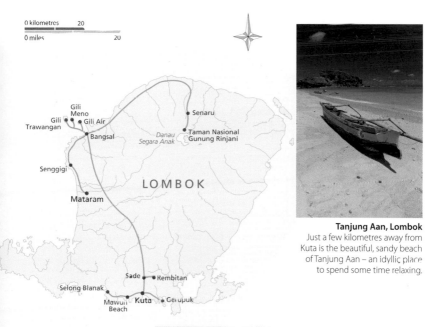

0 kilometres 20

0 miles 20

Gili Meno
Gili Trawangan
Gili Air
Bangsal
Senaru
Danau Segara Anak
Taman Nasional Gunung Rinjani
Senggigi
LOMBOK
Mataram
Sade
Rembitan
Selong Blanak
Mawun Beach
Kuta
Gerupuk

Tanjung Aan, Lombok
Just a few kilometres away from Kuta is the beautiful, sandy beach of Tanjung Aan – an idyllic place to spend some time relaxing.

Seven Days in Lombok

- Start your trip in peaceful **Kuta**, gateway to some beautiful beaches, including **Tanjung Aan** and **Selong Blanak**.

- Hire a surfboard and catch the breaks at the village of **Gerupuk** before treating yourself to a lobster dinner.

- Island-hop between the enchanting **Gili Trawangan**, **Gili Meno** and **Gili Air** until you find your favourite.

- Diving, snorkelling and beachside barbecues are highlights, regardless of which of the Gili Isles you opt for.

- Check out the impressive **Batu Bolong** temple shrine, or take advantage of the gusty breezes and go **windsurfing**.

- Dedicate a day to exploring the volcanic **Gunung Rinjani National Park**, ideal for hikers and wildlife-watchers.

Key

— Three Days in Bali

— Seven Days in Lombok

— Two Weeks in Central, East North and West Bali

Three Days in Bali

- **Airports** Arrive at and depart from Ngurah Rai International Airport.
- **Transport** A car is handy, but not essential. A combination of taxis and travel on foot or by bicycle will suffice.

Day 1
Morning Drive or take a taxi from the airport to your hotel in **Kuta**, **Legian**, **Seminyak**, **Canggu** or **Nusa Dua** (pp68–77). After settling in, head to the fascinating **Bali Museum** (pp66–7) in the capital, Denpasar, for an insight into the island's history and culture. For lunch, try the nearby **Babi Guling** restaurant (p182), which serves succulent roast suckling pig.

Afternoon Head to **Kuta Beach** (p72) or one of the **Nusa Dua beaches** (p77) for a swim, surf or sunbathe. For dinner, visit **Jimbaran** (p78), and sample the local fish and seafood in one of the thatched beachside eateries.

Day 2
Morning Pamper yourself with a massage or treatment at one of South Bali's many **spas** (pp172–3). Take lunch at one of Kuta's cafés and restaurants – such as the classic **Made's Warung I** (p182) – and wander down the main drag, Jalan Legian, to the **Bali Bomb Memorial** (p73).

The unusual arched doorway of the sacred Pura Luhur Uluwatu

Afternoon Head to one of Bali's most sacred places, the beautiful **Pura Luhur Uluwatu** (pp80–81). After exploring the temple complex, find a good spot to enjoy the sunset. The famous kecak dance is performed here daily at 6pm.

Day 3
Morning Start the day by browsing in the myriad craft shops, clothing boutiques and homeware stores in **Seminyak** (p73), then stop for lunch at one of the many health-conscious cafés. For something more cultural, stroll north along the beach to the 16th-century **Pura Petitenget** temple.

Afternoon Visit **Pura Tanah Lot** (p132), one of the island's most famous landmarks, to look around before the crowds arrive for sunset. Return to Seminyak for a romantic dinner at one of the area's top restaurants, such as **Sarong** or **Sardine** (p184).

Seven Days in Lombok

- **Airports** Arrive at and depart from Praya Airport, which has regular flights to and from Bali, other Indonesian cities, and Singapore and Malaysia.
- **Transport** A car is useful, but you can get around mainland Lombok by using a mix of taxis and shuttle buses. Regular boats travel to and from the Gili Isles, which are easily navigable on foot or by bicycle.

Day 1: Kuta
Drive or take a taxi from the airport to your hotel or guesthouse in **Kuta** (p166), a tranquil but fast-developing village on Lombok's south coast. After settling in, head west to the beautiful Mawun beach or east to the equally attractive Tanjung Aan. Beyond the latter is **Selong Blanak** (p167), a fishing community with colourful outrigger canoes lined up on its beach.

Day 2: Kuta
Take a day trip down the coast to the village of **Gerupuk** (p166), which is home to one of the island's most popular surf breaks. There are several places to rent boards, and a number of inexpensive joints serve fresh fish and lobster. Alternatively, head inland to the farming villages of **Rembitan and Sade** (p166) for a glimpse of traditional Sasak life. Keep an eye out for the traditional lumbung bonnet-shaped rice barns.

Day 3: Gili Isles
Drive or take a taxi or shuttle bus to Bangsal harbour, on the northwestern edge of Lombok, from where public and charter boats head to the three **Gili Isles** (p160): Gili Trawangan is the largest and most developed of the islands; Gili Meno is the smallest and least frequented by tourists; and Gili Air is

Pura Tanah Lot, sitting on an island off the southwest coast of Bali

For practical information on travelling around Bali and Lombok, see pp224–5

Lounging chairs lining the beach and awaiting tourists at the picturesque Gili Trawangan

the most populous of the three but still very tranquil. All of the Gili Isles are perfect for relaxing and taking a break from the pressures of modern life.

Day 4: Gili Isles
The Gili Isles are famous for **diving** *(p198)*. There are more than 3,500 species of marine life in the surrounding waters, including turtles and reef sharks, and numerous companies on the islands offer half- and full-day diving (and snorkelling) trips. After you return, sate your appetite with a hearty seafood barbecue at a beachside restaurant such as **Scallywags** *(p187)*.

Day 5: Gili Isles
The daily boats that island-hop between Air, Meno and Trawangan are great for exploring. If you're looking for more freedom, you can charter your own boat. After swimming and sunbathing in the after-noon, head for a sundowner at one of many low-key beach bars that dot the islands.

Day 6: Senggigi
Catch a morning boat back to Bangsal and then a taxi or shuttle bus south to the beach resort of **Senggigi** *(p160)*. In the afternoon, take a stroll along the beach to the charming temple of **Pura Batu Bolong**, go windsurfing or

head south to Lombok's capital, **Mataram** *(p159)*, which boasts museums, the Mayura Water Palace, traditional Sasak architecture and several good places to eat.

Day 7: Taman Nasional Gunung Rinjani
Get up early and spend the day at **Taman Nasional Gunung Rinjani** *(pp162–3)*, which offers stunning views of the eponymous volcano, as well as a range of wildlife, including the distinctive black-naped oriole. You can hire a guide and visit independently or take an organized tour. A trip to **Senaru** *(p161)* offers the option of a gentle walk along the river valley to two breathtaking waterfalls: the 40 m (132 ft) tiered waterfall and natural spring known as Sendanggile,

and the awesome Tiu Kelep. At the base of Tiu Kelep falls is a deep pool. If you feel like having a dip in the refreshingly cool water, you should allow yourself to drift in a circle behind the main waterfall. It is believed to be blessed with youth-enhancing properties, and according to local legend, each time you encircle it, you will emerge one year younger. Stay overnight in the trailhead of Senaru, or return to Senggigi.

> **To extend your trip...**
> For those with more time, there are plenty of rewarding, multi-day treks in the **national park** *(pp162–3)*, including up to the summit and to the blue-green **Danau Segara Anak** lake.

The stunning view across lake Danau Segara Anak, at Taman Nasional Gunung Rinjani

Two Weeks in Central, East, North and West Bali

- **Airports** Arrive at and depart from Ngurah Rai International Airport, or continue your trip by road and then public ferry to Java.

- **Transport** A car is handy but not essential, since taxis, shuttle buses and (for Nusa Lembongan) boats can take you around.

Day 1: Ubud

Drive or take a taxi or shuttle bus over to your accommodation in **Ubud** (pp92–3). After settling in, explore the town centre, making sure to stop off at the **Museum Puri Lukisan** (pp96–7), home to a collection of 20th-century Balinese paintings and sculptures. In the afternoon, stroll down to the **Monkey Forest Sanctuary** or **Puri Saren** royal palace (pp92–3), or visit the **Neka Art Museum** in **Sanggingan** (p100). For dinner, try the cutting-edge **Locavore** (p185).

Day 2: Ubud

In the morning, visit the **Bali Bird Park** (pp88–9), which boasts more than 250 different species from around the world. Back in Ubud in the afternoon, visit one of the many **spas**, take a **yoga class** (pp172–3), or see the nearby villages of **Peliatan**, **Sanggingan**, **Pejeng** or **Petulu**

(pp100–101). Finish the day with a show in the atmospheric grounds of **Puri Saren** (p94).

Day 3: Ubud

Make an early start, and head to **Gunung Batur** (pp124–5), Bali's most active volcano, surrounded by a dramatic caldera and overlooking glimmering Lake Batur. Several hikes can be completed in a day (or longer, if you wish), and a number of agencies offer exhilarating downhill **mountain-biking tours** (p201).

Day 4: Ubud

Wake up with arguably Bali's best coffee at the achingly hip **Seniman Coffee Studio** (p185). Suitably fortified, follow this with a picturesque walk in the **Ubud countryside** (pp98–9), before heading back to base.

Day 5: Candidasa

In the morning, indulge in some retail therapy. Ubud has some of the island's finest arts, crafts and clothing shops, as well as the bustling **Pasar Ubud market** (p94), perfect for souvenirs. The narrow, crowded alleyways here are crammed with paintings, wooden artifacts, batik quilts and much more. Striking a bargain is part of the fun. Afterwards, drive or take a taxi or shuttle bus to **Candidasa** (p112). In the afternoon, visit the Pura Candi Dasa temple, then climb up to Pura Gomang for stunning views of the surrounding area.

Day 6: Candidasa

Rise early, and take a guided tour – or travel independently and hire your own guide – to **Gunung Agung** (p118), the dominant feature in East Bali. If you are feeling energetic, you could scale the summit, but note that this requires advance planning and a 2am start. In the late afternoon, visit **Besakih** (pp120–21); Bali's most venerated temples, located on the slopes of the volcano. They are said to have been founded in the late 8th century.

Day 7: Candidasa

Work your way up the coast to the village of **Tulamben** (p117), where numerous agencies offer diving trips to the wreck of the American cargo ship Liberty, just 30 m (33 yd) offshore. The area is also ideal for snorkelling. Alternatively, stay on dry land and visit the remains of **Klungkung's Royal Palace** (pp110–11), which dates back to the 18th century, or **Tenganan** (pp114–15), the best preserved of Bali's Aga villages and an excellent place to buy fine textiles or basketware.

Day 8: Nusa Lembongan

Take a morning taxi or shuttle bus to the port at **Padang Bai** (p112), from where fast boats and ferries make the short crossing to **Nusa Lembongan** (p78). In the afternoon, explore the island's pristine coves, go for a swim, visit the Cavehouse – an

The road to the remains of the Royal Palace, Klungkung

For practical information on travelling around Bali and Lombok, see pp224–5 underground house dug by a Balinese priest – and soak up the peaceful atmosphere once the day-trippers return home at the end of the day.

Day 9: Nusa Lembongan

Start the day with a morning ferry trip from the village of Jungutbatu to the settlement of Toyapakeh on the neighbouring larger island of **Nusa Penida** (p79). Check out the carvings – some of an erotic nature – in the Pura Ped and Pura Kuning temples, the impressive decorative reliefs of the Batumadeg village temple, and the sacred Goa Karangsari cave.

Day 10: Munduk

Catch a fast boat or ferry back to Padang Bai and, from there, a taxi or shuttle bus to the highland village of **Munduk** (p144), set among orange groves, hydrangea fields and pink bougainvillea. Here, a hilltop restaurant affords a breathtaking vista of palm trees, deep valleys, jungle and mountains. Spend the afternoon at the relaxing hot springs of nearby **Banjar** (p143), or cycle around the surrounding countryside, taking in the coffee and clove plantations, rice paddies, mountainous countryside and waterfalls.

Day 11: Munduk

Spend the day touring around **Lake Tamblingan** (pp144–5), beautifully located in a volcanic caldera, and its surrounding area. Highlights include the Pura Ulun Danu Tamblingan temple and the tropical rainforests near Lake Buyan. The region is abundant with birdlife and popular with bird watchers. You may spot babblers, woodpeckers, ground thrushes and malkohas; and even if you don't see them, you will most certainly hear them. From here, you might be able to arrange for one of the local villagers to row you across the tranquil waters in a *pedau ukit*, which is a traditional, simple double canoe.

If you have the time, consider travelling on to **Lake Bratan** (p145), which offers parasailing and water-skiing. Alternatively,

Padang Bai – a relaxed beach resort that is popular as a base for exploring East Bali

wander through Kebun Raya's **Eka Karya Botanic Gardens** (see p145), a cool, shady park on the slopes of Gunung Pohon, with more than 2,000 species of plants, including 650 species of tree and hundreds of varieties of orchid. The adjacent daily market, Bukit Mungsu, is busy, vibrant and colourful. Although it caters largely to tourists, it also offers a tempting and diverse collection of locally grown fruit, vegetables, spices and plants, including orchids.

Day 12: Lovina

Drive or take a taxi north to the seaside resort of **Lovina** (p151). Off the coast are some pristine coral reefs that are ideal for snorkelling. Alternatively, hike inland to the Singsing Waterfall, or head east along the coast past **Singaraja** (pp148–50), the region's main commercial centre, to the **Pura Meduwe Karang** (pp152–3) temple.

The Hindu temple of Pura Kahyangan Jagat Segara Rupek, in Taman Nasional Bali Barat

Day 13: Taman Nasional Bali Barat

After rising early for a dawn dolphin-spotting boat trip, travel west to **Taman Nasional Bali Barat** (pp140–41). Stay in one of the resorts inside the park on **Menjangan Island** (p142), which is linked to Labuhan Lalang on the mainland by daily boats. Spend the afternoon diving or snorkelling.

Day 14: Taman Nasional Bali Barat

Spend your final day exploring the rest of the national park. Take a guided nature walk through rainforests, and visit the fertile grasslands, savanna, mangroves and wetlands, keeping an eye out for sambar deer and Bali starlings.

Complete your adventure by visiting the Bali Tower at **The Menjangan** resort (p176), an extraordinary feat of engineering. Standing 27 m (88 ft) high and built entirely from wood, the structure has five floors and tapers to a peak with a thatched roof. Order sunset drinks at the very top, and soak up the glorious sight of a mangrove-fringed coastline stretching out along the sea. Here, way above the treetops, you can enjoy an uninterrupted view of the monsoon and African-forested terrain to the south, as well as the mountains of Java to the east. To the north, you will see Menjangan Island, in perfect alignment with Java's Mount Baluran. To the east is the landscape of Bali laid out like a map – nothing but trees, sky, sea and nature.

Putting Bali and Lombok on the Map

The island of Bali lies east of Java, separated from it by the Bali Strait.
Bali is 5,633 sq km (2,253 sq miles) in area. Lombok lies east of Bali,
with an area of 5,435 sq km (2,098 sq miles). Bali (population
4.2 million) is more developed than Lombok (population 3.3 million).
Lombok now has an international airport, but international flights
are limited, so the main airport for both islands is Ngurah Rai
International Airport near Denpasar in Bali; most onward travel
to Lombok is by domestic flight, or by ferry or fast boat from
Padang Bai, Benoa Harbour, Sanur Beach or Serangan Island.
The road network reflects the islands' mountainous nature;
many of the most important routes run along the coasts.

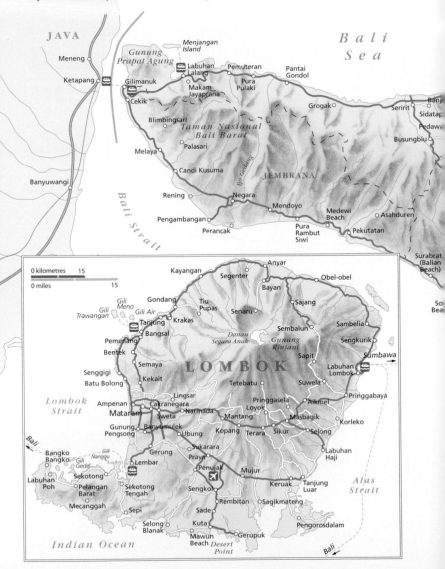

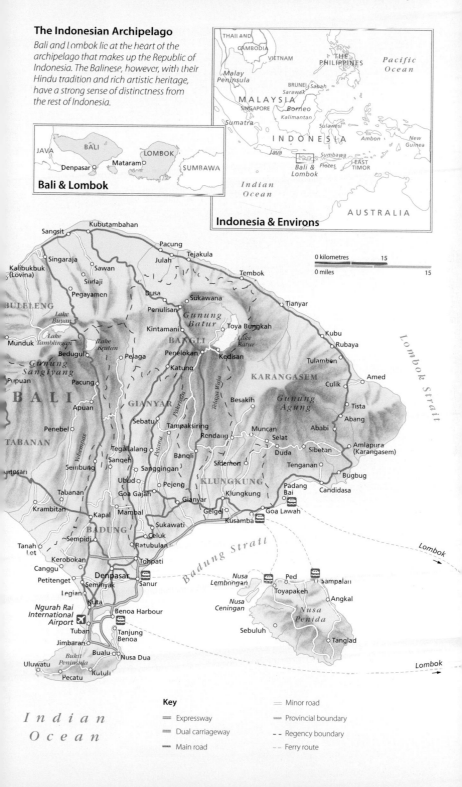

The Indonesian Archipelago

Bali and Lombok lie at the heart of the archipelago that makes up the Republic of Indonesia. The Balinese, however, with their Hindu tradition and rich artistic heritage, have a strong sense of distinctness from the rest of Indonesia.

Bali & Lombok

Indonesia & Environs

Key

— Expressway
— Dual carriageway
— Main road
— Minor road
— Provincial boundary
-- Regency boundary
--- Ferry route

A PORTRAIT OF BALI AND LOMBOK

The islands of Bali and Lombok are sufficiently close to be visible to each other on a clear day. They are both volcanic, are of similar size and have much else in common. However, they offer the visitor very different experiences. Bali – noisy, colourful, crowded and glamorous – is one of the world's most celebrated destinations while quiet Lombok was, until recently, a travellers' secret.

Geographically, Bali and Lombok are at the centre of the Indonesian Archipelago. This is a vast chain of islands stretching from the Indian Ocean to the Pacific. It lies across the ancient trade routes between Europe, the Middle East, India and China, and has absorbed influences from all these civilizations.

Bali is a province within the Republic of Indonesia, with its provincial capital at Denpasar. Lombok is part of the province of West Nusa Tenggara; Mataram, the provincial capital, is on the island. Both are mainly rural societies, despite the urbanization of southern Bali in the 1980s and 1990s. Facilities such as electricity and television came to most places only in the last quarter of the 20th century (despite this, the Internet is already widely used).

In daily life on Hindu Bali and mostly Muslim Lombok, great importance is attached to community matters, including social harmony. With Indonesia's move in the late 1990s from dictatorship to democracy, there is great awareness of the importance of religious tolerance, while at the same time each society takes pride in its own identity. Bali eagerly shares its flamboyant religious culture; the people of Lombok, however, are generally more reticent.

The Mayura Water Palace in Mataram, a legacy of Balinese rule in Lombok (see p159)

◄ Balinese religious statues

A Balinese family group carrying holy water to their house temple

The Balinese Way of Life

At the core of Balinese society is the village, a cohesive religious community organized around a group of temples. Village members are required to take part in temple rituals and assist in the community's funerary rites.

Religious practice in Bali entails music, theatre and elaborate offerings. The labour-intensive nature of rituals requires a high degree of social organization, which is visible in the village layout. Family house compounds are usually laid out on a north–south axis. The village core is dominated by temples, market, civic structures and often *puri*, houses of the nobility.

On Lombok, most of the indigenous Sasak people are orthodox Muslims *(see p27)*, and their social life is organized around the family and village mosque.

Painting of rice terraces

Economic Development

Bali and Lombok were both prime rice producers until land began to become scarce in the mid-20th century. Since then the government has encouraged crop diversification, particularly into commodity crops such as coffee, vanilla, cloves, tobacco and citrus fruits. Today, land is increasingly being used for tourism. There seem to be few alternatives. Marine and coastal resources have never been energetically developed, perhaps because of the more salubrious climate of the rice-growing regions; until the advent of tourism, the coasts produced little more than coconuts and salt. Fishing remains generally a poor man's occupation.

There has been little true industrialization. Some artisanal manufacturing has emerged in South Bali, particularly in the garment industry around Kuta; but although this does absorb some local labour, it also attracts workers from other, poorer islands who are willing to work for lower wages, compounding problems of unemployment with new social challenges.

On the other hand, cottage industry, in particular handicrafts, has allowed local economies within Bali and Lombok to shift away from agriculture without a great rural exodus.

A roadside food stall near Candidasa

Arts and Handicrafts

Handicrafts and the production of art objects for secular use have become a vigorous export industry in Bali. Styles of painting, wood sculpture, jewellery and textiles have been adapted for sale to visitors and to export markets *(see pp40–41)*, and this has opened up creative opportunities.

A sizeable expatriate community in Seminyak, Canggu, Sanur and Ubud has played an important role in developing this sector together with local entrepreneurs. Bali is also a marketplace for handicrafts, antiques and reproduction furniture from other islands of the Indonesian Archipelago.

Lombok has a venerable tradition of making low-fired domestic pottery *(see p158)*. The artisans are generally women, often aided in the marketing by their husbands or male relatives. Lombok's hand-woven textiles and shapely rattan baskets have also found an eager international market. There are great hopes that tourism will further strengthen the island's local economy.

A beach in South Bali, the tourist centre of the island

Tourism

Tourism came to Bali much earlier than to Lombok *(see p55)* and is far more developed here. On both islands there is awareness of tourism's economic importance. On Bali, it has created an almost urban density in Kuta, Seminyak, Sanur and Ubud, and heavy road traffic has become a problem. On Lombok, tourism is concentrated on the fertile west coast around Senggigi and the unspoiled Gili Isles *(see p160)*. The south coast of Lombok has splendid beaches that are still relatively pristine, although development is taking place around Lombok's Kuta village *(see p166)*, where tourism is growing. For most travellers, even from outside Indonesia, access to Lombok is mainly by way of Bali.

Despite sporadic internal disturbances associated with broader political changes in Indonesia, Bali and Lombok remain places where social harmony is greatly prized and visitors are regarded as welcome guests.

The rural landscape of central Bali

Landscape and Wildlife of Bali and Lombok

Bali and Lombok have a rich flora and fauna. Human activity, including agriculture and tourism, has caused some loss of habitat diversity. Nevertheless, large areas are still unspoiled, and some are officially protected. There are few places better for the nature lover than Bali and Lombok, where conditions for walking and exploring range from arid mountain slopes and high natural forests to the margins of rivers and ricefields and the seashore.

Giant golden orb weaver, common in lowland areas

Forests

Much of Bali and Lombok was once covered in forest, including large areas of lowland rainforest. Much has been destroyed; causes include volcanic eruptions, coffee and coconut cultivation and collection of firewood. Lush forests still grow on Bali's southern and western mountain slopes. On the drier, northern slopes the forest is deciduous.

Volcanic Peaks

After volcanic ash is deposited by an eruption, centuries pass before the formation of soil capable of sustaining a rich plant life. However, the slopes are soon colonized by mosses, grasses and ferns, and there is a diverse birdlife. On the arid northern and eastern slopes grows a grassland vegetation often punctuated by lontar palms.

The long-tailed macaque monkey is often seen in forests, on roadsides and around temples.

The mountain white-eye gathers in treetops, uttering a characteristic high-pitched call.

The black-winged starling is an endangered species that lives in the deciduous forests of northwest Bali, as well as in open grasslands.

The helmeted friar bird inhabits the arid mountain areas of Lombok.

The senduduk flower, with its exotic pink petals, is found in mountain scrub.

Wallace's Line

Alfred Russel Wallace (1823–1913), a British naturalist, noted differences between the wildlife of the former tectonic landmasses of Asia and Australia – marked by a line that passes between Bali and Lombok at its southern extremity. The Australian group includes birds of paradise, and species such as the orange-banded thrush, which is seen in Lombok but not in Bali. The Asian group includes monkeys and the tiger (the latter last seen in Bali in the 1930s). Another example is the fulvous-breasted woodpecker, more often seen in Bali than in Lombok.

Orange-banded thrush

Wallace's Line

Rivers and Ricefields

Some 150 rivers flow through the gorges of Bali and Lombok, assisting irrigation of the rice crops. Here birds, frogs, toads and spiders can live on plant hoppers and other small pests which cause damage to the rice itself. The birds include egrets, herons, ducks and small finches.

The Java sparrow, a red-billed native of Java and Bali, is found around river gorges and ricefields.

Toads live in damp habitats such as ricefields; here they survive on a diet of insects, including grasshoppers, beetles and crickets.

Coastlines

The beaches, coral reefs and shallow waters around these islands support a huge variety of marine life, even in developed areas such as Sanur. Although little true mangrove forest remains, mangroves still absorb the force of waves, helping to reduce coastal erosion.

The lionfish, while visually attractive, is poisonous to touch. It lives in waters off the smaller islands around Bali.

The green turtle is endangered; it is hunted for its meat, sometimes used in Balinese ritual.

Rice Cultivation

The mountain lakes, the gentle climate and the volcano-enriched soils of Bali and Lombok are ideally suited for the growing of rice (*Oryza sativa*). Although some of the islands' rice-farming land is being converted to other uses, terraced ricefields are still the dominant feature of the rural landscape, and the cult and cultivation of rice remain much as they were in Neolithic times. Steep terrain makes mechanization difficult and poses a particular problem for "wet rice farming" – water flows far below the arable land, in deep river gorges. The Balinese solution, which dates from as early as the 9th century AD, is an ingenious and complex network of irrigation channels, tunnels and aqueducts that diverts water from sources high up in the mountains to water-sharing communities known as *subak*.

Padi Bali is the generic term for several strains of traditionally grown rice, a tall, strong plant with a growing cycle of 210 days.

The paddy field is a basin of packed earth reinforced with intertwining grassroots. Irrigation water is let in and out of each field individually through a small gap in the earthen wall that can be opened or closed with a hoe. The water is drained off through channels that empty into rivers.

Rice plants nearing full growth

Ricefield Ceremonies

Across the island of Bali and among traditional farmers in Lombok, offerings are made in the ricefields at significant stages of the rice-growing cycle. These rituals reflect the central importance of rice cultivation in the traditional life of the islands. The most elaborate ricefield ceremony takes place when the rice grain begins to form on the stalk. A small shrine to honour Dewi Sri, the rice goddess (*see p29*), is built by the farmers in a corner of their ricefields and decorated with handmade palm-leaf festoons.

Bamboo shrines where offerings are given to the rice goddess

The Rice Barn, once a common feature of houses in Lombok and Bali, is where sheaves of the older strains of rice are stored. The grain is threshed by hand as needed. These buildings are less frequently seen than in the past.

Coconut, banana and bamboo grow along high ridges above the river valleys, concealing small village communities.

The Rice-Growing Cycle

1. Rice seed is planted in a protected bed. While the seedlings mature, farmers prepare the fields.

2. The planting basin is prepared by flooding, ploughing and levelling the field.

3. Seedlings are transplanted into flooded fields by hand. As the plants mature, the fields are alternately flooded and dried at specific stages to maximize growth, and they are periodically weeded.

4. Harvesting is done by women, who cut the stalks with a small knife concealed in their palms so as not to frighten the rice goddess.

5. High-yield varieties of rice are threshed directly in the fields and put in bags to be taken to a rice mill. Older strains of rice are kept on the cut stalks and gathered into bundles to be stored in a rice barn until needed.

Rice Terraces

Bali's terraced ricefields have been described as an "engineered landscape", a collaboration between nature and human beings. Terracing allows rice to be planted on steep slopes and protects the land from erosion. Each terrace is irrigated by a complex series of channels, controlled by small dams.

River gorges can often be seen below rice terraces.

6. After harvest, fields are burned off, producing a soil-protecting alkaline ash.

The Islands' Religions

The majority of the Balinese are Hindu. Most of the Sasaks, the indigenous people of Lombok, practise orthodox Islam. However, permeating religious practice on Bali and Lombok are animistic beliefs and a sense of the supernatural *(see p28)*. Ancient agricultural and mountain cults are reflected in temple and village architecture, and in rural rituals. There are Muslim and Christian minorities in Bali's towns and coastal areas and a smaller number of Buddhists.

Temple offerings are a prominent aspect of Hindu observance in Bali *(see pp42–3)*.

Traces of Ancient Cults

In architecture and ritual practice, the forms and beliefs of prehistoric Indonesian societies are still visible today in modern Hindu Bali and the traditions of rural Lombok.

Temple shrine

A temple in stepped-pyramid form suggests that a site predates Hindu times.

Rice cult image made from palm leaves

A shrine at the grave of folk hero Jayaprana, near Labuhan Lalang *(see p142)*, draws petitioners for supernatural favours.

Hinduism

Balinese Hinduism has elements not only of the Shivaite cult, but also of animism and Buddhism. Deities are believed to visit the human realm on ritual occasions. Temples hold *odalan* (anniversary festivals), during which gods are honoured with offerings, music and dance *(see pp42–3)*.

Offerings of palm leaf and flowers

Sprinkler made of grass

Consecrated rice grains

Holy water, the medium of the gods, is sprinkled on offerings and distributed along with rice grains to worshippers after prayers.

Villagers carrying a temple effigy in a portable "ancestral spirit house" during a temple festival

Islam

Most people on Lombok are Muslims. Like the majority of Indonesians, they follow a traditional form of Islam which often incorporates underlying folk traditions. In some of the more isolated parts of the island, the Sasaks adhere to a form of Islam known as Wetu Telu, mixing Islamic beliefs with pre-Islamic, indigenous and Hindu-Buddhist elements. Like Balinese Hinduism, Wetu Telu ascribes great powers to the spirits that dwell within nature.

A village mosque in Lombok

Many Muslims in Bali and Lombok can be seen wearing the traditional *peci* cap, particularly on Friday, the day of prayer.

Buddhism

Although certain Buddhist cults flourished in Bali at around AD 1000, it was not until late in the 20th century that mainstream Buddhism gained any signifi-cant presence here. Buddhists are still a small minority.

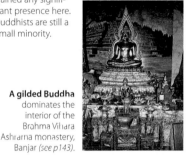

A gilded Buddha dominates the interior of the Brahma Vihara Ashrama monastery, Banjar *(see p143)*.

Christianity

Small communities of Protestants and Catholics are to be found in West Bali, where they resettled after conversion by missionaries in the early 20th century. Many Balinese people of Chinese descent are Christian.

The Catholic cathedral at Palasari has architectural features which echo Balinese temples.

Religion in Community Rituals

In Bali and Lombok religion plays a part in rituals such as weddings, funerals and coming-of-age ceremonies, which require the participation of an entire village *(see pp32–3)*. In Muslim Lombok, the most festive rituals are circumcision rites, undergone by boys around the age of eleven.

This palanquin (ceremonial litter) is in the form of a painted lion.

A gilded offering bowl holds ritual implements.

Hindu high priests conduct a ceremony as part of the preparation for a royal cremation.

At a circumcision rite, a Sasak Muslim boy is paraded through the streets.

Traditional Beliefs

Animism and ancestor worship are a strong undercurrent in Balinese life, even in local Hindu observance. The Balinese term *sekala niskala* ("visible-invisible") sums up the idea that the physical world is penetrated by a spirit world. The spirits, loosely described as "gods" and "demons", are honoured almost everywhere with offerings made of flowers and other materials. The invisible world is represented in many vivid symbols. Ancestors are deified in complex rituals and venerated at domestic and clan temples *(see p30)*.

Figure of Rangda at Puri Saren, Ubud's royal palace *(see p94)*

Animism

Large stones, trees and other powerful-looking natural objects are believed to be favoured dwellings for invisible beings. To keep these spirits content, a shrine or small temple may be erected for them. *Buta kala* (ground spirits) are demonic energies that cluster at crossroads, graveyards, rivers, in certain trees, or wherever there is an important life event such as a birth, a death or an accident. They are appeased with offerings that contain meat or strong drink.

Keris (dagger)

Parasols indicate that a deity is present.

The effigy of the god is presented with offerings.

Guardian spirits reside in demonic statues.

Objects such as daggers and consecrated masks are seen as imbued with great spiritual power, and can give rise to trance possession.

A shrine by a sacred tree, decorated on holy days when holy water and offerings are placed here

Magic

Fear of the supernatural feeds a widespread fear of witchcraft. Practitioners of Balinese "black" and "white" magic may engage invisible powers such as *buta kala* (ground spirits) to heal or harm. Household offerings are made to the spirits daily.

Daily flower offerings known as *canang*

A *tumbal*, a type of magical drawing often prepared by a witch doctor, is shown as protecting a man against the influence of a *buta*, or spirit.

Tumbal (Magical Amulet) (1938) by Anak Agung Gede Sobrat, Ubud

The Rice Goddess

The Hindu goddess of prosperity, Dewi Sri, became identified in Bali with the rice spirit of local belief, and she is honoured in the fields, the granary and the rice basket. Her image in offerings and textiles is known as the *cili* motif. According to tradition, after the daily meal has been cooked, tiny rice offerings must be set out before food can be consumed.

Wooden ornament with *cili* motif
representing the head of the rice goddess

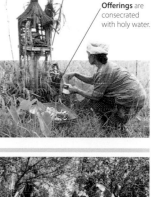

Bamboo shrines are built in the fields to honour the rice goddess during the growing cycle.

Offerings are consecrated with holy water.

Barong and Rangda

The dragon-like Barong (representing order, harmony and health) and his demonic counterpart Rangda (associated with chaos, illness and harm) are guardian effigies. They are periodically "awakened" to restore the spiritual balance of a village by means of a ritual battle culminating in wild trance. Devotees of the Barong attack Rangda with their *keris* (daggers). Rangda's power turns the daggers against the attackers; the Barong's power prevents the blades from piercing their bare skin.

Rangda, identifiable by her fangs, striped breasts and necklace of entrails

The Barong's beard is made of human hair.

The magical power of the Barong and Rangda is concentrated in their masks, which are kept in a village temple and given offerings.

"High" and "Low" Spirits

The Balinese believe that human beings can help keep "high" and "low" spirits in balance through making ritual offerings to both. For the Balinese, the universe is dualistic in nature, a play of ever-shifting opposites. This opposition is symbolized by the black-and-white chequered textile known as *poleng*, in which statues and other objects thought to be magically charged are often wrapped.

The ubiquitous *poleng* cloth

Guardian statues wrapped in *poleng* cloths, as often seen in Balinese temple forecourts

Balinese Temple Architecture

A Balinese *pura* (public temple) is a holy enclosure where Hindu deities are periodically invited to descend into *pratima* (effigies) kept in shrines. During *odalan* (festivals), temples are alive with music, dance and offerings *(see p42)*. Otherwise they are rather quiet. Temples include the *kahyangan tiga* (the three village temples – *see pp32–3*), clan temples, market temples, irrigation temples, temples to nature deities, and "state" temples of former kingdoms. Temples are usually open to visitors during daylight hours.

The *padmasana* shrine ("lotus throne"), in the most sacred corner of the temple, has an empty seat at the top open to the sky, signifying the Supreme God.

The *jeroan* (inner courtyard) has shrines to the temple's core deities and often to deities of the mountains, lakes and sea. It is often closed to visitors, but can usually be viewed from outside the walls.

The *bale gong* is a pavilion where ritual *gamelan* music may be played *(see p36)*.

The *bale agung* is the village council pavilion.

Pelinggih are shrines or "seats" of the gods. The dark fibre used for the roof, which resembles human hair, is a product of the sugar palm.

Temple Layout

The arrangement of Balinese temples follows a generally consistent pattern, with individual structures orientated along a mountain–sea axis. Degrees of sacredness are reflected in proximity to the mountain.

The *kori agung* is a grand gateway usually reserved for gods and priests.

The *meru* shrine has 3, 5, 7, 9 or 11 tiers, depending on the importance of its deity. It symbolizes the Hindu holy Mount Meru, but can also represent other sacred peaks.

Bali's Main Temples

There are tens of thousands of temples on Bali, perhaps 200,000 including house temples. The locations of the most important ones are shown here. Visitors should observe temple etiquette (*see p215*).

Sights at a Glance

① Besakih Temple Complex (*pp120–21*)
② Pura Goa Lawah (*p112*)
③ Pura Kehen (*p108*)
④ Pura Luhur Uluwatu (*pp80–81*)
⑤ Pura Meduwe Karang (*pp152–3*)
⑥ Pura Taman Ayun (*pp134–5*)
⑦ Pura Tanah Lot (*p132*)
⑧ Pura Tirta Empul (*p103*)
⑨ Pura Ulun Danu Batur (*pp126–7*)

In the *jaba tengah* (middle courtyard) are secondary shrines and pavilions for a variety of practical purposes.

The *candi bentar* (split gate) is often used as a courtyard entrance. It represents the cosmic mountain split into the positive and negative forces of the universe.

Entrance

The *kulkul* is a watchtower with a drum which is struck when deities are thought to descend to the temple.

The *bale piasan* is a sacred pavilion for placing religious offerings.

Village Life

The Balinese village is one of the island's most visually distinctive features. It is essentially a religious community, organized around a core of temples. Village land is considered to be a bequest of the founding ancestors, who are worshipped as local deities. Private life is largely ruled by *adat* (village customary law). Every married couple is obliged to belong to the *banjar* (community association); among the *banjar*'s duties are funerary rites for village members. Not to belong to a *banjar* is to risk perdition in the afterlife.

Funerary rites involve all village members, who will congregate in the spirit of *banjar suka duka* ("together in happiness and woe").

Village streets are usually aligned with the mountain and the sea, an arrangement which the Balinese call *kaja-kelod* (mountainward-seaward).

Balinese Village Layout

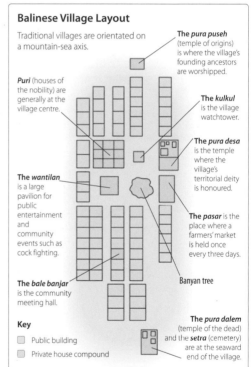

Traditional villages are orientated on a mountain-sea axis.

The *pura puseh* (temple of origins) is where the village's founding ancestors are worshipped.

Puri (houses of the nobility) are generally at the village centre.

The *kulkul* is the village watchtower.

The *pura desa* is the temple where the village's territorial deity is honoured.

The *wantilan* is a large pavilion for public entertainment and community events such as cock fighting.

The *pasar* is the place where a farmers' market is held once every three days.

The *bale banjar* is the community meeting hall.

Banyan tree

Key

☐ Public building
☐ Private house compound

The *pura dalem* (temple of the dead) and the *setra* (cemetery) are at the seaward end of the village.

The slit-log drum in the *kulkul* tower summons *banjar* members to village duty, announces a death, and serves traditionally as a general alarm bell.

The *warung*, a family-run coffee-stall-cum-mini-shop, is at the heart of village social life, although it has no special location.

A Village House Compound

Village land is divided into uniform residential plots or compounds enclosed on all sides by a wall of clay or brick. Living quarters are enclosed pavilions for sleeping and storage, with large verandas for work and socializing. The courtyards are generally floored with packed earth, and kept free of vegetation except perhaps for a few ornamental flowers or a decorative tree. Most compounds house extended families of the male line. They may not be sold. Upon the death of the occupant, if there is no heir the property reverts to the village.

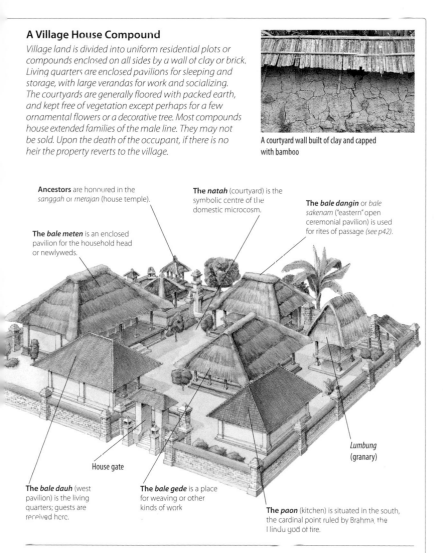

A courtyard wall built of clay and capped with bamboo

Ancestors are honoured in the *sanggah* or *merajan* (house temple).

The *natah* (courtyard) is the symbolic centre of the domestic microcosm.

The *bale dangin* or *bale sakenam* ("eastern" open ceremonial pavilion) is used for rites of passage *(see p42)*.

The *bale meten* is an enclosed pavilion for the household head or newlyweds.

Lumbung (granary)

House gate

The *bale dauh* (west pavilion) is the living quarters; guests are received here.

The *bale gede* is a place for weaving or other kinds of work

The *paon* (kitchen) is situated in the south, the cardinal point ruled by Brahma, the Hindu god of fire.

House Gates

The range of gates lining the narrow streets is one of the most striking features of a Balinese village. The gate is traditionally positioned towards the kelod (seaward, or downhill) end of the house compound. The degree of architectural elaboration generally reflects the material status of the family living in the house.

Simple house gate with *alang alang* grass thatch

Gate with tiled roof and minimal decoration

Gate with decorated roof and brickwork

Traditional Dance and Drama

The roots of Balinese dance are trance ritual and the Javanese theatrical forms known as *wayang*. Various performances take place at religious ceremonies, often late at night and several hours long. Shorter versions are put on for visitors in more convenient circumstances. In Lombok, the dances of the Sasak are ritual performances, often involving men in competition or combat. Islam has favoured literary rather than performing arts, one reason why dance is less common in Lombok than in Bali.

Arja is a dance-opera in which choreography, music, costume and singing styles are strictly defined for twelve core character roles.

Theatrical Performance

Various forms of dance and drama can be seen at the annual Bali Arts Festival (see p45). Some tell a story; some are non-representational. Modern genres such as sendratari often contain elements of older traditions.

Servant-clowns   Stage entrance   Offerings

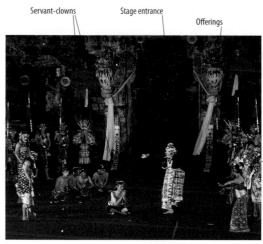

The **oleg tambulilingan**, a dance created in the 1950s, is performed to the accompaniment of the Gong Kebyar *gamelan* orchestra *(see p36)*.

Noble hero

Sendratari was devised in the 1960s as an art form without ritual function. The name is a contraction of the words for "art", "drama", and "dance".

Ritual and Trance

Ritual-based performances range from dances performed for temple deities to complex dramas. They often contain elements of trance (see p28). Even trance dances for visitors require ritual offerings.

Baris gede is an old ritual dance performed by a regiment of soldiers to protect the deities.

Kecak is based on a *sanghyang* (trance) chorus formerly used in times of epidemic.

Mask and Puppet Theatre

Bali evolved its own style of the Javanese wayang kulit *puppet theatre and* wayang wong *masked dance drama. Both are vehicles for the Indian epics* Mahabharata *and* Ramayana. *In* topeng, *the performer changes masks and costumes to show different characters.*

Wayang kulit (shadow puppet theatre) uses flat leather puppets which cast shadows on a screen. The puppet master manipulates the puppets with sticks.

Masks are often carved by the dancer

Servant-clowns interpret the *Kawi* (Old Javanese) speech of "high characters".

Topeng dancers recount genealogical histories of dynasties through a series of masks. Players may be a troupe of three or more, or may perform solo.

Servant-clowns in *topeng* amuse the audience and make moral commentaries.

Wayang wong characters wear masks and move like puppets. This is Garuda, a mythical bird.

Wayang kulit characters are distinguished by headdress and manner of speech. These are the "prince" and the "demon".

Sasak Dances

In Lombok, the performing arts reflect both indigenous Sasak rites and Balinese traditions. Dances in Lombok are very often accompanied by drums; they often consist of a sequence of energetic movements alternating with slower actions and graceful poses. *Peresehan*, a dance which is often performed for festivals, is the ritual enactment of a duel between two Sasak warriors.

Peresehan, a traditional fight using poles and shields made of rattan.

Puspawresti is a modern creation inspired by *rejang*. A dance addressed to the gods, *rejang* is performed by females, usually either young or past child-bearing age.

Musical Instruments of Bali and Lombok

In Bali and parts of Lombok, traditional music is performed by a *gamelan* orchestra. This is a percussion ensemble consisting largely of bronze metallophones (instruments with tuned metal keys), led by drums; there are a few wind and stringed instruments. The music is based on rhythmic and melodic cycles punctuated by gongs. Many orchestras play for tourists. Most villages in Bali own at least one set of *gamelan* instruments for ritual occasions. Some sets are considered sacred and are played only during religious ceremonies.

The *gamelan tingklik*, with bamboo keys, accompanies traditional dances.

Instruments of the Gamelan

Most of the orchestra is made up of pairs of metallophones, which are tuned to a very slight but precise dissonance which gives the gamelan *its piercing, shimmering sound. Each* gamelan *has its own unique internal tuning; instruments are not interchangeable between orchestras.*

Bamboo resonators amplify sounds made by the bronze keys.

Metal keys

Wooden mallet

Gangsa, which are keyed metallophones of various sizes, are played in syncopation to create a complex melodic texture.

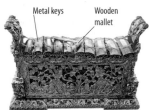

A pair of "male" and "female" *kendang* (drums) conduct the orchestra.

Bronze material is recycled from old gongs to make new ones.

Carved *pelawah* (instrument stands) are custom-designed for each orchestra.

Gongs

Bronze gongs of various sizes form the heart of the gamelan orchestra. They are struck with padded mallets or sticks to produce resonant sounds which punctuate the melodies made by keyed instruments.

Carved wooden frame

Pot gong

Kemong gong

Kempur

Kempli

Gong Ageng

Balaganjur, a walking orchestra of cymbals and drums, has an exciting, crashing sound intended to scare off evil spirits in its path.

The **terompong** is a series of inverted kettle gongs played by a single musician.

The **reyong** is a row of small gongs played by a group of two, three or four musicians.

Drums in Lombok

Drums play an important role in the music of Lombok. The island's main musical traditions reflect Hindu-Buddhist forms which originated in Java and Bali, and others which developed from the traditions of Islam.

Kendang beleq ("big drum") at a cultural festival in Lombok

Celebration of a special occasion with the aid of drums

The use of drums and ceremonial dress at a wedding

The Gamelan Orchestra

The Gong Kebyar is Bali's most popular and most complex form of gamelan. Its sound has been described as a "cascade of blazing gold".

Large bamboo musical instruments are used by *gamelan jegog* orchestras, a type of ensemble associated particularly with West Bali.

Suling are bamboo flutes of various degrees of thickness and length. The players use a special breathing technique to produce a continuous stream of sound.

Balinese Painting

Balinese art is a rich tradition very much alive today, especially in the villages of the Ubud-Mas-Batuan area of Central Bali. During the 20th century the influence of Westerners *(see p92)* was a factor in Balinese painting. However, themes and images still show traces of Bali's Javanese heritage, including Indian themes which predate the arrival of Islam in Java *(see p49)*. In the late 20th century, when some artists were educated in academies, what is known generally as "modern art" began to appear.

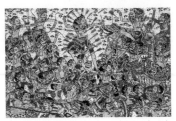

The "wayang" style dominated pre-colonial painting; this anonymous canvas from Kamasan dates from the 19th century.

One of the most gifted Balinese artists of the mid-20th century was I Gusti Nyoman Lempad, who created expressive and stylized works such as *The Tantri Stories* (1939). Lempad took the art of drawing in Bali to new heights.

Batuan style

The Batuan style, as in this work painted by Ida Bagus Made Togog in 1932, is typical of much Balinese painting in its full occupation of the canvas, repetition of patterned iconographic elements, fine detail and slightly monochromatic quality. Balinese painters often tell a story by showing scenes of everyday life. The basis of this story is not known.

Garuda, the mythical bird

A busy market scene

Regional Styles

The Pita Maha association, which was centred around Ubud, led to the creation of the "Ubud Style". This stimulated the emergence of other local styles, such as that of Sanur in the south. The villages of Pengosekan and Penestanan, though both in the Ubud area, also developed distinct artistic identities.

The Community of Artists in Pengosekan uses subtle colours, as in I Dewa Nyoman Batuan's *Cosmic Circle* (1975).

The Sanur School flourished in the 1930s. *Fighting Horses* (undated) by I Gusti Ketut Rundu is essentially decorative rather than narrative in nature.

Modern Art in Bali

Academic art education has introduced a different, more analytical approach to Balinese art. Some painters have opted for academic realism; others have chosen a modernist look. I Nyoman Gunarsa combines the free brushstrokes of American Expressionism with exotic Balinese themes, such as traditional dancers and *wayang* figures. Painters such as Made Wianta and Nyoman Erawan have also produced art which is modern yet at the same time strongly Balinese in feeling.

Three Dancers (1981) by I Nyoman Gunarsa

A battle scene provides a sharp contrast to the peaceful scenes of daily life shown in the rest of the painting.

The Pita Maha association was founded in 1936 by Cokorda Gede Agung Sukawati and European painters Walter Spies and Rudolf Bonnet. It encouraged local artists to create non-religious art using their own imaginative resources.

The river at the centre of the painting gives it a strong graphic structure.

Farmers are shown working with their cows in the ricefields.

The Ubud Style, as in *Balinese Stone-Craftsmen Working* (1957) by I Nyoman Madia, is characterized by themes of daily life and a way of showing anatomy that was influenced by Rudolf Bonnet.

The Young Artists School of Penestanan, influenced by Dutch artist Arie Smit, typically uses bright colours, as seen here in *Jayaprana Ceremony* (1972) by I Nyoman Kerip.

Crafts and Textiles

Gold- and silversmithing, stone carving, woodcarving and weaving are all crafts that have survived from the age of Bali's opulent kingdoms. Today, a thriving handicraft industry produces goods mainly for tourism and export. Crafts are generally practised in specialist villages, and Bali is an important market for goods made on other Indonesian islands. Lombok has a long tradition of domestic pottery, and produces colourful hand-woven textiles *(see p165)*.

Garudas (mythical birds) carved in wood and painted in the villages around Ubud

Carved Architectural Elements

The virtuoso carving of architectural elements, still practised today in Bali, blurs the distinction between crafts and fine arts. The works of craftsmen can be seen adorning many temples, palaces and houses; an industry has also developed producing items for general decoration.

Wall ornamentation such as this example from Pura Tirta Empul *(see p103)* is carved from volcanic stone *(paras)*.

Chinese-inspired motifs decorate this door in Puri Agung *(see p116)*, the work of Chinese artisans in the 19th century.

Stone sculpture is a thriving industry as a consequence of strong local demand in the restoration of Bali's temples.

Wooden mallet and locally forged chisel

Lombok Pottery

Renowned for its simple designs and fine craftsmanship, Lombok pottery is made using simple, age-old techniques and fired in straw on open ground. Sasak women have been making pottery since the 14th century, when the skill was probably introduced by Majapahit migrants. Among Lombok's most prominent pottery villages are Penujak *(see p165)*, Banyumulek *(see p158)* and Masbagik Timur.

Domestic pottery, such as this water jar, is widely used in Lombok households for storage, cooking and bathing.

Forms are built by hand.

Clay material comes from local riverbeds.

Lombok pottery, ranging from a terracotta colour to rich reddish-brown and black

Artshop Ware

A large cottage industry has grown up in Bali, based on craft work. It provides employment to thousands of rural families who can no longer make a living by farming. The level of skill demonstrated by a sizeable part of the Balinese population is remarkable. Some craftsmen have an "artshop" in their home.

Painted wooden trinkets

Lacquer-painted baskets woven in Bali

Basketware is widely made in Lombok using rattan, grass, bamboo and lontar. Designs vary between villages. Sometimes palm leaves are used for smaller boxes.

Gold and silver are imported to Bali from other islands and worked by members of the metal-smithing Pande clan.

Traditional Hand-woven Textiles

The most common textiles are *endek* or warp *ikat* (made by dyeing the threads before weaving) and the more costly *songket* (gold tapestries). The Balinese are the only weavers in Southeast Asia to master double *ikat*, in the form of *geringsing* made in the village of Tenganan *(see pp114–15)*. Most of this work is woven on simple backstrap looms in the home.

The traditional hand-operated loom is supported by the weaver who leans back to maintain the tension of the threads. Very complex pieces can take years to complete.

Silk sarong made in North Bali in the 19th century, showing a mythological story enacted by shadow puppets

Detail of flower motif, part of a *geringsing* from Tenganan

Prada, a gold-painted fabric made in Bali

The rich design of *songket*, with a pattern of gold or silver thread

Festivals and Holy Days

Bali's holy days, often the occasion for extravagant celebrations, are calculated according to either a lunar calendar or the 210-day Balinese calendar. *Odalan* (temple festivals) are the anniversary celebrations of particular temples. There is almost always a temple festival taking place somewhere. Rites of passage and other religious holidays are mostly celebrated with guests at home in the family temple. Outsiders may watch more public occasions such as *odalan* and even cremations, provided they show due respect.

The ingredients of offerings include palm leaves, flowers, fruit and other foodstuffs.

Female devotees are dressed with a ceremonial waist sash and flowers for the occasion.

Offerings are made by the women in the household. This skill is passed from mother to daughter. Older women are highly respected as *tukang banten* (offerings experts).

Temple Festivals

At an odalan, *the deities of a temple are honoured with offerings, prayers, and entertainment. Temples sometimes strike the visitor as rather quiet places, but they come alive during temple festivals, which generally last three days. The whole occasion has a carnival atmosphere, and demands elaborate preparations. All village members contribute labour and materials.*

Male devotees, shown here praying, wear a white formal costume which includes a white headcloth.

In a Balinese cremation, the corpse is placed in an animal-shaped sarcophagus.

Balinese Rites of Passage

Rites of passage ease a soul along the cycle which runs from before birth to after death. A person's *oton* is his or her birthdate on the Balinese calendar, and so occurs once every 210 days. A child's first and third *oton* are usually lavish occasions. A tooth-filing ceremony, in which the front teeth are filed even, marks the coming-of-age of an adolescent. A wedding ceremony takes place in the family home of the groom, where a high priest conducts prayers; a ritual bath is followed by a feast. A ritual cremation usually involves elaborate preparations by the community.

This guardian statue has been elaborately decorated with flowers, cloth and offerings in preparation for a temple festival.

Offerings are brought by worshippers from home and placed on a special platform.

The Balinese Calendar, each day represented by an appropriate image

The Balinese Calendar

Certain Balinese holy days are calculated according to the complex 210-day *pawukon* calendar. This is made up of 30 seven-day *wuku* (weeks), along with nine other overlapping *wewaran* (cycles) of different lengths. The most common *wewaran* are the three-day "market" cycle, the five-day cycle and the seven-day cycle. Many festivals fall when these cycles cross.

Saraswati and Renewal of the Cycle: On the last day of the 210-day cycle, Saraswati, the goddess of learning, is worshipped. Certain books are honoured with offerings laid on them and sprinkled with holy water. Children make offerings at school while adults bring gifts to healers and traditional teachers.

Banyu Penaruh: The first day of the 210-day cycle is one of ritual cleansing with holy water, usually at a spring temple or at the house of a high priest.

Pagerwesi: This is a day for spiritual strengthening; it is celebrated elaborately in North Bali with *penjor* and feasting as at Galungan. The name means literally "fence of iron".

Tumpek: Once every 35 days, offerings are made to specific categories of valued things, such as metal objects, trees, books, musical instruments, livestock and *wayang* puppets; in modern Bali, motorcycles, cars, computers and refrigerators may be included. There are six Tumpek days in the 210-day calendrical cycle.

Devotees receiving holy water during a religious festival

Decorated bamboo poles known as *penjor* adorn Bali's village streets at Galungan.

Galungan and Kuningan

Galungan occurs every 210 days, in the 11th week of the cycle. This holiday celebrates the creation of the universe. A period of festivity culminates ten days later in Kuningan, the Balinese "All Saints' Day".

BALI AND LOMBOK THROUGH THE YEAR

The seasons in North Bali, South Bali and Lombok do not coincide precisely. In very broad terms the coastal areas are generally drier than those at higher altitudes. Any particular day can often differ from place to place: the situation in Ubud may well be different from that in Sanur. For precise dates of religious holidays and cultural festivals, visitors should check with tourist information offices or consult the Internet – and be prepared for slight discrepancies. Many temples have festivals on the *purnama* (full moon). A few are mentioned below. The high season runs through July and August; the long weekends around Chinese New Year, Easter, Christmas and New Year are also particularly crowded. If you plan to travel then, book well in advance and expect to pay higher rates for accommodation.

Ogoh-ogoh (demonic effigies) in a Nyepi procession in April

Dry Season

From April to October, occasional rain, generally at night, is normal. July and August are relatively cool and pleasant months, and nights in the highlands can even be chilly.

April

Nyepi *(Mar/Apr)*. Falls on the day after the ninth new moon. A few days prior to Nyepi, temples hold *melasti* processions, carrying statues of gods to the sea or to holy springs. At midday on the eve of Nyepi, massive offerings are set out at major crossroads; they are believed to have the power to exorcise evil spirits. That evening, there are noisy torchlit processions of huge *ogoh-ogoh* (demonic effigies). These are created each year by village youth groups, who compete to make them as frightening, funny or outrageous as they can. At the end of the festivities, the effigies are burned.

On Nyepi itself, the Day of Silence, no one is allowed to go out on the street and no lights may be lit until 6am the following day.

The growing impact of tourism and modern lifestyle on religious culture has led some Balinese to become increasingly scrupulous about keeping the Day of Silence. Visitors are expected to observe these restrictions and remain indoors. Special arrangements are made to look after guests, and sometimes to include them in the festivities on the eve of Nyepi. During this 24-hour period airline travel is suspended and Bali's international airport is closed. Travellers should check for details ahead of time.

Purnama Kedasa *(two weeks after Nyepi)*. To mark this, the full moon of the tenth month, there are large festivals at important Balinese temples, especially at Besakih *(see pp120–21)*, Pura Ulun Danu Batur *(see pp126–7)* and Pura Samuan Tiga *(see p91)*. These are opportunities to see offerings, music and sacred dance in their full cultural context.

May

Waisak *(Apr/May)*. The small Buddhist community of Bali visits the few Buddhist temples of the island on this holiday, which takes place on the day of the full moon usually in May,

Balinese worshippers at a temple festival at Pura Taman Ayun

Average Daily Hours of Sunshine in Bali

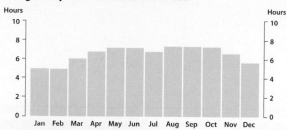

Sunshine Chart
The island of Lombok typically receives about an hour less sunshine each day compared to Bali. Daylight hours are fairly constant throughout the year on both islands as they are close to the equator.

The annual Bali Kite Festival in South Bali

according to the Buddhist lunar calendar.

Purnama Desta (full moon). Hindu temple festival held at Pura Maospahit in Denpasar (see p65), and Pura Segara, near Ampenan on Lombok.

June

Pesta Kesenian Bali (Bali Arts Festival) (mid-June to mid-July), Denpasar. The height of Bali's secular cultural calendar, this is a two- to four-week jamboree of mostly Balinese (but increasingly international) dance, theatre, music and cultural events at the Taman Werdhi Budaya (Bali Arts Centre) (see p65). The dates and duration vary from year to year. The opening-day parade is a spectacular procession in which the participating troupes perform as they move through the city streets.

July and August

This is the high season for visitors from Europe and North America. It is also thought to be an auspicious time for cremations.

Bali Kite Festival (Jun–Aug), South Bali. An annual, international event which draws participants from all over Southeast Asia and Japan, the Bali Kite Festival takes place at the time of year when winds are most suitable for kite-flying. The festival inspires children throughout the countryside; they construct kites from plastic bags or any other materials they can find, often decorating them too, and fly them from drying ricefields and village streets.

Indonesia's Independence Day (17 Aug). In the week leading up to Independence Day, which is marked by events throughout Indonesia, Bali's traffic may be held up by ranks of schoolchildren marching along the roads, in preparation for the military-inspired ceremonies held on the big day itself in the provincial capital, Denpasar.

Mekepung (Jul–Oct, dates variable). Buffalo races are held in Negara (see p138).

September

In September, the weather is hot and dry, bringing out flowers in profusion.

Purnama Katiga (full moon). Temple festival at the Gunung Kawi Royal Monuments at Tampaksiring in Central Bali (see p103).

October

Ubud Writers and Readers Festival (early Oct). Attracts writers and lovers of literature from all over the world.

Purnama Kapat (full moon). Festivals at many major temples, including Besakih (see pp120–21), Pura Ulun Danu Batur (see pp126–7), Pura Tirta Empul (see p103), Pura Pulaki (see p142) and Pura Tegeh Koripan (see p119).

Hari Raya Sumpah Pemuda (28 Oct). A working day commemorating the independence movement, associated with political reform in Bali and Indonesia.

Kuta Beach during the high season in July and August

Average Monthly Rainfall in Bali

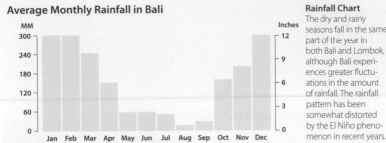

Rainfall Chart
The dry and rainy seasons fall in the same part of the year in both Bali and Lombok, although Bali experiences greater fluctuations in the amount of rainfall. The rainfall pattern has been somewhat distorted by the El Niño phenomenon in recent years.

Raindrops falling on an irrigated ricefield

Rainy Season

Monsoon weather brings rain from mid-October to mid-March. The wettest months of the year in Bali and Lombok are December and January. During these two months, according to local belief, people are at their most susceptible to illness. Several days of uninterrupted rain may be followed by a week without any rain at all. These are also the warmest months at the equator and rain brings ready relief from the scorching heat. Sunny days during this period are hot and humid.

Bali and Lombok are not subject to typhoons, but in February there is normally a week or two of southwesterly wind and rain before the monsoon shifts direction and brings in cooler, drier weather from the northeast.

November to December

Purnama Kalima *(Nov)*. The full moon of the fifth month of the Hindu calendar is the occasion when Pura Kehen in Bangli *(see p108)* holds its temple festival.
Purnama Kenam *(Dec)*. On the full moon of the sixth month, the

temple festival takes place at Pura Lingsar temple complex *(see p158)* in Lombok.
Siwa Latri *(Dec–Jan)*. "Shiva's Rite" is celebrated by Balinese Hindus two weeks after Purnama Kenam, on the night before the seventh dark moon (Tilem Kapitu). The celebrations involve a 24-hour vigil, usually held in a temple, fasting and silence.

February to March

Chinese New Year *(Jan/Feb)*. Crowds of Chinese come to Bali from Singapore and Jakarta. Like the Eve of Nyepi *(see p44)*, the Chinese

New Year is celebrated with great fanfare, particularly in Denpasar.
Bau Nyale *(Feb)*. Sasak courtship rites take place on Kuta beach *(see p166)* in South Lombok, on the appearance of the *nyale* seaworm, a traditional symbol of fertility.
Purnama Kesanga *(Feb/Mar)*. The temple festival of Pura Penataran Sasih in Pejeng *(see p101)*, near Ubud, takes place on the day of the full moon.
Bali Spirit Festival *(Mar)*. A spiritually charged event in Ubud that celebrates yoga, dance and music. It features health and wellness workshops

A street procession at a Muslim festival

Hindus praying during a temple festival at Pura Taman Pule in Mas

Average Monthly Temperature in Bali

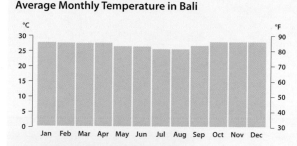

Temperature Chart
Bali has an average temperature which is higher than Lombok by about one degree Celsius. Temperatures on Bali and Lombok fluctuate only marginally throughout the year, but it is generally cooler in the hill regions than in the areas near the coast.

Moving a musical gong in preparation for celebrating Galungan in Ubud

Balinese Holy Days

Between the major religious holidays and annual temple festivals, the 12-month lunar calendar is the framework for regular ritual celebrations and religious observance.

On the *tilem* (new moon) and *purnama* (full moon) of each month, special offerings are prepared and presented within the household and at local public temples.

The monthly celebration of *purnama* is particularly lively at certain "state" temples, such as the Pura Jagatnatha in Denpasar, Pura Kehen in Bangli and other regional capitals. It is marked by

performances of shadow puppet theatre and readings of sacred poetry.

Other festivals are based on the 210-day Balinese Calendar (see p43). The most important of these is Galungan, which occurs in the 11th week. The whole of Bali is festively decorated, and people dress up in their best finery. Kuningan follows ten days after Galungan, on a Saturday, and marks the end of the holiday period. The day after Kuningan is Manis Kuningan, a big day for temple festivals at Pura Sakenan on Pulau Serangan, and Pura Taman Pule in Mas.

Ramadan – Muslim Month of Fasting

During Ramadan, the ninth month of the Islamic calendar, Muslims

Greeting cards for the Muslim festival of Idul Fitri

refrain from eating, drinking and smoking from dawn to dusk. Visitors to Lombok should avoid these activities in public in Ramadan.

At the end of Ramadan is **Idul Fitri**, a two-day holiday. Most Muslims return to their villages, causing massive air, sea and land traffic throughout the country.

Public Holidays

New Year's Day (1 Jan)
Nyepi (Hindu New Year; 6 Mar 2016, 28 Mar 2017)
Hari Paskah (Good Friday/ Easter; 25 Mar 2016, 14 Apr 2017)
Hari Waisak (Buddhist holy day; 20 May 2016, 10 May 2017)
Ascension of Christ (5 May 2016, 25 May 2017)
Christmas Day (25 Dec).
Hindu Holidays based on Balinese 210-day calendar:
Galungan (10 Feb and 7 Sep 2016, 5 Apr and 1 Nov 2017)
Kuningan (20 Feb and 17 Sep 2016, 15 Apr and 11 Nov 2017)
Saraswati (25 Jun 2016, 21 Jan and 19 Aug 2017)

Muslim Holidays based on Islamic 354- or 355-day calendar:
Idul Adha (11 Sep 2016, 1 Sep 2017)
Maulid Nabi Muhammed (11 Dec 2016, 30 Nov 2017)
Isra Miraj Nabi Muhammed Date varies
Idul Fitri (5 Jul 2016, 25 Jun 2017)

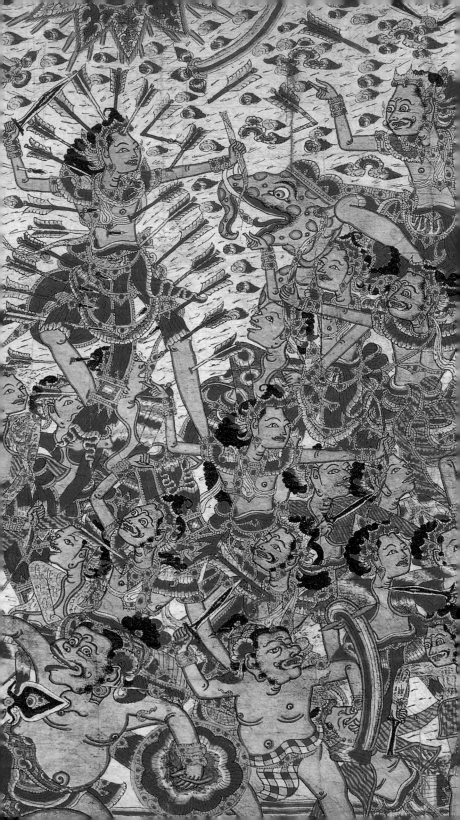

THE HISTORY OF BALI AND LOMBOK

Hilltops and mountain gods are both prominent in Balinese legend. The landscape of the islands has deeply influenced their cultural, political and economic life for thousands of years. Old traditions have persisted remarkably intact, despite the successive impacts of colonialism, political strife and the travel industry.

The Balinese, and the Sasaks (the indigenous people of Lombok), are thought to be descendants of migrants from southern China who arrived around 2000 BC. Their legacy is believed to include the growing of rice as a staple crop, the craft of metalworking and the prevalence of mountain cults. These cultural traits, still clearly observable in traditional Balinese life today, suggest broad affinities with other peoples of Southeast Asia and the Pacific Ocean.

Early Kingdoms

There are few written records of Bali and Lombok before the 20th century, and none of Lombok before 1365; but ancient artifacts tell of Hindu kingdoms and the continuous influence of Java. An inscribed pillar in Belanjong, Sanur, dated to AD 914, implies that relations had been established before that date between Bali and the Buddhist Sanjaya dynasty of Central Java. In Central Bali there are relics of a Hindu-Buddhist kingdom, dating from the 10th–13th centuries, whose seat was near today's Pejeng and Bedulu. During the 11th century, the Gunung Kawi Royal Monuments (see p103) were built in order

to commemorate the king Anak Wungsu and his queen Betari Mandul. This king's edicts have been found in Sangsit on the north coast and as far as Klungkung in the south, implying that he was ruler of the entire island. Pura Teqeh Koripan (see p119) may have been built to venerate him. Anak Wungsu's reign, which began around 1025, was a period of close contact with Java. His mother was a Javanese princess; his father was the Balinese king Udayana; and his older brother was the great Airlangga, who ruled a large kingdom in East Java.

A contemporary of Anak Wungsu, Mpu Kuturan, is thought to have established the three-temple system common in Balinese villages (see p32): the pura puseh (temple of origins), the pura desa (village temple), and the pura dalem (temple of the dead).

There was substantial Chinese influence in early Bali. Kepeng (Chinese coins) were in circulation from the 7th century onwards; the dragon-like Barong effigy (see p29) is thought to be of Chinese origin; and King Jayapangus of Bali married a Chinese princess in the 12th century.

250,000 BC	10,000 BC	2,000 BC	1,000 BC	AD 1	AD 1000

250,000–10,000 BC Upper Pleistocene era

Ancient pillar in Pura Belanjong, Sanur

AD 914 First written inscription, on a pillar in Pura Belanjong, of a Balinese royal name

2000 BC Migrations from China to Indonesia

Prehistoric bronze spearheads

AD 960 Holy spring temple of Pura Tirta Empul built

◀ The Death of Abhimayu, from the epic *Mahabharata*; late 19th century, Kamasan style (detail; artist unknown)

Shrine in Denpasar's Pura Maospahit, a temple established in the Majapahit era *(see p65)*

Majapahit Bali

Bali maintained its independence from the kingdoms of East Java until 1284. In that year the Singasari king Kertanegara sent a hostile expedition to Bali, and as a consequence brought the island into the Javanese political sphere.

Kertanegara's successor in East Java, Raden Wijaya, founded the kingdom of Majapahit, which over the next two centuries became the largest empire ever in Southeast Asia. Bali was not truly subjugated by Majapahit until 1343, when the Javanese prime minister, Gajah Mada, defeated the king in Bedulu. Majapahit sovereignty was eventually established at Gelgel.

The Gelgel kings ruled with the help of local chieftains under a Majapahit lord. The people of some villages declined to adopt Majapahit's religious and social customs. These people, now known as the Bali Aga ("original Balinese"), remained isolated in

Ceremonial bowl from around the 15th century

their village settlements, and became a culturally distinct minority *(see p125)*. Majapahit shaped the culture that has survived in Bali to the present day, including architectural, dance and theatrical forms; literature written in Kawi script; and painting and relief sculpture influenced by *wayang* puppet theatre *(see p35)*. However, with time the imported culture gradually took on certain features of the more rustic Bali.

Majapahit also ruled Lombok. A 1365 Javanese chronicle mentions Lombok as a dependency. Lombok histories tell of Majapahit princes being sent to Bali, Lombok and Bima (present-day Sumbawa). The old Hindu-Buddhist elements in Lombok's culture can be traced to this period.

Bali's Golden Age

By the end of the 15th century Bali had recovered its independence. Majapahit was seriously foundering, a decline accelerated by the rise of Islam in Java. The Balinese kingdom of Gelgel flourished in the mid-16th century under King Waturenggong, who extended it westward to Java, and over Lombok to Bima. Some Hindu Javanese nobles migrated to Gelgel, bringing a fresh infusion of Majapahit court culture. Waturenggong's reign was a time of rebirth in the Hindu arts, literature and religion.

Around the 1540s, two new streams of religious thought spread eastward from Java: Islam, which was never to become widely established in Bali; and a Hindu reformation movement led by Waturenggong's priest, Dang Hyang Nirartha. This

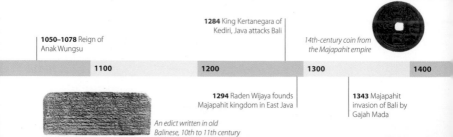

1050–1078 Reign of Anak Wungsu

1284 King Kertanegara of Kediri, Java attacks Bali

14th-century coin from the Majapahit empire

| 1100 | 1200 | 1300 | 1400 |

1294 Raden Wijaya founds Majapahit kingdom in East Java

An edict written in old Balinese, 10th to 11th century

1343 Majapahit invasion of Bali by Gajah Mada

Javanese brahman was a poet, architect and religious teacher. Among his reforms was the introduction of the *padmasana* shrine *(see p30)*, an altar to the Supreme God. He established, inspired or renovated many temples in Bali, including Pura Tanah Lot *(see p132)*. He preached in Lombok; and he is considered to be the ancestor of Bali's Brahmana Siwa clan, the island's main priestly kinship group.

Kulkul tower at Pura Taman Ayun, built in Mengwi around 1740

Meanwhile, from the 16th century Lombok was embracing Islam. Two of the most important figures in the process were Sunan Prapen, a disciple of the Islamic saint Sunan Giri; and the possibly mythical Javanese prince, Pangeran Sangupati, who the Sasaks consider founder of the mystical Islamic sect Wetu Telu *(see p27)*.

Rise of New Powers

By 1597, which saw the first recorded visit to Bali by Europeans, the court at Gelgel was decadently rich. The dynasty was soon displaced by a new branch, founded around

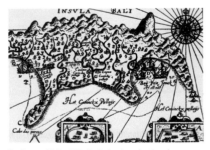
Dutch map of Bali, c.1597, clearly showing volcanic peaks

1650 at Klungkung, the kings taking the title Dewa Agung ("great lord"). Soon, the Klungkung dynasty began to break into smaller kingdoms. Over the next 250 years, warfare and intermarriage created a complex political landscape.

The 18th and 19th centuries saw the rise of other kingdoms that foreshadowed the regencies of Bali today. These were Klungkung, Karangasem, Buleleng, Jembrana, Bangli, Badung, Gianyar, Tabanan and Mengwi. Buleleng became a major power under Panji Sakti, who ruled from 1660 to 1704; in the 18th century it was rivalled by Mengwi and Karangasem. Mengwi was split up among its enemies in the late 1890s, but a trace of its former glory remains at the royal temple complex Pura Taman Ayun *(see pp134–5)*. Although the territory ruled by Klungkung was smaller than the other great kingdoms, the Dewa Agungs retained prestige because their realm included the important temple at Besakih *(see pp120–21)*.

The kingdom of Karangasem in eastern Bali occupied Lombok in 1740; Balinese settlers lived in the western part of the island. There was resistance in the centre and the east from the Sasak nobility and Bugis migrants *(see p139)*. Conversely, contacts with Islam increased in Bali itself. By the end of the 18th century all of the kings on Bali had hired Muslim mercenaries. This is why many "Balinese-Muslim" villages still exist near what were formerly important court centres.

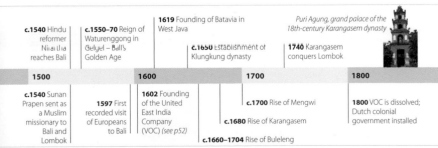

c.1540 Hindu reformer Nirartha reaches Bali	c.1550–70 Reign of Waturenggong in Gelgel – Bali's Golden Age	1619 Founding of Batavia in West Java		*Puri Agung, grand palace of the 18th-century Karangasem dynasty*
		c.1650 Establishment of Klungkung dynasty	1740 Karangasem conquers Lombok	
1500	**1600**	**1700**		**1800**
c.1540 Sunan Prapen sent as a Muslim missionary to Bali and Lombok	1597 First recorded visit of Europeans to Bali	1602 Founding of the United East India Company (VOC) *(see p52)*	c.1700 Rise of Mengwi	1800 VOC is dissolved; Dutch colonial government installed
			c.1680 Rise of Karangasem	
		c.1660–1704 Rise of Buleleng		

Arrival of the Europeans

The 17th century saw a new player on the scene. The Dutch set up the United East India Company (VOC) in 1602, a trading company succeeded in 1800 by the Dutch East Indies colonial administration.

Until the mid-19th century, Dutch colonial attention was concentrated in Batavia (now Jakarta), on the island of Java. Bali had little contact with the Dutch, except for trade in opium and slaves. Balinese kings sold debtors and prisoners of war; the Dutch sold opium.

The raja of Buleleng, mid-19th century

British interregnum in Java (1811–16), a consequence of the Napoleonic Wars – this caused some concern to the Dutch. The Dutch were to become far more militant after their victory over the Javanese, who were led by the prince Dipanagara, in the Java War of 1825–30. They also found themselves in conflict with Balinese kings over salvage from shipwrecks: the kings regarded cargo as a just reward for saving ship and crew. One such dispute with the king of Buleleng in 1845 led to the landing of Dutch troops on Balinese soil. The Balinese, led by the brilliant tactician Gusti Jelantik, resisted three military expeditions before they were finally defeated in 1849 at Jagaraga; Jelantik fled to Karangasem where he was killed in a palace intrigue.

The Dutch now had direct control of the northern Balinese kingdoms of Buleleng and Jembrana. Rivalry prevented a lasting alliance among the other kingdoms; most aspired to

A Tumultuous Century

The 19th century brought enormous suffering to Bali and Lombok, as a consequence of volcanic eruption, famine, disease and war. There were military incursions by the Dutch and petty wars between the kingdoms. Thomas Stamford Raffles (later the founder of Singapore) showed some interest in Bali during the

View of the harbour of Ampenan, Lombok, c.1850

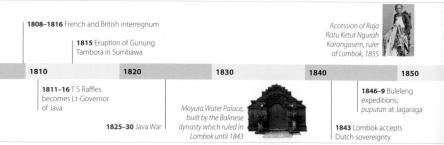

1808–1816 French and British interregnum

1815 Eruption of Gunung Tambora in Sumbawa

Accession of Raja Ratu Ketut Ngurah Karangasem, ruler of Lombok, 1855

1810	1820	1830	1840	1850

1811–16 T S Raffles becomes Lt-Governor of Java

1825–30 Java War

Mayura Water Palace, built by the Balinese dynasty which ruled in Lombok until 1843

1846–9 Buleleng expeditions; *puputan* at Jagaraga

1843 Lombok accepts Dutch sovereignty

Dutch cavalry in Lombok, 1894

Dutch help against their neighbours. The Balinese ruler in Lombok during this time had accepted Dutch sovereignty in 1843. In 1849 he sided with the Dutch against Buleleng by attacking Buleleng's ally Karangasem, his own ancestral home. Thus Karangasem became a vassal of Lombok.

The Fall of Bali's Old Kingdoms

Dutch control over Lombok was not fully asserted until the end of the 19th century. In 1894, seizing the pretext of a Sasak revolt against their Balinese masters, the Dutch attacked and subdued the whole island, in the process acquiring Karangasem as well. In 1900, Gianyar put itself under Dutch control, while Bangli hesitated. Three kingdoms remained independent – Badung, Tabanan and Klungkung.

The occasion for the next and decisive Dutch attack was another dispute over a shipwreck – the pillage of a small Dutch ship which had run aground off Sanur. The matter escalated and became a

political stand-off. In September 1906, a large Dutch fleet arrived. In Denpasar, kings, princes and brahmans dressed in white and had their ritual weapons blessed. As the Dutch advanced towards the town, they were met by hundreds of men, women and children emerging from the Denpasar palace. The Balinese ran towards the Dutch guns and were mown down. The survivors turned their weapons on themselves in an orgy of suicide *(puputan)*. That afternoon a similar tragedy took place at the nearby Pemecutan palace. The king of Tabanan surrendered with his son; two days later they committed suicide in their cell. In Klungkung, the Dewa Agung and his court were shot down in another *puputan* in 1908. Bali was then wholly incorporated into the Dutch East Indies.

Colonial Rule

Royal houses were stripped of property and power as the Dutch recruited surviving "rajas", as junior personnel, into their bureaucracy. With a *modus vivendi* established, The Netherlands were to conserve Bali as a "living museum" of classical culture, a showcase for enlightened

Interior of the Karangasem royal palace, built c.1900

1860–88 Epidemics and plagues in Bali

The Ruins of Denpasar (1906) by W O J Nieuwenkamp

| 1860 | 1870 | 1880 | 1890 | 1900 |

1882–1900 Inter-kingdom wars in Bali

1888 Major earthquake in Bali and Lombok

1894 Dutch conquest of Lombok

1906 Dutch expedition against Badung; *puputan* in Denpasar; Tabanan falls

Dutch colonialism. The restoration of the role of the rajas as custodians of ritual matters gave the appearance of cultural continuity.

At the same time the Dutch used compulsory labour, formerly a royal prerogative, to improve irrigation and build a network of roads across the island. They streamlined village laws and class structure; new taxes rewarded loyal nobility but impoverished the peasantry, and were especially harsh on Lombok. These actions created tensions that were to erupt later, when post-colonial governments raised popular expectations but were not able to resolve certain fundamental social problems.

King and visitor at the gateway of Puri Gianyar, 1910

The Last Paradise

To visitors from abroad, however, Bali was a paradise. Early images by Dutch illustrator W O J Nieuwen-kamp, and German photographer Gregor Krause, inspired Westerners to visit the island. The Dutch cautiously encouraged tourism. Some visitors stayed on more permanently, settling mainly in Ubud and Sanur, and presented to the outside world an image of Bali as "the island of the gods" where "everyone is an artist".

Meanwhile, a modern bureaucracy was growing, whose members soon constituted, with Chinese, Arab and Muslim traders, the core of a new urban intelligentsia. Together with other Indonesians from Java, Sumatra and the eastern islands, they formed the pan-archipelago political networks which later gave rise to Indonesian nationalism. In 1928, the *lingua franca* of the archipelago, Malay, was declared the official language of the Dutch East Indies, Bahasa Indonesia.

War and Independence

In 1942 Japan invaded and occupied the Dutch East Indies. Requisition of crops led to deprivation and non-Indonesians were imprisoned by the Japanese or deported. The occupation spurred on the forces of nationalism. Leading the nationalists was Javanese intellectual Sukarno, who proclaimed independence on 17 August 1945, two days after the Japanese surrender. However, the Dutch returned to reclaim their

Photograph of Balinese people, taken by G P Lewis in the 1920s and coloured for publication

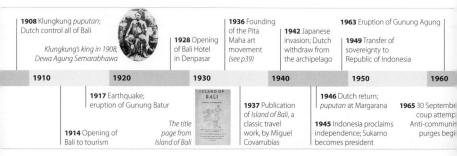

1908 Klungkung *puputan*; Dutch control all of Bali

Klungkung's king in 1908, Dewa Agung Semarabhawa

1928 Opening of Bali Hotel in Denpasar

1936 Founding of the Pita Maha art movement *(see p39)*

1942 Japanese invasion; Dutch withdraw from the archipelago

1963 Eruption of Gunung Agung

1949 Transfer of sovereignty to Republic of Indonesia

1910	1920	1930	1940	1950	1960

1917 Earthquake; eruption of Gunung Batur

The title page from Island of Bali

1914 Opening of Bali to tourism

1937 Publication of *Island of Bali*, a classic travel work, by Miguel Covarrubias

1946 Dutch return; *puputan* at Margarana

1945 Indonesia proclaims independence; Sukarno becomes president

1965 30 Septembe coup attemp Anti-communis purges begi

Balinese judges under the colonial regime, 1935

colonies, meeting fierce resistance. In Bali they achieved a political foothold among the former nobility. Pro-republican youths waged guerrilla war until November 1946, when a band of 94 freedom fighters, led by Gusti Ngurah Rai, died in a *puputan* at Marga *(see p136)*. Despite this victory, the Dutch were in an unsustainable position. Three years later they withdrew from Indonesia, transferring sovereignty on 27 December 1949.

The prosperity promised by independence did not materialize for many years. Guerrilla bands roamed the islands of the archipelago. Successive governments, powerless or over-nationalistic, deterred foreign investors. Thought to be extinct, Bali's highest volcano, Gunung Agung, erupted in 1963, killing thousands of people, devastating East Bali and causing famine. Political polarization worsened.

Suharto in Bali, 1979

Autocracy and Reform

On 30 September 1965, an alleged coup attempt took place in Jakarta. Sukarno was displaced by the little-known general Suharto, who then led a "cleansing" campaign in which thousands of communists and suspected communist sympathizers were murdered, and countless internal conflicts brutally settled. Suharto's "New Order" eventually brought prosperity to Bali with the resurgence of tourism.

The first modern tourists were travellers on the "hippie trail" of the late 1960s and 1970s. The Australians discovered Bali as a nearby holiday destination. The coconut groves of Kuta were gradually replaced by "artshops" and small hotels. In the 1980s and 1990s, South Bali was transformed by a building boom. There were just a few hundred hotel rooms in 1965, and 30,000 by 1999.

In the Suharto era, development took place at the expense of civil liberties, a trade-off destroyed by the financial crisis of 1997. In May 1998, Suharto was forced to resign. Suppressed social pressures erupted.

Pro-democracy banner, 1999

In Bali, after the 1999 elections, some public buildings were burned down. Later, Lombok suffered unrest, apparently provoked by outsiders; tourists were unharmed. Megawati Sukarnoputri, favoured by the majority of Balinese as presidential candidate, became vice-president. Terrorist bombings in 2002 and 2005 brought tragedy to Bali in the new millennium; the two men responsible for the 2002 attack were executed in 2008.

Nusa Dua Beach Hotel

1966 Bali Beach Hotel is opened

1983 Opening of Nusa Dua Beach Hotel, part of a 5-star resort complex

1967–98 Suharto's New Order; dramatic rise of tourism

1998 Economic crisis causes riots in Jakarta; Suharto resigns

1999 PDI-P party led by Megawati Sukarnoputri wins 80 per cent of vote in Bali; Abdurrahman Wahid becomes president of Indonesia

2009 Susilo Bambang Yudhoyono is the first Indonesian president ever to be re-elected

2002 On 12 October a terrorist bomb in Kuta kills over 200 people

2014 Joko Widodo elected seventh president of Indonesia

Number of foreign tourists visiting Bali reaches a record 3.6 million

2015 Indonesia executes eight drug smugglers by firing squad

2008 The bombers responsible for the 2002 terrorist attacks are executed

| 1970 | 1980 | 1990 | 2000 | 2010 | 2020 |

BALI & LOMBOK AREA BY AREA

Bali and Lombok at a Glance

The attractions of Bali and Lombok are varied, appealing to visitors with an interest in cultural heritage, natural beauty and sports. South Bali has the greatest concentration of beach resorts and nightlife; Central and East Bali are particularly rich in history and artistic interest. Throughout both islands there is wonderful scenery, from volcanic peaks and lakes to rice terraces and a beautiful coastline, in many areas quite undeveloped.

Pura Meduwe Karang *(see pp152–3)* is a temple noted for its stone sculptures, wall carvings and reliefs.

Bali Bird Park *(see pp88–9)* is home to nearly 1,000 birds of over 250 species displayed in a fine tropical garden.

Singaraja *(see pp150–51)* retains the atmosphere of an old port and colonial capital.

Ubud *(see pp92–9)* and the nearby villages are at the heart of Bali's cultural life.

Taman Nasional Bali Barat *(see pp140–41)* is a large nature reserve which includes the Bali Starling Breeding Facility and the coral reefs of Menjangan Island.

Gilimanuk

Singaraja

NORTH AND WEST BALI
(See pp128–153)

Negara

CENTRAL BALI
(See pp82–)

Antosari

Mengwi

U...

Denpa...

Pura Taman Ayun *(see pp134–5)* is a royal temple with an inner and an outer moat.

Kuta

Sar...

Nusa Dua

Bali Museum *(see pp66–7)* is noted both for its fine collection of artifacts and for its architecture.

Denpasar *(see pp64–5)* is Bali's administrative capital and commercial centre.

0 kilometres	20
0 miles	10

Pura Luhur Uluwatu *(see pp80–81)* is set high on the edge of a cliff at the end of South Bali's Bukit Peninsula.

Kuta *(see pp70–73)*, the most developed tourist centre in Bali, is crowded with hotels, shops, bars and restaurants.

◄ Verdant ricefields outside the woodcarving village of Tegallalang

Taman Nasional Gunung Rinjani *(see pp162–3)* is a national park and trekking area encompassing Lombok's highest volcano and the crater lake Danau Segara Anak.

Gunung Batur *(see pp124–5)*, an active volcano, and Lake Batur are enclosed within a spectacular caldera within which are several historic temples and some trekking routes.

Besakih Temple Complex *(see pp120–21)* contains 22 temples built on the lower slopes of the sacred volcano Gunung Agung.

Senggigi *(see p160)* is a popular beach resort area set in a sandy bay.

EAST BALI
(See pp104–127)

ıglı

Amlapura

Klungkung

Tenganan *(see pp114–15)* is a village where the minority Bali Aga ("original Balinese") still live according to their own, ancient traditions.

Senggigi

LOMBOK
(See pp154–167)

Labuhan Lombok

Mataram

Selong

Toyapakeh

Praya

SOUTH BALI
(See pp60–81)

Sepi

Gerupuk

Taman Gili *(see pp110–11)* is a royal compound with beautiful ceiling paintings in its two main pavilions.

Pura Lingsar *(see p158)* in Sweta is a temple with 300 years of history. Apart from the temple's importance to worshippers, the lotus ponds in the precincts give pleasure to local children.

SOUTH BALI

A blend of history, culture and tourism, South
Bali offers many contrasts. Budget travellers
have flocked to the beaches here since surfers first
arrived decades ago, while at the other extreme, lavish
hotels and resorts have created a more glamorous and
exotic version of Bali. Meanwhile, despite modern development, temples
and village communities still maintain their cultural and artistic traditions.

At the heart of South Bali is Denpasar, the
island's provincial capital since 1958 and
today a busy, modernizing city, Bali's
administrative and commercial hub.
Denpasar used to be a royal capital –
the kingdom of Badung dominated the
southern part of Bali from the late 18th
to the beginning of the 20th century,
and its heritage is to be seen in several
of its older buildings. Two important
cultural centres are here: the Bali Museum
(see pp66–7) and Taman Werdhi Budaya
(Bali Arts Centre) *(see p65).*

The city lies within Bali's most important
tourist area, a triangle formed by the
beach resorts of Kuta, Legian, Seminyak
and Canggu on the west coast, Sanur
on the east coast, and Nusa Dua to
the south.

Kuta is Bali's leading tourist centre; the
beaches are famous. There are hotels of
every standard, exciting restaurants and

bars, water sports, pulsating nightlife and
shops to suit every budget. Sanur has
many of the attractions of Kuta, but in a
gentler, less raucous style. Nusa Dua, a
development planned specially for
visitors, offers the manicured gardens of a
5-star resort-hotel complex complete
with an 18-hole golf course.

The highland peninsula of Bukit in the
far south is arid and stands in stark
contrast to the verdant gardens and rice
terraces that enriched the rajas of old.
One of Bali's holiest temples, Pura Luhur
Uluwatu, is set high on a cliff at the Bukit's
southwest extremity, with a spectacular
view of the ocean.

The sea is never far away in South
Bali. Surfers come for the waves, divers
and snorkellers for the reefs and underwater life. Everyone comes for the
beach life, which has few rivals in
Asia or further afield.

Fishermen off the South Bali coast in their light outrigger boat

◀ Dragon statues at the Bali Museum in Denpasar *(see pp66–7)*

Exploring South Bali

Most visitors arrive at Denpasar's airport at the centre of
South Bali. The most important resort areas, with their
beaches and nightlife, are only a short taxi ride
away. Some people feel no need to venture
further afield, but communications are good
to other parts of Bali, and to Lombok. South
Bali is therefore a good base for further
exploration; it is easy to make all the practical
arrangements here. This is the least mountainous part
of the island, but much of the landscape is lush with
gardens and ricefields, and the Bukit Peninsula in the
south offers a more rugged contrast. Offshore to the east
lie the islands of Nusa Lembongan, Nusa Ceningan and
Nusa Penida, usually reached from Benoa Harbour or Sanur.

Sights at a Glance

1. *Denpasar pp64–5*
2. Canggu
3. Sanur
4. *Kuta pp70–71*
5. Seminyak
6. South Kuta Beach
7. Benoa Harbour
8. Pulau Serangan
9. Tanjung Benoa
10. Nusa Dua
11. Jimbaran
12. *Pura Luhur Uluwatu pp80–81*
13. Nusa Lembongan
14. Nusa Penida

Kuta Beach, a popular spot for sunbathing, surfing and
other water sports

Getting Around

All flights to Bali land at Ngurah Rai
International Airport, near Tuban,
south of South Kuta Beach. Bali's first
dual carriageway, Jalan Bypass Ngurah
Rai, runs from Nusa Dua to Kuta (via
the airport), up to Tohpati (via Sanur)
before continuing its coastal route as
far as Kusamba. Transport is plentiful,
in the form of *bemo*, taxis and tourist
shuttle buses. Buses run from Denpasar to other parts of the island, and
to the inter-island ferry terminals at
Gilimanuk and Padang Bai. These
cater more for locals than visitors.

For hotels and restaurants in this region see p174 and pp182–4

Mengwi ↑
Gaji
Celuk
Kangkang
Kayutulang
Kulibul
Kerobokan
Anyarbelodan
2 CANGGU
Umalas
Semor
Petitenget
Pengubengan
Taman
Basang
A
SEMINYAK **5**
Kuta Bay
Pel
4
KUTA
SOUTH **6**
KUTA BEACH
Jimbaran Bay
JIMBARAN **11**
Tegalwangi
Tegalsari
Indian Ocean
Simpangan
Garuda Wisnu Kencana
Labuansait
Suluban
Banket
A PURA LUHUR
12 ULUWATU
Bukit Peninsul
Ungasan
Kutuh
Uluwatu
Pecatu
Nyang Nyang

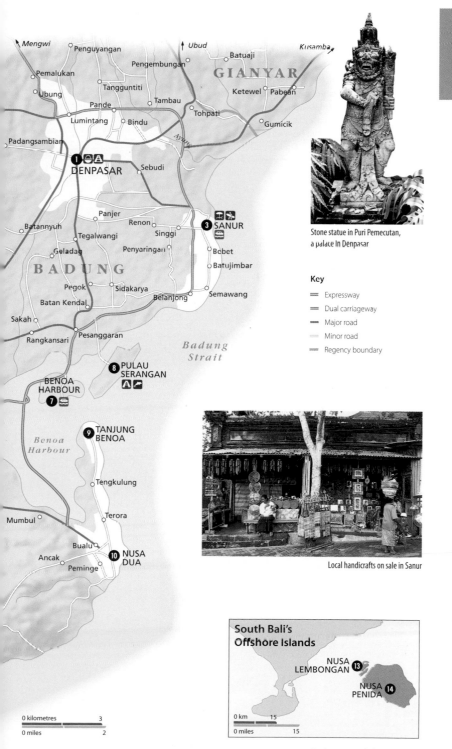

Mengwi
Penguyangan
Pemalukan
Pengembungan
Ubung
Tangguntiti
Pande
Lumintang
Bindu
Padangsambian

↑ Ubud
Batuaji
GIANYAR
Ketewel
Pabean
Tambau
Tohpati
Ayung
Gumicik

→ Kusamba

1 ⬛🅰
DENPASAR
Sebudi

Panjer
BADUNG
Batannyuh
Tegalwangi
Renon
Singgi
3 🏖✈
SANUR
Geladag
Penyaringan
Bebet
Batujimbar
Pegok
Sidakarya
Semawang
Batan Kendal
Belanjong
Sakah
Pesanggaran
Rangkansari

Badung Strait

8 PULAU
SERANGAN
🅰↗

BENOA
HARBOUR
7 ⬛

Benoa Harbour

9 TANJUNG
BENOA

Tengkulung

Mumbul
Terora

Bualu
Ancak
10 NUSA
DUA
Peminge

Stone statue in Puri Pemecutan,
a palace in Denpasar

Key

— Expressway
— Dual carriageway
— Major road
— Minor road
— Regency boundary

Local handicrafts on sale in Sanur

South Bali's Offshore Islands

NUSA
LEMBONGAN **13**
NUSA
PENIDA **14**

0 km   15
0 miles   15

0 kilometres   3
0 miles   2

For keys to symbols *see back flap*

● Denpasar

Denpasar is Bali's bustling provincial capital. Some older buildings predate the Dutch invasion of 1906 *(see p53)*, and there are still some white-walled, red-tiled structures dating from colonial times. On the streets can be seen several statues commemorating heroes of Indonesia's struggle for independence. Around the main street, Jalan Gajah Mada, are shophouses built by Chinese, Arab and Indian traders. Shopkeepers from all over Bali buy wholesale here.

Bronze statues in Taman Puputan commemorating *puputan* heroes of 1906

⌂ Pasar Badung
Jalan Gajah Mada. **Open** daily.
This is a lively, open-air market full of colour and excitement; sellers from all over Bali do a brisk trade all day. The extensive flower section is not to be missed – exotic blossoms used in religious offerings *(see p42)* are a major commodity on Bali.

The fruit, vegetable and fish market is full of spectacular tropical harvests. Bargains can be found among the textiles, baskets, mats and traditional dancers' costumes.

⌂ Jalan Hasanudin
Gold jewellery in Balinese, Indonesian and Western designs is sold here.

⌂ Jalan Sulawesi
This three-block stretch houses a myriad of fabrics and textiles. Everything from cheap batiks to imported silks and brocades can be found here. This is where the Balinese come to buy their temple clothing, and the delicate lace used for *kebaya* (a traditional tight-fitting ladies' blouse).

Colourful textiles for sale on Jalan Sulawesi

⌂ Jalan Gajah Mada
Several interesting Chinese apothecaries with an array of herbal medicines can be found on this busy street. One of the largest is Toko Saudara. Other stores sell electronics, sporting goods, handicrafts, batik and *ikat* textiles. Many traders of Arab and Indian descent have businesses here.

🏛 Taman Puputan

Jalan Udayana and Jalan Surapati.

Puputan translates as "ritual fight to the death", and this large square in the middle of town (once the site of Denpasar's palace) has a huge bronze statue which commemorates the *puputan* of 1906 (*see p53*). Nowadays the square is much more peaceful, making a pleasant green oasis amid the bustle and noise of Denpasar.

Statue of Ngurah Rai
(*see p55*)

🏨 Inna Bali Heritage Hotel

Jalan Veteran 3. **Tel** (0361) 225 681.
🌐 innabali.com

Built in 1928, and once the only luxury accommodation in Bali, this hotel has welcomed famous guests such as Charlie Chaplin and Noel Coward. The open pavilion on the opposite side of Jalan Veteran was built to stage dances for guests. Seen here were many great performers who helped to make Balinese dance world-famous.

Denpasar

① Pasar Badung
② Jalan Hasanudin
③ Jalan Sulawesi
④ Jalan Gajah Mada
⑤ Taman Puputan
⑥ Catur Muka
⑦ Inna Bali Heritage Hotel
⑧ Pura Jagatnatha
⑨ Bali Museum
⑩ Pasar Burung
⑪ Pura Maospahit
⑫ Taman Werdhi Budaya

🏛 Catur Muka

Northwest corner of Taman Puputan.

On the traffic island adjacent to Taman Puputan is a representation of Wisnu, the four-headed Hindu god, shown in the form of a stone statue 20 m (65 ft) tall, dating from the 1970s. The name means "four faces".

🏛 Pura Jagatnatha

Taman Puputan, Jalan Letkol Wisnu. **Open** daily. 🎁 donation.

This temple was built in the 1970s for the worship of Sang Hyang Widhi Wasa, the Supreme God. It is crowded on the full and new moons, and on Kajeng Kliwon, which falls every 15 days in the Balinese calendar (*see p43*). It has a very tall *padmasana* shrine (*see p30*).

Bali Museum

See pp66–7.

🐦 Pasar Burung

Off Jalan Veteran. **Open** daily.

At this lively bird market many species of birds and other animals can be seen. The Balinese love songbirds, and those with exceptional voices can sell for very high prices. There is also trade in dogs, tropical fish, fighting crickets and fighting cocks.

VISITORS' CHECKLIST

Practical Information
Road Map C4.
ℹ️ JL Raya Puputan 41 Renon, Denpasar, (0361) 225 649.
Bali Arts Festival: Taman Werdhi Budaya, Jun–Jul (*see p45*).

Transport
from Kuta, Sanur & Nusa Dua.

🏛 Pura Maospahit

Jalan Sutomo, Grenceng.
Closed to public.

This temple dates from the time between the 13th and 15th centuries, when the Majapahit ruled over Bali (*see p50*) – the style of the statuary and brickwork developed at that period, and the restrained ornamentation is delightful. Although the temple is closed to visitors, the architecture can be seen from outside.

Pura Maospahit, one of Bali's oldest temples

🏛 Taman Werdhi Budaya

Jalan Nusa Indah. **Tel** (0361) 227 176. **Fax** (0361) 247 722. **Open** 8am–5pm Tue–Sun. **Closed** public hols.

Also known as the Bali Arts Centre, this is an attractive if under-used complex with extensive gardens, an art museum, several indoor theatres and an outdoor amphitheatre. There are frequent dance and music performances, but no set programme.

The centre is a good place to come to during the heat of the day. The permanent collection of sculptures and paintings reflects the art world of the 1970s and 1980s. More recent works are shown in rotating exhibitions.

Information can be found in the *Bali Post* newspaper and tourist magazines.

Denpasar: Bali Museum

The Bali Museum houses one of the world's best collections of Balinese art. Completed and opened in 1931 by architect P J Moojen, its attraction is not only the items on show but also the buildings and setting. The exterior walls, gates and courtyards were executed in the manner of an old Denpasar royal palace, while the Tabanan, Karangasem and Buleleng *gedung* (pavilions) are built in the style of the regions after which they are named.

Ceremonial Gate
Fine brickwork without mortar is combined with volcanic-stone reliefs.

Carved Palace Doors
On display are these carved, gilded doors from the 19th century.

★ **Stone Sculptures**
Lining the veranda of the pavilion are stone statues from the 16th to the 19th centuries. The one shown here depicts motherhood.

Masks
Ritual masks, such as this 19th-century example from South Bali, are shown with puppets and musical instruments.

Bronze Cannons
This 17th-century gun, with monster-head muzzle, is one of a pair made for a Denpasar prince.

The gazebo has a base decorated with fine stone motifs.

★ Excavated Artifacts
The collection ranges from the
Bronze Age to the 19th century.
These *prasasti* (inscribed bronze
plaques) praise 10th-century
Balinese princes.

VISITORS' CHECKLIST

Practical Information
Jalan Letkol Wisnu, on east side
of Taman Puputan. **Tel** (0361) 222
680. **Open** 8am–2:45pm Tue–Sat
(to 3:45pm Sat). **Closed** public
hols.

The arched gateway
is richly decorated with
stone carvings.

Main entrance

The *kulkul* is a
multilevelled
tower which
houses a slit-log
alarm drum.

Entrance to Timur Pavilion
In front of the pavilion is a landscaped
courtyard with an ornamental pool.

Gallery Guide
*The collections are housed in four
pavilions: Tabanan is noted for
its theatrical masks and musical
instruments; Karangasem has a
display of sculptures, woodcarvings
and paintings; Buleleng has a
collection of textiles; Timur contains
prehistoric finds and, upstairs, some
antique woodcarvings.*

★ Textiles
The collection contains pieces woven
in the Bali Aga villages *(see pp114–15)*,
such as this gold brocade from North
Bali, and examples of *geringsing*
double *ikat* from Tenganan.

Key to Floorplan
- Tabanan Pavilion
- Karangasem Pavilion
- Buleleng Pavilion
- Timur Pavilion
- Library

❷ Canggu

Road Map C4. **ℹ** Denpasar (0361) 756 176. 🎿 📧 🏄

Canggu used to be little more than a sleepy coastal village, celebrated among the surfing fraternity for its famous beach breaks. However, the 2006 arrival of the international Canggu School and The Canggu Club, with sports and leisure facilities and a kids' water park, started drawing a more family-oriented expat community. Canggu is now fast becoming Bali's hippest beachside spot.

Behind the beach is a landscape of coconut palms, ricefields and luxurious private villas. Those interested in the use of traditional elements in architectural design will appreciate the holiday homes and villas, which combine Balinese style with modernity.

Canggu is popular for its cool bars, busy live-music venues, coffee shops and cafés serving healthy cuisine. For fitness fans, there is a surf school, some yoga studios and three riding stables. There are also massage and beauty parlours, beachwear boutiques and a deli.

Well worth a visit is Hotel Tugu (see p174), a "museum hotel" furnished with Asian antiques. Two villas here take as their theme artists who lived in Bali – Walter Spies (see p92) and Adrien Le Mayeur – while an 18th-century Chinese temple serves as a private dining room.

Farmers harvesting rice in Canggu with holiday homes nearby

❸ Sanur

Bali's longest-established resort, Sanur has a quiet charm. At its heart is an old Balinese community. The simple layout of Sanur's streets and its tranquil atmosphere appeal to families and those seeking a relaxed vacation with the convenience and facilities of a beach resort, but without the intrusiveness of Kuta's hawkers and traffic. The shops are pleasant and sell goods from Bali and elsewhere in Indonesia. Many of the unpretentious cafés and pubs aim to attract visitors of a particular nationality or lovers of a particular sport. The nightlife is enjoyed by both visitors and locals.

Exploring Sanur

Jalan Danau Tamblingan, Sanur's main artery, is lined with restaurants, and shops selling locally made fashion and craft goods. It runs some 5 km (3 miles) parallel to the beach from old Sanur village, to the formerly distinct villages of Blanjong and Mertasari. Halfway is Bale Banjar Batu Jimbar, a community centre where musicians practise and women make flower and palm-leaf offerings. At Pasar Sindhu, sarongs and other products can be bought at bargain prices; it operates early in the morning.

🅰 Pura Desa

Jalan Hang Tuah. **Open** daily.
This fine village temple was probably built early in the last century, although its brickwork has been restored since. It is in Sanur's oldest neighbourhood, which is famous for the spiritual power of its priests.

Museum Le Mayeur

Jalan Hang Tuah, via Grand Bali Beach Hotel. **Tel** (0361) 286 164. **Open** 9am–4pm daily (to 1pm Fri). 🎿 📷 🐾
Built in the 1930s by Adrien Jean Le Mayeur – Belgian painter and one of Sanur's first European residents – the house became a museum and gallery on the artist's death in 1958. Now a little faded, some of the buildings are wooden, with interesting carved decorations. The courtyard garden features in Le Mayeur's work. Le Mayeur's wife, the famous Balinese dancer Ni Polok, is the subject of several paintings on show.

Typical laid-back café at popular Sanur Beach

🏨 Grand Bali Beach Hotel

Jalan Hang Tuah. **Tel** (0361) 288 511.
w innagrandbalibeach.com
Bali's only high-rise hotel was refurbished after a fire in 1992 and is now adorned with giant Balinese-style statues. After it was built in 1964, the religious authorities issued a famous edict outlawing structures taller than coconut palms. Such buildings were deemed offensive due to the spiritual value attributed to the trees.

🏖 Sanur Beach

The beach runs virtually the full length of the town; along much of it is a paved walk.

Grand Bali Beach Hotel complex – Bali's only high-rise hotel

For hotels and restaurants in this region see p74 and pp182–4

Sanur Beach – a popular spot for watching the sunrise

Offshore, enormous breakers crash into a reef. The calm waters between the reef and the white sands are good for swimming except at low tide. Beyond the reef the currents are strong. Activities include diving, fishing trips and an evening sail on a *jukung*, a traditional outrigger. The beach is a place to explore for marine life, such as sea grass, starfish, sea cucumbers, hermit crabs, *Fungia* corals and sea urchins. It is regarded as an excellent place to watch the sunrise.

🅰 Pura Segara

Jalan Segara Ayu, or from Sanur Beach. **Open** daily. 🛐 donation.

Set in the grounds of Segara Village Hotel, but accessible to the public, this is one of the best of several beach temples built of coral. The pyramid shape of the offering houses is unique to Sanur, and suggests origins in prehistoric times.

🅰 Pura Belanjong

Jalan Danau Poso. **Open** daily. 🛐 donation.

In this plain-looking temple is an ancient stone column,

VISITORS' CHECKLIST

Practical Information
Road Map C4. 🅸 Denpasar (0361) 756 176. 🖼 traditional dance at some restaurants. 🖼
🖼🖼🖼

Transport
🚌 🚢 to Nusa Penida & Nusa Lembongan.

the Prasasti Blanjong. On it is carved the oldest edict so far found in Bali (AD 914). The inscription is written in a form of Sanskrit, although it is not all decipherable. It suggests Sanur was a lively trading port more than 1,000 years ago.

🔲 Bali Orchid Garden

Jalan Bypass Tohpati, Kasamba 1. **Open** 8am–6pm daily. **Tel** (0361) 466 010. 🆆 baliorchidgardens.com

This beautiful botanical garden is a serene tropical haven, with a huge variety of orchids that bloom throughout the year. For those keen to take home a piece of paradise, many of the flowers are also available to buy.

Sanur Town and Beach

① Pura Desa
② Museum Le Mayeur
③ Grand Bali Beach Hotel
④ Sanur Beach
⑤ Pura Segara
⑥ Pura Belanjong

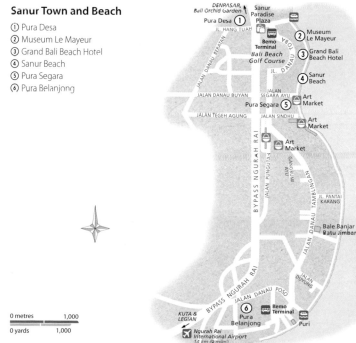

0 metres 1,000
0 yards 1,000

For keys to symbols see back flap

❹ Street-by-Street: Kuta

Kuta is the most developed visitor destination in Bali. Forty years ago the beach was set against coconut groves and banana plantations. It is still a great attraction today; however, a few steps away, there are now streets lined with businesses catering for visitors – bars, restaurants, hotels, nightclubs and department stores. Packed along the narrow lanes are shops and stalls selling many kinds of product likely to appeal to travellers from around the world, as well as *losmen* offering budget accommodation *(see p170)*. Commercialized Kuta may be, but it is a vibrant place, and caters for all budgets.

A local artisan at work on one of the many handicraft stalls in the area

★ **Poppies Lane II**
Along this narrow alley are shops, stalls, restaurants and reasonably priced accommodation.

★ **Kuta Beach**
The sandy beach, which stretches northwards towards Seminyak and beyond, is a place to surf, swim, and relax in the sun.

To Legian →

JALAN PANTAI KUTA

POPPIES LANE II

JALA

POP

★ **Poppies Lane I**
This is a good area for travellers on a budget, with several inexpensive hotels as well as casual dining places.

VISITORS' CHECKLIST

Practical Information
Road Map C5. *i* Jalan Raya
Kuta, **Tel** (0361) 756 176; Jalan
Pantai Kuta 2, (0361) 756 176.

Transport

Made's Warung I
One of Kuta's first and most famous restaurants serves
local and international dishes (see p182).

To Jalan Bypass Ngurah Rai,
Denpasar, Sanur and Nusa Dua

★ Kuta Square
This is a major shopping complex
housing hundreds of small retailers,
the large Matahari emporium and
Kuta Galleria (see p191).

Key
— Suggested route

To South
Kuta Beach

0 metres 100
0 yards 100

**Hard Rock
Café and Hotel**
This, the only
Hard Rock hotel
in Asia, has the
largest swimming
pool in Bali.

Kuta Art Market
Here it is possible to buy basketware and other craft goods made
in Bali and the nearby islands of
the Indonesian Archipelago.

Kuta and Legian

The beach at Kuta is long and sandy. However, the dollar-a-night homestays that attracted young backpackers and surfers in the 1970s have been replaced by a resort strip, which is now world-famous (see Street-by-Street, pp70–71). Besides the beach and water sports, the principal attractions are shopping and nightlife. Development has spread beyond the original Kuta Beach, including Legian, and has now enveloped the South Kuta Beach area in the south and Seminyak in the north.

Surfers at Kuta Beach, a location suitable for all levels of ability

Exploring Kuta and Legian

As Bali's main tourist hub, Kuta is a good base for relaxation and organizing trips to other parts of the island. Away from the beach, shopping is perhaps the most tempting activity around these parts; there are no major cultural or historic sights in either Kuta or Legian. A good rest-stop is **Made's Warung I** (see p182), casual and cool, and one of Kuta's most famous restaurants. Both Legian and Seminyak (see opposite) are now as built up as Kuta proper. However, Legian's labyrinth of back streets offers a wide range of low-priced accommodation options.

Relaxing on the golden sands of Kuta Beach

🏖 Kuta Beach

The beach is flat and sandy, and stretches for over 3 km (2 miles), backed by some sizeable hotels. Hawkers sell their wares and refreshments are available all day long. Surfboards can be rented – this is a good place for the novice surfer, although one should watch out for the rip tides. Because of currents, swimmers should stay between the safety flags. Kuta Beach becomes Legian Beach north of Jalan Melasti. Kuta's famous night-spots are Sky Garden, Paddy's, M-Bar-Go and The Bounty.

Kuta and Legian

① Sky Garden
② Bali Bomb Memorial
③ Kuta Beach
④ The Bounty
⑤ Made's Warung I
⑥ Bemo Corner

0 metres	500
0 yards	500

Key

🟦 Street-by-street See pp70–71

For keys to symbols see back flap

Poppies Lanes I & II

These two narrow lanes are lined with small shops, stalls, hotels and bars. One of the first hotels was Poppies, from which the lanes took their name. The network of alleys in this part of Kuta offers a refuge from the traffic, pollution and noise of the main streets.

Jalan Legian

This is the commercial artery of Kuta, running parallel with the beach. At the southern end is **Bemo Corner**, a busy inter-section. Jalan Legian is the place to find banks, travel agencies, car-rental outlets and the like. Pubs, bars and nightclubs proliferate – some, such as **The Bounty** and **Sky Garden**, are land-marks in themselves. Also on Jalan Legian, the **Bali Bomb Memorial** is a poignant reminder of the 202 victims of the Kuta bomb blast of October 2002.

Bima monument on Jalan Bypass

Environs

On the outskirts of Kuta, beside the underpass on Jalan Bypass Ngurah Rai at Simpang Siur, is an ornate modern statue of Bima, hero of the Hindu *Mahabharata* epic. It is one of several public monuments erected by the authorities for the benefit of visitors.

Shop in Jalan Legian, selling craft goods from Bali and elsewhere

Pool volleyball at the Waterbom Park & Spa

❺ Seminyak

Road Map C5. 🚌 from Kuta. ℹ️ Kuta, (0361) 756 176.

Seminyak extends north of Kuta and Legian. The further northward one goes, the more peaceful the atmosphere becomes, although Seminyak is now an important tourist centre. Some good fashion boutiques can be found here, selling stylish clothes made in the region.

The luxurious **Oberoi Hotel** (see p177) has very attractive gardens overlooking the beach. Further north still, in the Petitenget area, you'll find Potato Head Beachclub and the glamorous W Retreat.

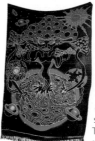
Colourful scarf for sale in Seminyak

Environs

A short walk up the beach north of Seminyak is the **Pura Petitenget** ("magic chest") temple, raised some 8 m (26 ft) above road level. Founded by the 16th-century priest, Dang Hyang Nirartha (see pp50–51), it is considered one of Bali's most mystically charged temples.

The area from Seminyak to Kerobokan, 5 km (3 miles) to its north, is a furniture-making centre (see p190). Galleries line the main road.

Pura Petitenget

Jalan Kayu Aya. **Open** daily. donation.

❻ South Kuta Beach

Road Map C5. 🚌 from Kuta. ℹ️ Kuta, (0361) 756 176.

It is hard to know where Kuta ends and the South Kuta Beach area begins. However, the streets of South Kuta are laid out on a slightly larger scale, and the effect is a sense of greater order than in Kuta. By the beach is a series of large luxury hotels with spacious gardens. Shopping in South Kuta has an inter-national feel, especially in the modern beachfront Discovery Mall. Some people may find it a welcome respite from the bustle that often accompanies shopping in Bali. The northern limit of South Kuta is Kuta Square and the Matahari department store, selling a huge range of practical items, T-shirts and handicraft goods.

Near Kuta Square it is possible to take a ride on a *dokar*, one of the colourful carts pulled by small, hardy horses originally brought in from Sumba Island.

A very popular attraction for visitors is the **Waterbom Park & Spa** (see p197) which has an array of slides and pools. It is also a good place to relax and eat.

South Kuta Beach is one of the departure points for surfers trav-elling to the break at Kuta Reef, off Jimbara (see p78). Fishermen with motorized outriggers can be chartered for the trip.

For hotels and restaurants in this region see p174 and pp182–4

Cruise vessels in Benoa Harbour

❼ Benoa Harbour

Road Map C5. 🚌 from Denpasar (shuttle bus services available to Benoa from hotels). 🚢 to Lembar on Lombok. 🖥

Linked to Nusa Dua by a scenic highway across the Benoa Bay, Benoa Harbour will appeal to boat-lovers. Among the commercial and privately owned vessels, there is often an interesting variety of traditional craft from the Indonesian Archipelago. These include *pinisi*, broad-beamed sailing cargo boats from South Sulawesi; and brightly coloured fishing boats from Madura, off northeast Java. There is a multitude of boat charters and tours on offer. Day trips to Nusa Lembongan *(see p78)* are recommended. A yacht or traditional Bugis ship can be hired for a day; longer trips go as far as Komodo and the Lesser Sunda Islands.

Nearby, on the Jalan Bypass Ngurah Rai, is the Mangrove Information Centre (tel 0361 728 966), which aims to preserve the 15 species of coastal mangrove in its natural forest.

❽ Pulau Serangan

Road Map C5. 🏄

The island of Serangan is separated from the southern curve of Sanur Beach by a mangrove area known as Suwungwas. The name "Turtle Island" is sometimes used, because of the sea turtles that used to lay their eggs here. The island has been greatly extended by reclamation during construction works for a hotel. A causeway now links it to mainland Bali. Local people maintain an unofficial guard post, and charge visitors a small fee for access to the island. Besides the Balinese, there is an old Bugis community *(see p139)*; their ancestors migrated from South Sulawesi, in the 1600s.

Here also is one of the six most sacred temples in Bali, **Pura Sakenan**, said by some to have been founded by the 16th-century reformist priest Dang Hyang Nirartha *(see pp50–51)*. Others believe the temple was founded in the 11th century by the Javanese Buddhist priest Mpu Kuturan. Within the inner courtyard is a stepped pyramid built of white coral, reminiscent of temples in Polynesia. During Manis Kuningan *(see p47)*, a vibrant festival takes place here on the temple's anniversary.

The island is a good vantage point from which to watch vessels returning to Benoa Harbour at the end of the day. There are views of the islands and great sunsets.

🅐 Pura Sakenan
Pulau Serangan. **Open** daily. 🏄 donation. 🎫 Manis Kuningan

❾ Tanjung Benoa

Road Map C5. 🚌 from Nusa Dua. 🛈 Badung, (0361) 756 176. 📶 🖥 📷 🏄

Tanjung (meaning "Cape") Benoa is a long, narrow, sandy spit, with a small fishing village built on it. The cape is separated from Benoa Harbour by a narrow stretch of water. The village was once a trading port, and some Chinese and Bugis as well as Balinese still live here. There are some Balinese temples built of carved limestone, as well as a mosque. At an ancient Chinese temple built by sailors and traders, fishermen of all religions consult with the fortune-teller in the hope of finding a good catch.

There is now a modern road leading to the tip of the peninsula from Nusa Dua. Hotels, spas and restaurants specializing in grilled seafood have grown up along both sides of the road. One quirky landmark is the stone pineapple motif marking the entrance to the Novotel.

Wall motif in a mosque in Tanjung Benoa

A beach restoration project here has resulted in a series of attractive, crescent-shaped stone piers, complete with open-sided gazebos. There are facilities for water sports, such as water-skiing, banana boat rides, fishing and parasailing. Cruise operators offer trips out to sea for snorkelling in waters rich in corals and tropical fish.

An ancient Chinese temple on Tanjung Benoa

◀ The *kecak* dance, in which a chorus of men chant an accompaniment as the *Ramayana* story is enacted

The world-renowned Bali National Golf Club, and beyond it the resorts of Nusa Dua and the sea

⑩ Nusa Dua

Road Map C5. 🚌 ℹ️ Denpasar (0361) 225 649. 🚫 🅿️ 🏨 🚻 ⛵

The Nusa Dua (literally "Two Islands") area is named after the two peninsulas along its coast. It consists primarily of luxury resorts run by major hotel chains. The beaches are sandy and clean. The entrance road is lined with rows of statues; it leads through a large *candi bentar* (split gate), on each side of which carvings of frogs serve as guardian figures.

Inside, there is an air of gentility and order. The hotels are built on a big scale. Their grandiose entrances have been described as "Bali Baroque" or "expanded traditional" in style – they are of interest to architecture enthusiasts. Young visitors will love the fish ponds of the Ayodya Resort, where thousands of brightly coloured *koi* (a type of carp first bred in Japan) swim among water lilies.

The Bali National Golf Club (*see p200*) has a championship course over three types of terrain (highland, coconut grove and coastal). Other facilities at Nusa Dua include the Bali International Convention Centre, the Bali Collection Mall, restaurants and the Pasifika Art Museum. There are also regular dance and other cultural activities held here.

Environs

Bualu is a bustling village outside the gates of the Nusa Dua complex. Several streets are lined with restaurants offering fresh fish and shops selling handicrafts.

Between the Sheraton Laguna and Grand Hyatt hotels, a headland with native flora and several Balinese shrines juts out into the sea. The views from here are good. Geger Beach is sheltered by a reef but is now the playground of guests at the massive Mulia Resort. Camel safaris through the arid hills are offered at the Nikko Hotel. One beach near the Nikko is popular with surfers.

Beautiful beaches line the southern coast. Most require a hike or climb; many are popular surfing spots, but they can be dangerous for beginners, with big waves and strong currents.

West of Nusa Dua, on the road to Uluwatu, is the **GWK** (Garuda Wisnu Kencana, or "Golden Garuda Vishnu") cultural centre. The main feature is a statue of the head of the mythological bird Garuda and the upper body of the Hindu god Vishnu. There are regular exhibitions and performances here.

🎭 GWK

Jalan Raya Uluwatu, Bukit Ungasan, Jimbaran. **Tel** (0361) 703 603. **Open** 10am–9pm daily. 🚫 🅿️ 🏨 **W** gwk-culturalpark.com

The Amanusa, a boutique hotel overlooking the golf course at Nusa Dua (*see p174*)

For hotels and restaurants in this region see p174 and pp182–4

Sun loungers at the Four Seasons Resort, Jimbaran (see p173)

⓫ Jimbaran

Road Map C5. 🛈 Kuta, (0361) 756 176. 🖉 🏠 🔁

Jimbaran is a large village consisting of many family compounds laid out on traditional Balinese lines (see pp32–3). There are no individual buildings of great interest to visit, but Jimbaran is a good place for those who like to see scenes of local everyday life. Several of Bali's most luxurious resorts have been built nearby. The most famous is the Four Seasons Resort (see p173).

There is a very attractive beach, from which the sunsets and the views are spectacular. On a clear day the profiles of all Bali's volcanoes and hills are visible from here, including the three peaks of Gunung Batukau to the west (see p137), and Gunung Batur (see pp124–5), Gunung Agung (see p118), Gunung Abang (see p125) and Gunung Seraya (see p116) to the east. On the beach itself, it is possible to rent sailing-boats and take part in other water activities.

Surfing at Kuta Reef, off the west coast of South Bali

Jimbaran is a good place to eat. The beach is lined with thatch-roofed eating places, where customers choose their fresh seafood which is then grilled over coconut husks and delivered to the table.

There is a large fishing settlement here, consisting of simple huts built near the waterfront. Many of the fishermen are not of Balinese origin, but migrants from the islands of Java and Madura. The brightly painted boats with their impressive bows and sterns can be seen all day long bobbing at anchor in the surf off the coast. As the sun begins to set, the fishing craft set off into the dusk with lamps burning – it is an unforgettable sight.

Environs
Kuta Reef is one of Bali's famous surfing points. The reef break which lies off the coast of South Kuta Beach is one of the surfing spots in the sea around the Ngurah Rai International Airport. It can be reached by paddling for some time, or chartering an outrigger at South Kuta Beach (see p73) or at Jimbaran.

The **Bukit Peninsula** is the southernmost part of Bali, making up most of the area south of Jimbaran. Much of the coast is a series of limestone cliffs. The Bukit is now home to some of the most luxurious holiday rental villas and boutique hotels on the island.

⓬ Pura Luhur Uluwatu

See pp80–81.

⓭ Nusa Lembongan

Road Map E4. 🚢 from Sanur, Kusamba & Padang Bai. 🛈 Klungkung, Jalan Untung Surapati 3 (0366) 21 448. 🖉 🏠 🔁

This small island has pristine beaches for sun-lovers and good coral reefs for divers and snorkellers. Bird-lovers will find a variety of species.

Day trips to the island have been available since the early 1990s. In operation now are several jet catamarans, the best known of them being the Bali Hai (see p203); as a consequence the island is visited by larger groups than hitherto. Trips to the island are also offered by some local boat owners. The boats include *pinisi*, a type of Indonesian sailing vessel originating in the island of Sulawesi to the northeast.

Most boat operators rent water-sport equipment, and snorkelling and diving gear.

On the island is an extensive underground house, known as the **Cavehouse**. It was dug by a Balinese priest after he was instructed in dreams to live in the belly of Mother Earth. He has passed away but the cave remains a popular curiosity.

For those who like pristine islands with no cars, Nusa Lembongan is a good place to stay a night or two. Accommodation ranges from budget to luxury options. After the day-trippers go, silence reigns; only some overnighters and the locals remain.

Ideal conditions for snorkelling off Nusa Lembongan

0 kilometres   10

0 yards   6

The coastal temple Pura Batu Kuning, on Nusa Penida

⑭ Nusa Penida

Road Map E5 & F5. 🚤 from Sanur, Kusamba & Padang Bai. 🛈 Klungkung, (0366) 21 448. 🚲 🏝 🚤

This quiet, undeveloped island, once the penal colony of the Raja of Klungkung, appeals mainly to hardy adventurers. Here, Balinese language and art have been less subject to change than on the mainland. The island is the legendary home of Ratu Gede Mecaling, the Balinese "King of Magical Powers". It is somewhat feared by many Balinese.

In general the landscape is dry, even arid, resembling the limestone hills of the Bukit Peninsula. Towards the south coast, with its tall white cliffs, there are a few lusher hills.

Some cotton is grown here. From it is woven the *cepuk*, a form of *ikat* textile (see p41) thought to have magical, protective powers. Other local occupations include seaweed farming.

There are several interesting temples here. One is the **Pura Ped**, in the village of Toyapakeh. The temple is built on an island in a large lotus pond. Among the carvings in **Pura Kuning**, near Semaya, are some explicitly erotic reliefs. The *pura desa*, or village temple, of the inland village of **Batumadeg** also has some interesting decorative reliefs. They show a number of sea creatures, including crabs and a variety of shellfish. The main gate is especially imposing.

Stone sculpture at Pura Ped

A short distance south of there is a sacred limestone **Goa Karangsari**.

In general there are few facilities of any kind on Nusa Penida. Visitors must take even basic supplies with them. Simple homestays are the only accommodation. The roads are not good. The best way to get about is by motorcycle or on foot. It is also possible to rent a car with a driver or take a *bemo*.

The waters off the coast of Nusa Penida are crystal-clear, although the currents are often strong. Here experienced divers will be able to see many large and rare species of underwater life. There are fine coral formations, especially off the south coast, where the sea is also famous for its rare but spectacular concentrations of giant sunfish (see pp206–7); in December and January they float in the water like large hot-air balloons. Sailfish and the whale shark can occasionally be seen. Off the northern half of the island the waters, while also clear, are shallower and calmer, especially in the strait between Nusa Penida and Nusa Lembongan. Most people who dive off these islands make their arrangements with operators in Sanur.

For those who want to explore Nusa Lembongan there is a public ferry that runs from Toyapakeh, and fast boats from Sanur and Serangan.

Diving off the coast of Nusa Penida

ra Luhur Uluwatu

Luhur Uluwatu is not only one of Bali's most sacred
ces of worship but also one of the most beautiful
xamples of classical Balinese architecture. It is connected in
legend to two figures important in the history of Balinese
religion, Mpu Kuturan, thought to have built it in the 11th
century, and the reformer priest Dang Hyang Nirartha, later
deified as Betara Sakti Wawu Rauh *(see pp50–51),* who rebuilt it
some 500 years later. Until the beginning of the 20th century
only the princes of Denpasar were allowed to worship here.
It is best to visit during the late afternoon
when the sea breezes rise, and then
enjoy the sunset.

★ **Three-tiered Meru**
The pagoda is dedicated to
Nirartha, who achieved
enlightenment here.

View of the Temple
From several points the temple
can be seen in its full glory as
the surf crashes onto the rocks
below. It is sometimes possible
to see turtles, dugongs and
dolphins in the sea.

KEY

① **This courtyard** is reserved
for worshippers.

② **The** *jero tengah,* or central
courtyard, offers spectacular views
of the sunset.

③ **This shrine** is dedicated to
Dang Hyang Nirartha, with images
of Brahma and Vishnu.

④ **The** *bale tajuk* are shrines for
the spiritual guardians of Nirartha.

⑤ **The** *astasari* is a shrine for
festival offerings.

Stairways
These stepped paths along the cliff rise
200 m (600 ft) above the sea.

★ **Main Gate**
The unusual arched doorway has the shape of Meru, the Cosmic Mountain of Hinduism. Surmounting it are three finials and a *kala* head – this is a fanged demon with bulging eyes, thought to ward off evil spirits.

VISITORS' CHECKLIST

Practical Information
End of Jalan Uluwatu.
Road Map B5. **Open** 6am–7pm daily. **Closed** for festivals.
Kecak dance: 6pm daily.
temple anniversary (based on Balinese calendar).

Transport

Guardian Statues
These Ganesha, elephant-headed guardian statues, wearing a belt with a clasp in the form of a cyclops, are masterpieces of Balinese sculpture.

★ **Candi Bentar**
At the top of the stairs leading to the temple is a *candi bentar* (split gate) decorated with elaborate carvings.

② ③ ④ ⑤

Entrance

CENTRAL BALI

Bali's broad southern slopes, with their terraced ricefields and hundreds of villages, were the cradle of traditional Balinese society. This area coincides with the regency (and former kingdom) of Gianyar, made up of many *puri* (noble houses) whose former glory lives on in the courtly arts of sculpture, painting, gold- and silversmithing, music, dance and theatrical performance.

Gianyar is bounded on its western side by the tumultuous Ayung River and to the east by the Melangit River. A number of other rivers slice through the intervening landscape. Between the Petanu and Pakrisan rivers are the remains of one of Bali's oldest civilizations. Here is the village of Ubud, a cultural centre and former kingdom, which attracts many visitors today.

From the 9th to the 11th century, Bali was ruled by Hindu-Buddhist kingdoms centred near present-day Pejeng and Bedulu, a short distance from Ubud. After the Majapahit conquest in the 14th century, power shifted to Klungkung but it returned here in the 18th century. At that time branches of the Klungkung dynasty grew into rival kingdoms, two of which were based in Sukawati and Gianyar.

Satellite *puri* competed in architectural and ritual display.

Inter-kingdom warfare at the end of the 19th century gave Ubud much of Gianyar's land. Politically, Puri Gianyar remained on top, partly because of its early incorporation into the Dutch colonial regime.

Ubud became internationally famous as a gateway into Bali's cultural heartland, when several Western artists and intellectuals settled here in the 1930s. Today, many farmers are turning to tourism and handicrafts for economic reasons. Local cultural traditions are being preserved as a consequence.

The climate of Central Bali cools noticeably as one ascends from the coastal region into the foothills, and can be chilly north of Tegallalang.

cred Hindu temple, or *pura*, in Ubud

oly springs *(tirta empul)* at a Balinese temple

Exploring Central Bali

Central Bali, rich in history, is famous for craft production and the performing arts. Ubud is an important artistic centre, and a good base for exploring the area. Many other villages and monuments of historic and cultural interest are located on the roads running between the coastal plain and the slopes of Gunung Batur. The river gorges, separated by ridges and rice terraces, provide beautiful landscapes, and exciting white-water rafting. Near Singapadu are the attractively laid-out Bali Bird Park and Bali Reptile Park.

Pura Pengastulan, a temple in Bedulu

Getting Around

The main route through Central Bali leads through several arts and crafts villages: Batubulan, Celuk, Sukawati, Batuan, Mas and Ubud. A parallel, more westerly road runs through Singapadu. Most of these roads can be travelled by *bemo*. Taxis are not as frequent as in South Bali. North of Ubud three parallel roads climb, via the villages of Payangan, Tegallalang and Tampaksiring towards Gunung Batur and Kintamani. Bicycles and motorcycles are not pleasant ways of travelling on main roads south of Ubud, because of the density of traffic, although they are more satisfactory further north and on back roads. Public buses between Denpasar and Singaraja ply the main north–south route; however, tourist shuttle buses run frequently between South Bali's resorts and Ubud, and are much more comfortable.

For hotels and restaurants in this region see p175 and pp184–5

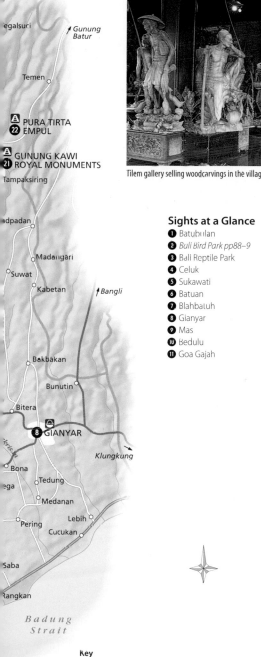

Tilem gallery selling woodcarvings in the village of Mas

Sights at a Glance

1 Batubulan
2 *Bali Bird Park pp88–9*
3 Bali Reptile Park
4 Celuk
5 Sukawati
6 Batuan
7 Blahbatuh
8 Gianyar
9 Mas
10 Bedulu
11 Goa Gajah

12 *Ubud pp92–99*
13 Peliatan
14 Sanggingan
15 Ayung River Gorge
16 Pejeng
17 Petulu
18 Tegallalang
19 Sebatu
20 Taro
21 Gunung Kawi Royal Monuments
22 Pura Tirta Empul

0 kilometres   3
0 miles   2

Coconuts being collected near Ubud

Key

━ Dual carriageway
━ Major road
━ Minor road
━ Regency boundary

For keys to symbols *see back flap*

Keris trance, one of the energetic ritual dance performances which can be seen in Batubulan

❶ Batubulan

Road Map C4. 🚌 *i* Gianyar, (0366) 93 401. 🖵 🏠 ♿

Although Denpasar's urban sprawl is enveloping Batubulan and the main road is lined with shops selling "antique" furniture, this large village is still a centre of traditional stone carving. Craftsmen can be seen in countless workshops sculpting mythological and religious figures or highly imaginative modern forms, apparently oblivious to the heavy traffic passing by on the main road.

The village temple, **Pura Puseh**, is a good example of the use of *paras*, Bali's ubiquitous grey stone, which is in fact volcanic tuff, quarried from river gorges. *Paras* is used both for sculpture and as a building material. Its soft texture makes it very easy to carve.

Batubulan is also home to several venerable Barong and keris dance theatre troupes. During alternate weeks the Pura Puseh is the pleasant venue of a daily Barong and keris dance performance by the celebrated **Denjalan** troupe; in intervening weeks the location is Batubulan's *bale banjar*, or community pavilion. A few other troupes perform at around the same time. Daytime performances were developed in the 1930s, in response to the desire of

visitors to take photographs. However, this exorcistic drama still has ritual significance.

🅰 Pura Puseh
Main Road, Batubulan. **Open** daily. 🏛 donation.

🎭 Denjalan
Tel (0361) 298 038 or (0361) 298 282. Performances: 9:30am daily. 🏛

❷ Bali Bird Park

See pp88–9.

❸ Bali Reptile Park

Jalan Serma Cok Ngurah Gambir, Singapadu. Next to Bali Bird Park. **Road Map** D4. **Tel** (0361) 299 344. **Open** daily. **Closed** Nyepi.
🅿 🖵 🏠 🛝

A visit to the Bali Reptile Park (Rimba Reptil) is combined with a visit to the Bali Bird Park next door, with a single entrance ticket. The two are conceived in a similar style. Although somewhat smaller in area than the Bird Park, the Reptile Park is also set in lush, botanically interesting gardens. The landscaping concept is that of an ancient archaeological site, excavated and restored to its former glory. All the significant reptile species of

Indonesia can be seen in the collection. They include Komodo dragons, four species of crocodiles, and what is claimed to be the largest known python in captivity. Many venomous snakes from around the world are well displayed in glass cages. Among them are a king cobra, a Malayan pit viper and a death adder.

❹ Celuk

Road Map D4. 🚌 *i* Gianyar, (0361) 943 401. 🖵 🏠 ♿ (limited).

The village of Celuk is devoted almost entirely to gold- and silversmithing. Much of the jewellery sold in Bali originates here. The workers belong to the caste clan of Pande Mas, traditionally practitioners of various metal crafts. Grand jewellery shops line the main road; smaller ones selling cheaper goods occupy the narrow side streets. Several studios produce traditional and modern designs of ornamental jewellery as well as *keris* daggers and religious items. Jewellery can be made to order. Buyers should be aware that at the larger outlets, prices may include a commission (often 40–60 per cent) passed on to tour guides.

Silver earrings from Celuk

❺ Sukawati

Road Map D4. 🚌 *i* Gianyar, (0361) 973 285. 🅿 🏠 ♿ (limited).

Sukawati is worth visiting primarily as a handicrafts centre. Opposite the farmers' market on the east side of the main road through the town is the **Pasar Seni** ("Art Market"). It is housed in a complex of two-storey buildings and is packed with stalls selling craft goods. Behind it is a market selling woodcarvings, open until 10am daily.

To the people of Bali, Sukawati is important as the ancestral seat of many of the region's *puri* (noble houses), and as a centre of the sacred shadow puppet theatre, *wayang kulit (see p35)*. In the early 1700s an offshoot of the royal house of Klungkung was established here. The palace, on the northeast corner of the main intersection, is much reduced; and the temples, further north on the main road and nestling in side streets to the east, are not generally open to visitors.

Stone sculptures of mythological figures in a shop at Sukawati

❻ Batuan

Road Map D4. 🚌 *i* Gianyar, (0366) 93 401. 🅿 🏠 ♿ (limited).

The history of Batuan goes back almost 1,000 years. The population contains more nobility than commoners; and it is celebrated for its artistic excellence not only in the field [of] dance but also in painting [and] architecture. Painters' [work]s are prominent in the

village. The Batuan school of painting is known for its dense graphics, dramatically restricted colour palette and astute observation of human life *(see pp38–9)*.

The **Pura Puseh**, the magnificent village temple, welcomes visitors. Extensively renovated, its opulent shrines and carvings are proof that Bali's traditional building arts are thriving. *Gambuh* performances are held at the temple on the 1st and 15th of each month, a rare opportunity to see this ancient court dance. Among the dance troupes of Batuan are practitioners also of *topeng* and *wayang wong (see p35)*. These are, like *gambuh*, performed to traditional music during temple festivals.

🅰 **Pura Puseh**
Open daily. 🎨 donation.
🎭 Gambuh dance: 7–9pm, 1st & 15th monthly. ♿

❼ Blahbatuh

Road Map D4. 🚌 *i* Gianyar, (0366) 93 401. 🅿 🏠 ♿ (limited).

The village of Blahbatuh is marked by a huge stone statue of a baby, which was erected in the early 1990s and said by some to be the village giant Kebo Iwa as an infant. Others whisper that the women of a nearby village urged their husbands to build the statue to placate a demon who they believed had been claiming the lives of their children.

Vihara Amurva Bhumi Blahbatuh, a large Chinese temple *(klenteng)* with Buddhist and Hindu elements which has undergone grand expansion, is a little-known but increasingly popular centre of worship for Chinese Buddhists from throughout South Bali.

Giant baby statue near Blahbatuh

Environs

On the main north–south road between Blahbatuh and the Bedulu road is the large workshop and showroom of the **Sidha Karya Gong Foundry**, established by the renowned gongsmith I Made Gabeleran. A full array of traditional musical instruments and dance costumes is on sale here.

At **Kutri**, 3 km (2 miles) north of Blahbatuh, is a hill at the base of which is the temple complex **Pura Bukit Dharma Kutri**. On the hilltop, from which there are good views, is a shrine that houses a partly effaced, but still fine, relief carving of the goddess Durga killing a bull. It is thought to be a portrait statue of an 11th-century Balinese queen.

Kemenuh, 1.5 km (1 mile) west of Blahbatuh, is a woodcarving centre where you can see woodcarvers at work and choose from a selection of ritual and ornamental pieces including effigies, masks and statues.

🅰 **Vihara Amurva Bhumi Blahbatuh**
Blahbatuh. **Open** daily. 👥

🏛 **Sidha Karya**
Jalan Raya Getas-Buruan, Blahbatuh. **Tel** (0361) 942 798.

🅰 **Pura Bukit Dharma Kutri**
Kutri. **Open** daily. 👥

Pura Bukit Dharma Kutri, a temple named after a hill near Blahbatuh

ali Bird Park

lt on what was originally an expanse of ricefields, Bali Bird
ark, or Taman Burung, is a place where visitors can see a
pr...sion of exotic wildlife at close quarters. There are almost
1,000 birds here, many of them in big, walk-in aviaries. There
are 250 species not only from Bali and Lombok, but also from
the rest of Indonesia, Kiira, Australia and the Americas. Many
of the birds are rare and endangered, and some of these are
bred here. Among the inhabitants is Bali's only endemic bird,
the Bali starling (see p141). Besides the birds, there are more
than 300 exotic trees and plants on display in a beautifully
landscaped setting.

★ **Birds of Paradise**
The lesser bird of paradise, from
New Guinea, has been hunted
close to extinction.

★ **Papua Rainforest Aviary**
This huge, walk-in aviary has a raised
walkway. The birds here include many
birds of paradise, the toco toucan, and
sun conures from South America.

Australian Pelican
This large waterbird
sometimes wanders as far
as Indonesia.

Victoria Crowned Pigeon
This aviary has one of the three
crowned pigeon species from
New Guinea; also the Nicorbar
pigeon; the pink-necked pigeon;
and the great argus pheasant.

Indonesian Owls

These nocturnal birds can rarely be seen in
the wild and the buffy fish owl and the
barred or Sumatran eagle owl are therefore
a highlight of the Bali Bird Park. They are
both large and feed on rodents. In all
there are 38 recognized species of
Indonesian owl – many of them found
only on small islands. Their secretive
nature and, in some cases, preference
for inhospitable habitats are reasons
why little is known about them.

Buffy fish owl

KEY

① Bali Aviary
② Entrance to Bali Reptile Park
③ Live shows
④ Breeding centre
⑤ Birds of South America
⑥ Parrots and cockatoos
⑦ Cassoary enclosure

Birds of Bali
The Bali Starling (*Leucopsar rothschildi*) is Bali's only surviving indigenous bird. An endangered species, it is being bred here.

Hornbills
The Asian pied hornbill has a very distinct, loud, raucous call.

Entrance

⑦

⑥

②

Ⓟ

③

④

⑤

0 metres 50
0 yards 50

★ **Turaja House**
This typical house from Sulawesi is nearly 100 years old. It was dismantled, moved and re-assembled here.

Major Mitchell's Cockatoo
Apart from this species from Australia, several parrots and cockatoos native to Indonesia (of which there are over 75 species) are bred in this bird park.

The African Grey Parrot
This species can often be trained to mimic.

Puri Gianyar, a palace of the royal family of the former kingdom of Gianyar, restored to its past glory

🖈 Gianyar

Road Map D4. 🚌 *i* Jalan Ngurah Rai 21, (0361) 973 285. 🖿 🏠 🖾 (limited). 🖾

This town is a centre of administration rather than of the tourist industry. The people of Bali shop here for farm produce, household appliances and paraphernalia for ceremonies; there is also a large market. This is a good place to buy jewellery and hand-woven and hand-dyed textiles, many of them made locally. During the day, there are food stalls at the Bale Banjar Teges (community association meeting hall) at the town centre; the *babi guling* (roast pig) is famous.

On the north side of the town square is the impressive **Puri Gianyar**. Although the palace is closed to visitors, its grand outer walls and gates give a sense of the power of

Local food stalls at the night market in Gianyar

the former kingdoms. After damage by an earthquake in 1917, the *puri* was restored as a replica of the original 17th-century construction.

Environs
Southwest of Gianyar are several villages whose livelihood is increasingly based on craft products from plant materials. Although these are sold for export and in shops around Bali, visitors can buy for better prices at source.
Bona, 3 km (2 miles) southwest of Gianyar, specializes in hand-woven objects made from the leaves of the lontar palm. About 2 km (1 mile) southwest of Bona is the village of **Blega**, which is a centre for the production of bamboo furniture.

🖈 Mas

Road Map D4. 🚌
i Gianyar, (0361) 973 285.
🖾 🖿 🏠 🖾 (limited). 🖾

The village of Mas is most famous not for teak furniture, as the number of roadside shops selling it might suggest,

but for fine wood sculpture and *topeng* masks (see p35). The brahmans of Mas have been master-carvers for many generations; sculpture has been produced for the art market since the 1930s (see pp40–41). Among the best-established studio-galleries are Siadja & Son, the Njana Tilem Gallery and Adil Artshop. Tantra Gallery and I B Anom (for masks) are well known. Brahmans come to Mas from all over Bali every Manis Kuningan festival (see p47) to honour their ancestor, the Hindu priest Dang Hyang Nirartha (also known as Dwijendra) at the temple **Pura Taman Pule**. The large old tree in the temple is regarded as holy. According to local belief, a gold flower once grew from it. The tree is dressed up in ceremonial colours during the festival. On the evening of the festivities there is usually a ritual performance of *wayang wong* (see p35).

Elaborately carved gateway at Pura Taman Pule, Mas

🅰 Pura Taman Pule
Open daily. 🖾 *Wayang wong*: during festivals. 🖾 Kuningan (see p47).

⑩ Bedulu

Road Map D3. 🚌 ℹ️ Gianyar, (0361) 973 285. 🛵 🖥️ 🦽 (limited).

This large, quiet village was at the centre of the Pejeng kingdom of the 10–13th centuries. The monumental relief carvings on a large rock wall at the **Yeh Pulu** spring, south of the village, are thought to date from the mid-14th-century Majapahit conquest *(see p50)*. The carvings – about 25 m (80 ft) long with an average height of 2 m (6 ft) – are thought to be the work of a single artist. Myth attributes the work to the legendary 14th-century giant Kebo Iwo. The stories can be "read" by looking at the vigorously carved images from left to right. Among them are heroic scenes showing humans fighting demonic beasts.

The large **Pura Pengastulan** temple *(see p84)* has grand gates built in the Art Deco style made fashionable by the artist I Gusti Nyoman Lempad *(see p38)*, who was born in Bedulu.

The village of Bedulu decorated for the Galungan festival

Lempad's style may be seen also in the nearby **Pura Samuan Tiga**. This name derives from a legend. In the 11th century, a meeting *(samuan)* is said to have been held here among the gods of three *(tiga)* warring religious sects after they had defeated the demon king Mayadanawa.

The annual festival around Purnama Kedasa *(see p44)* is a brilliant 11-day celebration; but even when empty, Pura Samuan Tiga has a great, quiet strength. The grand inner gate by Lempad is particularly impressive, as is the cockfighting pit on the east side of the first courtyard.

🚌 Yeh Pulu
Open daily. 🅿️ donation.

🅰️ Pura Pengastulan
Open daily. 🅿️

🅰️ Pura Samuan Tiga
Open daily. 🅿️ donation. 🎭 Perang Sampian: 1pm during festival. 🎭 Purnama Kedasa (Apr, variable).

Carved rocks at the entrance to Goa Gajah, the "Elephant Cave"

⑪ Goa Gajah

Bedulu. **Road Map** D3. 🚌 ℹ️ Gianyar, (0361) 973 285. **Open** daily. 🅿️ 🖥️ 🅿️ 🦽

The Goa Gajah ("Elephant Cave") became known to Westerners only in 1923. It is thought to date from the 11th century. Steps lead down to the temple and other monuments, about 15 m (50 ft) below road level. The large springs, excavated in 1954, were intended probably for bathing and as a source of holy water. The cave itself, with a large face in the exuberantly carved surrounding rock, is a small, rather airless, T-shaped chamber in which are niches containing Shivite and Buddhist statues.

Outside the cave is a shrine to the Buddhist child-protector Hariti, depicted as the Balinese Men Brayut, a poor woman with too many children. In a ravine a little to the south is a spring and more shrines.

The Legend of Bedaulu

The name Bedulu comes from the 14th-century sorcerer-king Bedaulu, who was said to remove his head *(hulu)* to achieve more efficient meditation. One day he was disturbed in this practice and hastily took the head of a passing pig *(beda* means "different"). Thereafter it was forbidden to look at the king, lest his ugly secret be discovered, and he ruled from a tower, raised above eye level. However, the Majapahit general Gajah Mada tricked him during a feast. As Gajah Mada tipped back his head to drink, he looked up, glimpsed the king's true nature and so was able to overpower him.

The King of Bedulu in his Tower (1934) by I Tomblos

⑫ Street-by-Street: Ubud

Almost everywhere in Ubud one is conscious of the town's artistic traditions. Since most shops stay open until around 9pm, the best time for strolling around is the early evening. By then the traffic has abated, the cafés and restaurants are invitingly lit, and the cool air is often filled with *gamelan* music from cultural performances. The main street, Jalan Raya Ubud, is the setting for several buildings of architectural interest. The streets running off it to the north and south lead to village neighbourhoods, and are lined with family-run shops, small businesses catering for visitors, and art galleries.

Pura Taman Saraswati is a stunning temple set by a lotus pond.

★ Museum Puri Lukisan
A fine collection of Balinese art is displayed here *(see pp96–7)*.

Ary's Warung
restaurant is run by a minor Ubud palace family, on land either side of the house gate.

Monkey Forest Road
is lined with galleries, restaurants and hotels.

To Monkey Forest Sanctuary

Influential Visitors of the 1930s

Bali owes much of its fame to foreign guests of Ubud's royal family in the 1920s and 1930s. Through their films, books and photographs, these visitors projected to the world an exotic image of Bali. Among the most influential were German painter and musician Walter Spies and Dutch painter Rudolf Bonnet, who helped found the Pita Maha artists' association *(see p39)*; and Mexican artist Miguel Covarrubias, who wrote the classic *Island of Bali* (1937). The anthropologists Margaret Mead and Gregory Bateson lived in Sayan, just outside Ubud; their neighbours were composer Colin McPhee and his wife, ethnographer Jane Belo.

Walter Spies, who settled in Ubud in 1927

0 metres 100
0 yards 100

Key

— Suggested route

★ **Puri Saren**
Ubud's palace has a shady forecourt where visitors can relax during the day and see traditional dance every evening.

VISITORS' CHECKLIST

Practical Information
Road Map C3. **i** Ubud Tourist Information, Jalan Raya Ubud, (0361) 973 285. Balinese performances: daily, details posted at Ubud.

Transport
from Denpasar & Kuta

Ubud Tourist Information Centre

The *wantilan* is a hall where locals can gather and cultural events take place.

★ **Pasar Ubud**
A produce market takes place here in the morning. Shops and stalls sell all kinds of crafts, snacks and sundries throughout the day.

JALAN SUWETA

JALAN RAYA UBUD

JALAN SRIWEDARI

To Peliatan and Bedulu

JALAN GAUTAMA

JALAN HANOMAN

Lempad House was once an artist's home and studio *(see p94)*.

JALAN DEWI SITA

To Pengosekan, Batubulan and Denpasar

Jalan Dewi Sita is a street brimming with popular boutiques, art galleries and restaurants.

Jalan Hanoman
Temples, shops, art studios and homestays can be found here.

Exploring Ubud

Ubud has long been known as the "village of painters". In the 1930s, the encouragement of the *puri* (royal family) attracted foreign artists and intellectuals seeking the "real Bali", and so the village's international reputation was born. A peaceful hamlet until the 1980s, Ubud developed rapidly into a village of "cultural tourism". Now it is a small town, packed with galleries, craft shops, restaurants, bars and hotels. However, Ubud spends much of its prosperity on ritual ceremonies and conservation of traditional art forms.

A palace gate in Puri Saren

ℹ️ Ubud Tourist Information Centre
Jalan Raya Ubud. **Tel** (0361) 973 285. **Open** daily.
The centre is a reliable source of information about tours, transport, dance performances, and current cultural events. It provides information about local ceremonies and encourages foreigners to observe dress etiquette when visiting temples or rituals *(see p214)*.

🏛️ Museum Puri Lukisan
See pp96–7.

🏛️ Pura Taman Saraswati
Jalan Raya Ubud. **Open** daily.
This temple was built in the 1950s by I Gusti Nyoman Lempad *(see p38)* at the command of Ubud's prince, in honour of Saraswati, the deity of learning and the arts. It is set in a water garden, with a lotus pond as the centrepiece. The temple has fine carvings by Lempad: a 3-m (10-ft) statue of the demon Jero Gede Mecaling; and the *padmasana* shrine in the northeast corner, dedicated

to the Supreme God *(see p30)*. The temple is normally closed, but admission may be gained via the adjacent Café Lotus.

🏛️ Puri Saren
Jalan Raya Ubud. **Tel** (0361) 975 057.
📺 Traditional dances 7:30pm daily.
🌐 ubudvillage.com
The grandeur of Ubud's royal palace dates from the 1890s, the time of warlord Cokorda Gede Sukawati. The present walls and resplendent gates are largely the work of master artist I Gusti Nyoman Lempad *(see p38)*. The *puri*, which owns several hotels, remains influential in Ubud's religious and cultural life, and spends lavishly on local ceremonies.

🛍️ Pasar Ubud
Jalan Raya Ubud. **Open** daily.
At the huge Pasar Ubud (Ubud Market) there are sellers of agricultural produce and dry goods on the ground floor and between the buildings. The main attraction for visitors is the all-day handicraft market. The food market is held every three days on *pasah*.

🏛️ Lempad House
Jalan Raya Ubud. **Tel** (0361) 975 618. **Open** daily.
This is the family compound of I Gusti Nyoman Lempad *(see p38)*, perhaps Bali's most celebrated artist. Some works by Lempad are on display in the courtyard, although the Neka Art Museum *(see p100)* holds a better collection of his work. Lempad was also an architect and builder in the traditional style, and the handsome north and east pavilions of the house were designed by him.

A group of woodcarvers at work near the Lempad House

Pondok Pekak Library and Learning Center
East side of the football field, Monkey Forest Rd. Tel (0361) 976 194.
Open Mon–Sat. 🌐 pondokpekak library.com 📧
The library here has more than 30,000 books, including bestsellers, philosophy titles and memoirs. The learning centre offers travellers private classes in traditional Balinese art and culture, such as dance, *gamelan*, Balinese offerings, fruit carving, silver jewellery making, woodcarving, masks and other crafts.

Pura Taman Saraswati facing Café Lotus across an ornamental pond

A Pura Gunung Lebah

Campuhan.

To the west of Ubud, Jalan Raya descends into the valley known as **Campuhan**, where two rivers meet *(campuh)*. A bridge built by the colonial Dutch survives next to the modern traffic bridge. From it can be seen the spring temple Pura Gunung Lebah (Pura Campuhan), which was founded in the 8th century. This has been a foreigners' residential neighbourhood since the 1930s, when Walter Spies *(see p92)* built his house at what is now the Tjampuhan Hotel and Spa.

Environs

At the end of a long street known as Monkey Forest Road is the **Monkey Forest Sanctuary**, offering protection to three troupes of long-tailed

A long-tail macaque in the Monkey Forest Sanctuary

Coconut palms surrounding rice plantations in the valley west of Ubud

monkeys *(Macaca fascicularis)*. It is advisable not to feed the monkeys – they can become aggressive. In the forest, there is an important temple complex and a graveyard. The large **Pura Dalem Agung** is a "temple of the dead"; its carved decorations are appropriately frightening. Close by is a spring temple, renovated in the 1990s with extra carvings.

Padang Tegal, on the southern outskirts of Ubud, is a large village notable for its many painters and intellectuals; it

offers numerous homestays. South of Padang Tegal is the small village of **Pengosekan**, home to many painters and woodcarvers. In the village of **Tebesaya**, east of Padang Tegal, there are many good places to eat, shop and stay. West of Pengosekan is **Nyuh Kuning**, a woodcarving centre.

Monkey Forest Sanctuary
Monkey Forest Road, Jalan Wana Wanara. **Tel** (0361) 971 304.
Open 8am–6pm daily.
W monkeyforestubud.com

Ubud

① Museum Puri Lukisan
② Pura Taman Saraswati
③ Puri Saren
④ Pasar Ubud
⑤ Lempad House
⑥ Pondok Pekak Library and Learning Center
⑦ Pura Gunung Lebah (Pura Campuhan)

0 metres   300
0 yards   300

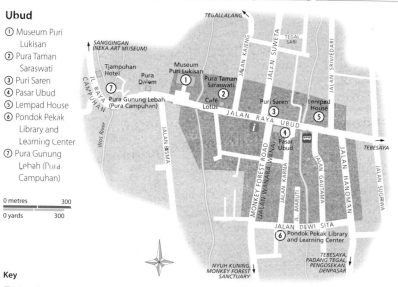

Key

Street-by-street *see pp92–3*

Ubud: Museum Puri Lukisan

Museum Puri Lukisan ("Palace of Painting"), was the brainchild of Ubud's prince Cokorda Gede Agung Sukawati, and Dutch painter Rudolf Bonnet *(see p92)*. It was conceived in 1953 out of concern that Bali's finest works of art were disappearing into private collections around the world. The museum's holdings are mainly 20th-century Balinese painting and wood sculpture, including important collections from the 1930s. The grounds, with their gardens and ponds, are a shady, tranquil oasis in the centre of Ubud.

★ Octopus (1955)
I Gusti Made Deblog is known for his fine ink-wash technique.

Dharmaswami (1935)
This work by Ida Bagus Gelgel is in the Balinese tradition of painting fables and tales.

★ Dewi Sri (1960)
The woodcarver Ketut Djedeng depicts the rice goddess with a grain of rice in her hand.

Birds Dancing the Gambuh (1940)
A bas-relief showing the *gambuh* dance inspired this painting by Ida Bagus Sali.

For hotels and restaurants in this region see p175 and pp184–5

Looking at Balinese Paintings

The density of Balinese painting is extraordinary. Even with little or no background in the arts, the viewer can enter the imaginative world of Balinese culture as represented by both traditional and modern painting. It is a good idea to look at a Balinese work from a distance at first, to see its graphic composition before moving nearer to inspect the details of the content. Close inspection reveals tiny scenes being enacted by the inhabitants of the canvas.

Tiger with Monkey (undated), artist unknown

VISITORS' CHECKLIST

Practical Information
Jalan Raya Ubud.
Tel (0361) 971 159.
Open 9am–5pm daily.
Closed public hols. 🎫 🏛 🏧
Ⓦ **museumpurilukisan.com**

Gallery Guide

Building I houses woodcarving and pre-World War II painting, including the Pita Maha and Lempad collections (see pp38–9). Building II has contemporary Balinese art. Temporary exhibitions are housed in Building III.

③

④

★ **Balinese Market**
(detail, 1955) Anak Agung Gede Sobrat, a leading Ubud school painter, explores a modern theme here.

Parking

Entrance steps

KEY

① **Building I**
② **Building II**
③ **Building III**
④ **Ticket office**

★ **Kala Rau** *(1974)*
I Ketut Budiana, of Padang Tegal, Ubud, paints the lunar eclipse of Balinese myth.

A Walk in the Ubud Countryside

The ricefields and ridges around Ubud are very suitable for walking. Two routes are shown here. They can be followed separately, or one after the other. The ricefield walk is 6 km (4 miles) long but can be shortened to 4 km (nearly 3 miles) by omitting the northern loop. The 9 km (5 mile) ridge walk runs between two rivers, the Wos Timur and the Wos Barat. Walkers may cross ricefields provided they behave with due consideration. Wildlife sightings may include the iridescent blue Java kingfisher among other birds, the golden orb weaver spider, and a colourful variety of butterflies.

View from Pura Ulun Sui

⑬ Jalan Raya Sanggingan
On this busy road, *bemo* transport can be found back into central Ubud.

⑫ Bridge
Near the bottom of the gorge, a bridge crosses the river to a steep road leading up to the village of Payogan.

⑪ Warung in Artists' Settlement
A small, isolated community of painters lives in this village, from which there are dramatic views along the Wos River gorges. Further north the landscape opens up to reveal ricefields.

⑩ Sari Organic Restaurant
A walk through the picturesque ricefields leads to this eatery, which uses organic ingredients to prepare dishes.

⑨ Alang Alang Grass
After Pura Campuhan, a setting for some important religious ceremonies, the path continues through alang alang, a grass used for thatching roofs.

⑧ Large Banyan Tree
The ridge walk starts near the Ibah Luxury Villas, leading past an old banyan tree to a footbridge hanging over the river gorge.

Bangkiang Sider

Payogan

Kedewatan

Sanggingan

Campuhan

Key

-- Ricefield walk route

-- Ridge walk route

▬ Major road

═ Minor road

═ Track

⑤ Rice Harvest
According to the season, rice farmers may be planting or harvesting. Across a narrow bridge carrying irrigation water is an attractive *subak* temple *(see pp24–5)*.

④ Pura Pejenenang
Crossing the Wos Timur River to this temple cuts off the northern part of the walk, creating an optional shorter route.

⑥ Pura Ulun Carik
From here there is a view of the Wos Timur gorge, where chestnut and black coucal birds abound.

③ Ricefield Shrines
Offerings are placed at these shrines to the rice goddess, who will bless the growing crops.

⑦ Jalan Raya Ubud
The path back to the main road passes a palace complex.

② Pura Ulun Sui
This is also known as Juwukmanis Temple. Adjacent to it is a *subak* office with a map explaining the irrigation system of Bali.

Tips for Walkers

Starting point: Café Lotus, in Ubud.
End point: Jalan Raya Sanggingan.
When to go: All year, but in the wet season, trails can be slippery.
Precautions: River gorges are prone to flash flooding and should be crossed by the bridges. Do not descend into gorges without an experienced guide. Avoid the small trails down to the stone quarries in the Wos River gorge – they are slippery and prone to landslides. Care should be taken walking along the edges of ricefields. Walking shoes and trainers are suitable footwear.

0 metres 500
0 yards 500

① Café Lotus
The ricefield walk starts at Café Lotus in central Ubud, running north along Jalan Kajeng towards the ricefields.

Ubud

Wos Timur River

Mumbul River

The south pavilion of the Agung Rai Museum of Art, Peliatan

❶ Peliatan

Road Map D3. 🚌 📞 from Ubud.
ℹ️ Ubud, (0361) 973 285. 🎭 *Kecak,*
Legong and *Barong* dance; women's
gamelan. 📷 💷 🏛️ 🛍️

The village of Peliatan, once the
seat of an offshoot of the royalty
of Sukawati, is renowned for
artistic activities. It was known
among foreigners for its artistic
traditions even earlier than
Ubud. Today, Peliatan's *gamelan*
and dance troupes *(see pp34–7)*
travel abroad as cultural
ambassadors, and perform
locally in traditional rituals
and for visitors.
 Peliatan is also a centre of
painting and woodcarving.
Many artists' studios can be
found along its main street and
back lanes. The collector Agung
Rai established the successful
Agung Rai Gallery and the
impressive **Agung Rai Museum
of Art** (usually referred to as
ARMA), in southwest Peliatan,
which has collections of
classical and contemporary
Balinese and Indonesian
painting as well as temporary
exhibitions. The Rudana

Museum houses an extensive
painting collection.
 The northern part of Peliatan,
known as Andong, has some
interesting craft shops.

🏛️ **Arma**
Jalan Pengosekan. **Tel** (0361) 975 742.
Open daily. 🅿️ 🛍️ 🍴 💷
🌐 **armamuseum.com**

🏛️ **Rudana Museum**
Jalan Cok Rai Pudak 44.
(0361) 975 779. **Open** daily. 🅿️

❶ Sanggingan

Road Map C3. 🚌 from Ubud.
ℹ️ Ubud, (0361) 973 285. 📷 💷
🏛️ 🛍️

The road running through the
village of Sanggingan is lined
with art shops, art galleries,
restaurants and small hotels.
 The excellent **Neka Art
Museum**, founded in 1976 by
local collector and former
teacher Sutéja Neka, houses one
of the best collections
of Balinese and Indonesian
paintings on the island. The
collection is displayed in seven
buildings numbered according

to the chronological sequence
of the works displayed. Moving
through the buildings gives a
good overview of Balinese art
history and its Indonesian
context today. Some works are
offered for sale. Of particular
interest to visitors are the
classical *wayang*-style paintings,
anonymous works of great
graphic sophistication; and also
the Lempad collection *(see p38)*,
consisting of superb pen-and-
ink drawings.

🏛️ **Neka Art Museum**
Jalan Raya Campuhan.
Tel (0361) 975 074. **Open** daily.
Closed public hols. 🅿️ 🛍️ 💷 🚻
🌐 **museumneka.com**

Portrait of Sutéja Neka (1991) by Arie Smit,
Neka Art Museum

❶ Ayung River Gorge

Road Map C3. 🚌 from Ubud.
ℹ️ Ubud, (0361) 973 285. 📷 🏛️ 🛍️

Between Kedewatan and Sayan,
the east bank of the
spectacularly beautiful Ayung
River Gorge, flanked by rice
terraces, is discreetly populated

The Ayung River Gorge viewed from the ridge at Sayan village

White-water rafting in the rapids of the Ayung River Gorge

with some attractive luxury hotels and private houses. Several companies offer white-water rafting from points on both sides of the river (see p199).

Environs
In the village of **Penestanan**, just east of the Gorge, there are studios making painted batik and beadwork. This is also the centre of the Young Artists movement (see p39) which emerged in the 1960s.

⑯ Pejeng

Road Map D3. 🚌 from Ubud & Gianyar. 🛈 Ubud, (0361) 973 285.
🚗 🖼 🍴 ♨ 🛍

Pejeng, a village on the road from Bedulu to Tampaksiring, lies at the heart of the ancient Pejeng-Bedulu kingdom, and there are many interesting relics from that time to be seen. The **Museum Purbakala** (Archaeological Museum) displays prehistoric objects in bronze, stone and ceramics, including several turtle-shaped stone sarcophagi.

A short walk from the museum are three temples of particular interest for their sacred stone sculptures. **Pura Arjuna Metapa** ("Arjuna Meditating" Temple) is a small pavilion standing alone in the ricefields, sheltering a cluster of stone sculptures that were probably once part of a spring temple. In accordance with the *wayang* tradition that recounts tales from the *Mahabharata*, Arjuna is attended by a stone-relief servant character. About 100 m (110 yards) north is **Pura Kebo Edan** ("Crazy Giant" Temple). The demonic statuary suggests that this was a cult-

Woodcarving in Bali
The surprising abundance of Balinese woodcarving reflects not only an intense decorative tradition but also the fact that Bali's wilderness is forest (still inhabited by tigers in the early 20th century). Trees have a ritual anniversary and must be given offerings before being felled. Traditional woodcarving is of two main sorts: ritual objects such as effigies and masks; and ornamental carving, especially of architectural elements. The liberalizing art movement of the 1930s (see pp38–9) encouraged woodcarvers to sculpt freely for a foreign market. The main centres of woodcarving today include Peliatan and several other villages in Gianyar regency, including Tegallalang (see p102) and Mas (see p90).

Sleeping Woman (1956), by Ida Bagus Njana

temple of Bhairava Buddhism. The chief figure is a masked 3.6 m- (12 ft-) high giant, dancing on a corpse. The beautifully proportioned **Pura Pusering Jagat** ("Navel of the World" Temple) has numerous pavilions housing similar tantric stone figures. The "Pejeng Vessel", a cylindrical stone urn carved with cosmological figures, is kept in a shrine in the southeastern corner of the temple.

About 2 km (1 mile) north of Pejeng, **Pura Penataran Sasih** houses the "Pejeng Moon" (*sasih* means moon), a bronze drum 186 cm (74 inches) long, of unknown age. Considered sacred, it is kept in a tall pavilion. Temple guides sometimes encourage visitors to stand on the base of an adjacent shrine; from here, you can glimpse the drum's fine geometric patterning. The design is associated with the

Dong-son culture of southern China and northern Vietnam of around 1500 BC.

🏛 **Museum Purbakala**
Pejeng. **Tel** (0361) 942 347. **Open** 8am–4pm Mon–Fri. 🖼 donation.

🅰 **Pura Arjuna Metapa**
Across the road from Museum. **Open** daily 🖼 donation.

🅰 **Pura Kebo Edan**
Pejeng. **Open** daily. 🖼 donation.

🅰 **Pura Pusering Jagat**
Pejeng. **Open** daily. 🖼 donation.

🅰 **Pura Penataran Sasih**
Pejeng. **Open** daily. 🖼 donation. 📷

⑰ Petulu

Road Map D3. 🚌 from Ubud & Pujung. 🛈 Ubud, (0361) 973 285.

This village is known for its white-plumed egrets and Java pond egrets, generically called *kokokan* in Balinese. It is not known why the birds suddenly settled in Petulu in 1965. According to local legend, they are the souls of the estimated 80,000 Balinese killed during the anti-communist massacres of 1965–6. The best place to see them is the road from the Jununqan direction through the ricefields; seen from here, the V-formations of birds at sunset are an unforgettable sight.

Prehistoric turtle-shaped stone sarcophagi at the Museum Purbakala in Pejeng

Woodcarver at work in Kenderan, a village near Tegallalang

⑱ Tegallalang

Road Map D3. 🚌 from Ubud.
ℹ️ Ubud, (0361) 973 285.
🚻 📷 🏨 🔄

The captivating village of Tegallalang, once the seat of a kingdom, is interesting as a centre of the woodcarving industry. Workshops and simple wholesale outlets line the road for 5 km (3 miles), selling a variety of wooden handicrafts at very low prices. There are several small cafés by the main road that overlook the spectacular emerald-green rice terraces sculpted into the side of the river gorge north of Tegallalang.

Environs
Kebon is a pretty village on a steep side road 3 km (2 miles) north of Tegallalang. At the junction with the main road is the excellent Kampung Kafe. **Kenderan**, also on a back road, is a former micro-kingdom with several small *puri* (houses of the nobility).

The village of **Manuaba**, about 4 km (2 miles) north of Kenderan, is notable for its Brahman temple **Pura Griya Sakti**, with its refurbished *wantilan* performance pavilion. A visit to see the huge intertwined trees behind the inner courtyard requires permission of the temple attendant.

There is an interesting holy spring, **Telaga Waja**, in Kapitu, 1 km (half a mile) south of Kenderan. Access is by way of a 200 m (220 yard) footpath and a long, steep flight of steps. There are traces of meditation niches which suggest that Telaga Waja was once a Buddhist retreat; it is possibly over 1,000 years old.

🅰 **Pura Griya Sakti**
Manuaba. **Open** daily. 🐾 donation.

⑲ Sebatu

Road Map D3. from Ubud.
ℹ️ Ubud, (0361) 973 285. 🚻 📷

Sebatu village, part of a larger area of the same name, is highly regarded among the Balinese not only for its painted wood sculpture but also for its dance, music and classical dance costumes. Easily explored on foot, the village is laid out on a grid of three north–south streets, with the temples and *bale banjar* (community pavilion) at the northern end. The westernmost street is lined with studios making woodcarvings for sale to visitors.

In a little valley on the western outskirts of Sebatu itself is the lovely spring temple **Pura Gunung Kawi**, not to be confused with the royal monuments of the same name near Tampaksiring *(see p103)*. The bathing springs are worth seeing (but should not be photographed if they are in use), as is the carp-filled spring pool in the northwest corner. In the centre of the pool is a handsome shrine. There are some interesting sculptures, some of them new and some old, among the small, colourfully painted pavilions in the central courtyard.

Stone sculpture in Pura Gunung Kawi

🅰 **Pura Gunung Kawi**
Open daily. 🐾

Pura Gunung Kawi, Sebatu's tranquil spring temple

⑳ Taro

Road Map D3. 🛈 Ubud, (0361)
973 285. 🚻 ♿

On a well-marked (but often
rough) road to the west of
Pujung is Taro, said to be one
of the very earliest settlements
in Bali.

At the village centre is the
large temple **Pura Gunung
Raung**. Over its walls it is
possible to admire the long *bale
agung* pavilion, and a glowering
three-tier *meru* pagoda. The
latter represents the East
Javanese mountain Gunung
Raung; from here the legendary
sage Rsi Markandya and his
followers set out in the 8th
century on a mission to Bali.

Taro is the source of Bali's
albino cattle; these animals are
valued for their
importance in large
rituals. Formerly
they were
sacrificed;
today they
are merely
borrowed for
the ceremony
and then
returned. The
herd has now
multiplied
greatly and wanders freely in the
forest south of the village.

An albino cow,
revered in Bali

The well-run **Elephant Safari
Park** *(see p202)*, created in the
late 1990s, enables visitors to
view the landscape from the
back of a Sumatran elephant.
Attractions include elephants
that have been trained to
paint, a museum of elephants
and their history, a large
restaurant, luxurious accommodation and a spa.

㉑ Gunung Kawi Royal Monuments

Tampaksiring. **Road Map** D3.
🚌 from Bedulu & Gianyar. 🛈 Ubud,
(0361) 973 285. **Open** daily. 🚻 🏛

To the east of the small town of
Tampaksiring, bordering the
Pakrisan River, is a valley into the
sides of which are carved nine
immense monuments. They are
shaped like *candi* (Buddhist-
Hindu shrines), and are carved

Gunung Kawi Royal Monuments, *candi* shrines set in natural rock walls

into niches in a natural rock wall
in the hill. At their heart are a
temple and a holy spring. A
flight of stairs leads to the
monument complex, which
straddles the river. Commonly
called "tombs", these are in fact
memorial shrines, associated
with the legendary 11th-
century king Anak Wungsu *(see
p49)* and his wives. To the south
of the main complex are the
"Second Cloisters" on the east
bank, and the "Third Cloisters",
which are believed to be
monuments dedicated to the
queens of Anak Wungsu or his
descendants. The "Tenth Tomb",
to the west, is reached by a
short walk along the edges of
some ricefields.

On the steps leading to the
tombs, craftsmen from
Tampaksiring sell their wares,
including some exquisite
bone carvings.

㉒ Pura Tirta Empul

Manukaya. **Road Map** D3. 🚌 from
Bedulu & Gianyar. 🛈 Ubud, (0361)
973 285. **Open** daily. 🚻 🏛 🚻

This sacred spring temple, near
the source of the river Pakrisan,
is a major tourist stop, but it
is a pleasant place to visit.
The main feature is a series
of courtyards containing rect-
angular bathing pools. The
spouts dispense specific kinds
of holy water, which devotees
request with elaborate ritual
offerings. The temple is
thought to date from the 10th
century; the present walls are
recent. The pavilions are in an
on-going state of restoration,
an indication of the temple's
importance. People come from
all over the island for holy
water and ritual ablutions,
particularly on the day of
the full moon *(purnama)*.

Pura Tirta Empul, a spring temple and source of holy water

EAST BALI

The old kingdoms of eastern Bali wielded influence and power beyond their lofty mountains and lush green valleys. What remains of their palaces and temples is still a window into a world of ceremony and tradition, focused around Gunung Agung, centre of the Balinese universe, and, high on its steep volcanic slopes, Besakih, one of the most important temples in Bali.

The East Bali area corresponds to the three regencies of Klungkung, Bangli and Karangasem. It is an area of natural beauty and stark contrasts. Not far from its high volcanic peaks are some of Bali's best beaches. Just over 3,000 m (almost 10,000 ft) high, the active volcano of Gunung Agung dominates the landscape, its foothills covered with green ricefields. East Bali was devastated by Agung's eruption in 1963 (see p119) and by an earthquake in 1974. In many places great lava flows transformed the landscape.

Some of the island's most important temples and palaces are in this region. Extravagant temple complexes stand on ancient sites endowed with cosmic significance, for example at Besakih and around the volcanic lake in the vast crater of Gunung Batur. At Tirtagangga, in the hills north of Amlapura, a luxurious water palace was built by descendants of the last king as late as the 1940s. This tradition of royal grandeur dates back ultimately to the 15th century, when the court of the first king of Gelgel was established. Around the courts and palaces of the region the arts flourished and villages of skilled artisans grew up. This tradition of craftsmanship survives in many places today.

In the 14th century the Javanese kingdom of Majapahit brought to Bali a new social order and caste system. Some communities resisted it, and their descendants, known as the Bali Aga (original Balinese), still live here in culturally distinct villages such as Tenganan and Trunyan.

Klungkung's royal house came to an end in 1908, when the king and members of his court committed *puputan* (see p53), rather than submit to Dutch colonial control. However, many architectural relics still remain as reminders of pre-colonial times.

Ricefields of East Bali overlooked by the sacred volcano, Gunung Agung

◀ Detail of a carved door at the entrance to a Hindu priest's house

Exploring East Bali

East Bali is dominated by the mighty volcano Gunung Agung, upon whose slopes is the important Besakih Temple Complex. To the west is Gunung Batur, with its own temples and a crater lake. To the south is historic Klungkung, and the royal pavilions of Taman Gili. From here the road runs eastwards to some good trekking country near Manggis and Tirta-gangga, and on to the dive sites of Amed and Tulamben on the coast. The arid, lava-strewn eastern slopes of Gunung Agung are austerely beautiful. Tenganan, not far inland from the resort area of Candidasa, is one of the island's Bali Aga ("original Balinese") villages, which are culturally distinct from the rest of Bali.

Sights at a Glance

1. Bangli
2. Iseh
3. Sidemen
4. *Klungkung pp109–11*
5. Gelgel
6. Goa Lawah Bat Cave
7. Padang Bai
8. Candidasa
10. *Tenganan Bali Aga Village pp114–15*
11. Ujung
12. Amlapura
13. Tirtagangga
14. Gunung Lempuyang
15. Amed
16. Tulamben
17. *Gunung Agung*
18. *Besakih Temple Complex pp120–21*
19. *Gunung Batur pp124–5*
20. Kintamani
21. *Pura Ulun Danu Batur pp126–7*
22. Pura Tegeh Koripan

Walk

9. Tenganan to Tirtagangga

0 kilometres 5
0 miles 3

Lush green ricefields around Tirtagangga

For hotels and restaurants in this region see pp175–6 and p186

Getting Around

A car, rented with or without driver, is the best way of getting around. Roads are mostly good, although signposting is poor. Because of the many bends, journeys often take longer than one anticipates. *Bemo* run between villages, but taxis are scarce. Although public buses ply the coastal roads, tourist shuttle buses are more comfortable. Public transport is virtually non-existent at night. Padang Bai, on the southern coast, is the ferry port for Lombok.

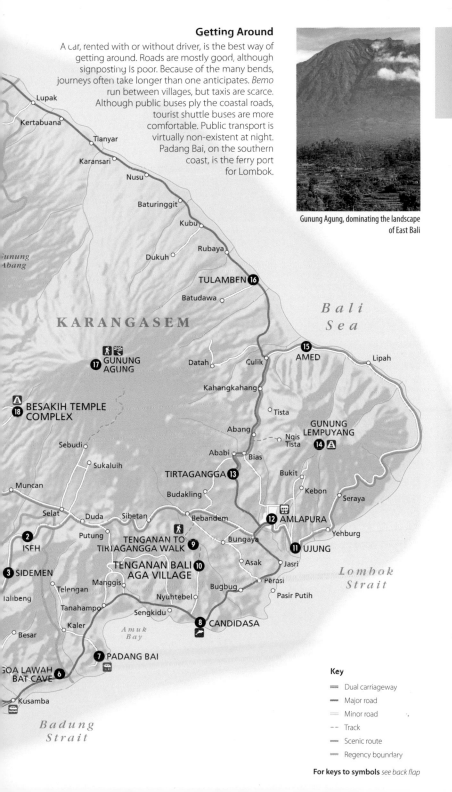

Gunung Agung, dominating the landscape of East Bali

Key

▬ Dual carriageway
▬ Major road
▬ Minor road
-- Track
▬ Scenic route
▬ Regency boundary

For keys to symbols *see back flap*

❶ Bangli

Road Map D3. 🚌 _i_ Jalan Brigjen
Ngurah Rai 30, (0366) 91 537. 🖉 🖳
🖳 🖳

A royal court city from the 14th
to the 19th century, Bangli is
one of Bali's oldest towns, a
small, well-ordered and tidy
community. Set some way up
the hills towards Gunung Batur,
the town is ideal for a walk in
the cool mountain air.

Pura Kehen, a place of worship
since the 12th century, steps
impressively up a hillside in a
series of eight terraces, enclosing
a huge banyan tree in the first
courtyard of the complex. High
in the banyan's branches is an
almost invisible _kulkul_ with
an alarm drum. Fine statuary
lines the steps leading to the
padmasana shrine _(see p30)_
where there is a multitiered _meru_
roof in the inner sanctuary. The
shrine is covered with elaborate
ornamentation. The gold-painted
doors of the temple are beautiful.

Pura Penyimpenan ("the
temple for keeping things")
contains three ancient bronze
inscriptions which imply that
the area was considered holy
long before the present temple
complex was built.

Images of heaven and hell,
the latter imaginatively grim,
cover the walls of **Pura Dalem
Pengungekan**, a temple

Mythological figure in Pura Dalem
Penungekan, a temple of the dead

dedicated to the dead, and
inside are shrines to Brahma,
Shiva and Vishnu.

🅰 Pura Kehen
Jalan Sri Wijaya. **Open** daily. 🖼
donation. 🖼 Pagerwesi (dates vary).

🅰 Pura Penyimpenan
Jalan Sri Wijaya. **Open** daily.
Closed for ceremonies. 🖼 donation.

🅰 Pura Dalem Pengungekan
Jalan Merdeka. **Open** daily.
Closed for ceremonies.

Environs
From the wooded **Bukit
Demulih**, some 4 km (2 miles)
west of Bangli, there are
glorious views of Gunung

Agung, and, on a clear day, as
far as Nusa Penida and Sanur. At
Bunutin, 7 km (4 miles) south of
Bangli, **Pura Penataran Agung**
has two small shrines on islands
in a lake filled with water lilies.

❷ Iseh

Road Map E3. 🚌 from Bangli and
Klungkung. _i_ Amlapura, (0363) 21
196. 🖳

The area around Iseh is
remarkable for glorious landscapes. Some of the best can be
seen on the road eastward from
Bangli via Muncan and Duda,
which carves its way east
through great volcanic valleys.
The terraced ricefields are lush
and green. Iseh itself is a small
village with little in the way of
tourist facilities. Walter Spies _(see
p92)_ built a house here, which is
still standing today, and it was
this location that inspired some
of his most beautiful paintings.

Environs
At **Putung**, 6 km (4 miles) east
of Iseh, there are some great
lookout points and a couple
of homestays _(see pp170–71)_.
A further 4 km (2 miles) to the
east is the village of **Sibetan**,
the best place to buy _salak (see
p193)_, a small, crisp, tart-tasting
fruit with a scaly exterior that
looks rather like snakeskin.

Ricefields and coconut groves at Iseh, a good setting for a walk

❸ Sidemen

Road Map E3. 🚌 from Bangli and Klungkung. ℹ️ Amlapura, (0363) 21 196.

Sidemen is set in some of the most beautiful country in East Bali. The views from the slopes of Gunung Agung stretch out like a green patchwork with an impressive mountain backdrop. The town is a retreat from the hustle and bustle elsewhere, and there are some good home-stays (see pp170–71) overlooking ricefields. In Sidemen one can visit workshops making songket. This work is historically the preserve of higher castes, and still implies high social status.

Street corner in the town centre of Klungkung

❹ Klungkung

Road Map D4. 🚌 ℹ️ Jalan Untung Surapati 3, (0366) 21 448. ♿ (limited).

Klungkung, also known as Semarapura, is a district capital and an important trading point. The most important historic sight in Klungkung is a pair of pavilions set in an ornamental moat, known as **Taman Gili** (see pp110–11). Adjacent to Taman Gili is the small **Museum Daerah Semarapura** in which you can see a collection of bronze and marble sculptures, and paintings by Italian modernist Emilio Ambron, as well as photographs of the royal family and the palace dating back to the early 1900s.

Wayang-style painting by an artist from Kamasan village

On the south side of Taman Gili is a large gateway, which is thought to be the entrance to the inner courtyard of the old palace. Legend has it that these massive wooden doors have remained stuck together since the puputan of 1908, when 200 members of Klungkung's royal court committed ritual suicide (see p53). This event is marked by the **Puputan Monument** across the road from Taman Gili. At the same road junction, a large indoor market sells temple and ritual paraphernalia, local handicrafts and food. It is one of Bali's best markets for textiles.

south of Klungkung is the "artists' village" of **Kamasan**; here painters can be seen at work. The artists of Kamasan have largely defined the style of traditional Balinese art (see pp38–9). As you travel from Klungkung to Kamasan, a turning on the left leads to **UD Kamasan Bali** (call 0366 24 781), where you can see kereng (Chinese coins) being forged. A small shop here sells all kinds of sacred coins and accessories. About the same distance to the northeast is the temple of **Pura Taman Sari**. In the temple's large, uncluttered compound is an eleven-roofed meru tower built on a stone turtle surrounded by a moat.

Environs
Less than 1 km (half a mile)

The Puputan Monument in Klungkung

Textiles of East Bali

In Bali great importance is attached to textiles and their making, and nowhere more so than in East Bali. This area is famous for a type of double ikat weave called geringsing, produced only in the Bali Aga village of Tenganan (see pp114–15). Geringsing cloths are credited by the Balinese with protective spiritual powers. In Sidemen, complex, decorative motifs in gold and silver threads are woven into cloth to create a rich brocade textile known as songket. This is often worn by the Balinese at religious or social events, and as part of the costume of traditional dancers.

Songket fabrics woven in a Sidemen workshop

Klungkung: Taman Gili

Built originally in the early 18th century, Taman Gili ("moated garden") is what remains of Klungkung's royal palace, most of which was destroyed in 1908 during the Dutch conquest. The main features are two raised, open meeting halls, or *bale*, with intricately painted ceilings. The paintings have undergone restoration and repainting several times in the last hundred years, but remain fine examples of the *wayang* style *(see p39)*, in which the figures resemble shadow puppets. The Kerta Gosa was originally the setting for the royal "high court". The present structure of the Bale Kambang dates from the 1940s.

The Moat
The surrounding moat gave the Bale Kambang its name, meaning "floating pavilion".

★ Kerta Gosa Ceiling Paintings
There are 267 painted panels arranged in several tiers. At the apex is a carved lotus flower surrounded by gilded doves, representing the goals of enlightenment and salvation.

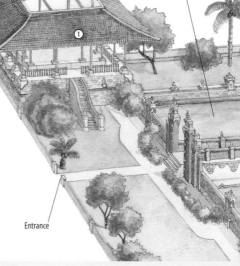

Entrance

Kerta Gosa Ceiling Paintings

The main series shows part of the *Bhima Swarga* narrative, which was incorporated into Balinese tradition from the Indian *Mahabharata* epic. There are also scenes from the *Tantri* stories (a Balinese version of a series of Indian moral fables), and some based on an astrological calendar, showing earthquakes and eruptions.

The demon Wirosa pursuing sinners

A scene from the *Tantri* stories

A stage in the ascent to enlightenment and salvation

★ **Bale Kambang Ceiling Paintings**
These depict scenes from Balinese myths, including the story of Sutasoma, a Buddhist saint symbolizing strength without aggression.

Carved Stone Wall Relief
The building is decorated with carved reliefs of mythical creatures.

KEY

① Kerta Gosa

② Roof made from hardwood shingles

③ Moat stocked with carp

④ Bale Kambang

Museum Daerah Semarapura
West of the Bale Kambang, the museum *(see p109)* has objects relating to the dynasties of Klungkung and Gelgel.

Temple entrance at the Goa Lawah Bat Cave

❺ Gelgel

Road Map E4. 🚌 from Klungkung.
ℹ Klungkung, (0366) 21 448.
🎎 Purnama Kapat (Oct).

The royal court of the Majapahit rulers of Bali *(see p50)* was established in Gelgel in the 14th century by Dewa Ketut Ngulesir, son of Bali's first Majapahit king. A reminder of the former kingdom is Gelgel's very ancient royal temple of **Pura Dasar**, with its large outer courtyard, and several tall *meru* towers.

The **Pura Penataran** is one of a number of other temples that can be seen along the village's broad streets.

❻ Goa Lawah Bat Cave

Road Map E4. 🚌 ℹ Klungkung, (0363) 21 196. **Open** daily. 🎎
🎎 ✐ 🏠

Thought to be more than 1,000 years old, Goa Lawah is important to temple rituals pertaining to the afterlife. The main feature of the temple is a cave inhabited by tens of thousands of fruit bats. Local legend has it that the cave stretches 30 km (19 miles) back into the mountain, as far as Besakih, *(see pp120–21)* and is the home of a giant dragon-like snake called Basuki who feasts on bats.

For visitors there are some good eateries outside the cave that have fine views over the ocean towards Nusa Penida and Lombok. However, it is also renowned for hawkers.

Environs

Kusamba, 4 km (3 miles) southwest of Goa Lawah, is a busy little fishing village with a black-sand beach. *Jukung* (outrigger fishing craft) line the shore, and are available for chartered day trips to nearby islands. The boats can feel vulnerable as the ocean swell picks up. Salt production pans can be seen on the coast here.

Colourful *jukung* (outriggers) on the black-sand beach at Kusamba

❼ Padang Bai

Road Map E3. 🚌 🚢 to Nusa Lembongan, Nusa Penida & Lembar, Lombok. ℹ Amlapura, (0363) 21 196.
✐ 🖥 🏠 🏖

This beach resort makes a good base for the exploration of East Bali. It is also the main port for ferries to Lombok, and therefore the traffic from Denpasar is quite heavy. In the village there are numerous restaurants, hotels, guesthouses, bars, tour guides and dive shops.

Environs

Within walking distance to the west of Padang Bai is **Biastugal**,

an unspoiled white-sand bay where sun-worshippers gather. A little further along the coast one can rent outriggers for diving and snorkelling. At the eastern end of the bay, a 20-minute walk away, there are several temples. They include **Pura Silayukti**, associated with Mpu Kuturan, who introduced the three-temple system to Balinese villages in the 11th century *(see p32)*.

🅰 **Pura Silayukti**
Open daily. 🎎 dates vary.

❽ Candidasa

Road Map F3 . 🚌 ℹ Jalan Candidasa, (0363) 21 002. 🖥 🏠 🏖

Originally a fishing village, Candidasa has now grown into a popular resort. However, since the reef which once lay offshore was largely destroyed by exploitation as a raw material, the beach has been almost completely eroded. Candidasa is still a good base for exploring the region, and for diving and snorkelling. There are some reputable diving schools, and good dive sites near the offshore islands. There is a wide range of *losmen*, hotels and other accommodation, restaurants and bars. The local dish is *bebek betutu*, succulent duck cooked with herbs and spices *(see p181)*.

The name Candidasa is said to be derived from the Balinese "Cilidasa", which means "ten children". In the centre of the village, overlooking a lagoon with water lilies, is **Pura Candi Dasa**, a temple dedicated to Hariti, the goddess of fertility.

🅰 **Pura Candi Dasa**
Jalan Candi Dasa. **Open** daily.

Environs

About 2 km (1 mile) east of Candidasa and up a steep flight of steps is **Pura Gomang**, where there are great views of the coast. Further east is **Pasir Putih**, a secluded bay hemmed in on one side by a sheer rock face, and used as a harbour by *jukung* outriggers.

❾ Walk from Tenganan to Tirtagangga

The walk from Tenganan to Tirtagangga reveals some of the most scenic terrain of Bali's interior, and many glimpses of traditional Balinese life along the way. The 6 km (4 mile) walk takes about three hours. From the higher points there are impressive views of Bali's mountains; the route passes also through terraced ricefields and peaceful hillside villages. This is a good way to see village temples, local schools, tiny mountain *warung* (shops) and weavers of basketware. In the early morning vendors sell *tuak*, a sour-tasting alcoholic drink made from the flower of the *jaka* palm tree. These trees can be recognized by the enormous grape-like buds jutting from their trunks.

④ Hillside Warung
A small café stands on the slope overlooking the rice terraces. The trail leads on to an irrigation dam and a ricefield shrine before crossing a shallow river.

③ Pura Puseh
At the Pura Puseh temple, a view to the far east of Bali is revealed; ricefields can be seen at various stages of cultivation. Gunung Lempuyang and Gunung Seraya are in the distance.

⑥ Budakling
This metal-smithing village is north of the main road, before one arrives at a lava trail.

⑦ Tirtagangga
The country road to Tirtagangga (see p116) offers good views of ricefields with the sea beyond.

⑤ Kastala
Across the river, the trail leads to this village near the main road. To cut short the walk, transport can be taken from Bebandem.

② Gumung Kaja
In the village of Gumung Kaja, baskets and mats are woven with the stems of the *ata*, a kind of palm tree.

Key
- ▬ Major road
- ═ Minor road
- ▪▪ Lava trail
- ▪▪ Walking route

0 kilometres 2
0 miles 1

① Tenganan Village Gate
From the village, a stone-paved path leads to a temple complex and then to the edge of the forest. Here a wall marks the beginning of a half-hour climb to the primary school at Gumung.

Tips for Walkers
Starting point: Tenganan.
End point: Tirtagangga
Getting there: *Bemo* to Candidasa, then own transport.
When to go: Any time, but trails are slippery in rainy season.
Walking time: 3 hours.

⑩ Tenganan Bali Aga Village

The Bali Aga, or "original Balinese" *(see p50)*, maintain a distinct cosmology and social organization. For example, villagers must marry in the community or live on the outskirts of the village. They make fine basketware, and this is the only place in Southeast Asia where *geringsing* double-*ikat* textiles *(see p41)* are made. Tenganan is the best preserved of the Bali Aga villages. It is closed to outsiders after dark.

Detail of double-*ikat geringsing* textile

Village Temple
In the village's "temple of origins", outside the village walls, the community joins in rituals reflecting a dualistic cosmology based on principles of complementary opposites.

Village Houses
A short flight of steps leads up to each house which also has a small courtyard.

The Legend of Tenganan

It is said that in the 14th century, King Bedaulu, the ruler of Bali, lost his favourite horse and offered a reward for its return. The horse was eventually found dead near Tenganan and the villagers asked to be granted land as a reward. The King sent his minister to draw the boundaries of the area to be given to them, instructing the minister to include all of the land where he could smell the dead horse. Accompanied by the village chief, who had hidden some of the rotting horse meat in his clothes, the minister performed his duties and drew generous boundaries which remain today.

Land at Tenganan, owned communally according to Bali Aga tradition

KEY

① **The *wantilan*** is a large, open pavilion where village members meet for social activities.

② **Public baths**

③ **Market**

④ **The *bale agung*** is the hall for meetings of the village council, composed of all the married couples.

⑤ **The kitchen** of the *bale agung* is where large numbers of pigs are killed and cooked for ceremonial purposes.

EAST BALI | **115**

★ **Bale Petemu**
This is the meeting hall of one of three associations of
unmarried village men.

VISITORS' CHECKLIST

Practical Information
Road Map F3. 🛈 Amlapura,
(0363) 21 196. **Open** daylight
hours. 🖼 donation. 🎭 *Rejang
Dewa* (dance) (Feb); *Usaba
Sambah* and *Mekare-kare* (stick
fight) (Jun–Jul). 🖵 📷 🏛

Transport
🚌 from Candidasa.

★ **Main Street**
The main streets are partly
cobbled and rise in tiers,
connected by ramps.

| 0 metres | 30 |
| 0 yards | 30 |

Fighting Cocks
Birds are often kept in cages in
front of the houses; most fights
take place outside the village.

Entrance

⑪ Ujung

Road Map F3. 🚌 from Amlapura.
ⅰ Amlapura, (0363) 21 196.

Ujung, meaning literally "at the end", is an appropriate name given the remote location of this fishing village. The **Puri Taman Ujung** is a water palace built in 1919 by the last raja of Karangasem, Anak Agung Anglurah Ketut. The buildings were all but destroyed in the 1976 earth-quake but have been restored to their former grandeur.

Environs

The narrow road winding east from Ujung around the eastern tip of Bali is very scenic, with spectacular views of the ocean and Gunung Seraya. Before taking this road, one should check its condition with the locals.

🏛 **Puri Taman Ujung**
Open daily. 🐾 donation. 🖥

Puri Taman Ujung, the royal water palace before renovation

⑫ Amlapura

Road Map F3. 🚌 ⅰ Jalan Diponegoro, (0363) 21 196. 🔲 🏛 🔲

The small but busy trading town of Amlapura is a district capital with an active market serving the area. The town was given its present name after recon-struction in the aftermath of the 1963 eruption of Gunung Agung. It is still often referred to by its former name, Karangasem.

Karangasem became an important power in the late 17th century. The royal families of Karangasem had strong political links with the nearby island of Lombok. In the mid-18th century they ousted the powerful kings of Sulawesi from Lombok and then divided the island up among themselves.

The Maskerdam Building, a royal residence furnished in Dutch style

The Balinese of Karangasem remained in power in western Lombok until 1894, although facing continuous challenges from the Sasak nobles. Karangasem became a vassal of Lombok in 1849, when the Lombok king attacked his own ancestral land. It placed itself under Dutch rule in 1894, after the Dutch conquest of Lombok.

Puri Agung, a royal palace of the kings of Karangasem, was built at the turn of the 20th century. It was the birthplace of the last king. The palace compound is no longer inhabited, descendants of the royal family preferring to live in the palaces of Puri Gede and Puri Kertasurahe across the road (unlike Puri Agung, they are not open to the public). Architecturally, Puri Agung is an eclectic mix of European and Balinese styles. It has a particularly impressive entrance gateway.

The main attraction is the **Maskerdam Building**, so called as a tribute to the Dutch ("Amsterdam" as pronounced by the locals). Behind its carved doors are pieces of furniture donated by Queen Wilhelmina of the Dutch royal

family. Another building in the compound is known as the Bale London, as some of its furniture bears the British royal family's coat of arms. There are two *bale* (open halls) beside orna-mental ponds in front of the Maskerdam Building. These were used for ceremonies and meetings.

Over one of the *bale* entrances is a photograph of the raja, taken in 1939 when the district was granted limited self-rule by the Dutch.

🏛 **Puri Agung**
Jalan Gajah Mada. **Open** daily. 🐾 🔲

⑬ Tirtagangga

Ababi. **Road Map** F3. 🚌
ⅰ Amlapura, (0363) 21 196.
Open daily. 🐾 🔲 🔲 🏛 🔲
(limited) 🐾

Tirtagangga (meaning "holy water from the Ganges") is the best surviving example of Bali's royal water palaces. It was built in 1947 by Anak Agung Anglurah Ketut, the last king of Karangasem, and restored after damage sustained in the 1963 eruption of Gunung Agung. The complex consists of a sacred spring, a cold spring-fed pool and several other ponds. Bathing is permitted in the pools. A small fee is charged at the spring-fed pool, which has simple changing rooms. The pools and fountains are set in well-maintained gardens.

Tirtagangga has a cool climate, and is a good base for walks in the area. There are several homestays here.

Gardens surrounding the bathing pools in Tirtagangga

Plantations beside the scenic route around Gunung Lempuyang

⑭ Gunung Lempuyang

Drive through villages of Tista, Abang and Ngis Tista. **Road Map** F3. 🚌 *i* Amlapura, (0363) 21 196. 🖥

At just over 1,000 m (3,300 ft), Gunung Lempuyang is worth a full day's trip, especially when there is a temple ceremony. Getting there is part of the attraction – the road from Tirtagangga runs northeast along a valley, with Gunung Agung to the west and Gunung Lempuyang to the east, carving its way through lush ricefields. The mountain itself is then reached via a side road.

At the top stands **Pura Lempuyang Luhur**. There has probably been a temple on this remote and sacred site since pre-Hindu times. The temple is important to Balinese today because of its location – at the top of the island's easternmost mountain. The temple is not large; there is just a single courtyard with a few simple *bale* (pavilions). The views of Gunung Agung are spectacular. Reaching the temple involves a two-hour climb up 1,700 stone steps, passing the smaller temple of Pura Telagamas at

the bottom. There are several strategically located resting places along the way.

🅰 **Pura Lempuyang Luhur Open** daily. 🎎 temple anniversary festival (Manis Galungan, 11 Feb 2016).

⑮ Amed

Road Map F2. 🚌 *i* Amlapura, (0363) 21 196. 🖉 🖥 🎎 🛶

The collective name for a string of fishing villages, Amed is of interest for its dive sites and salt production. In a simple evaporation process little changed for generations, salt is made from

Boats for diving or snorkelling trips off the coast around Amed

brine poured into wooden frames, gathered in sacks and laid out by the road for sale.

Divers come to this area, and in particular to the bay at Jemeluk to the east of Amed, for underwater views of colourful coral gardens and a spectacular variety of fish. It is also a great area to relax. There is plenty of accommodation, cafés and restaurants.

The east coast round Amed is hot, dry and economically rather poor. Barren hills pinned with thirsty-looking lontar palms stand in stark contrast to the green mountain slopes behind. The arid, harsh landscape is distinctly different from the lushness of most of East Bali.

Environs
Some 5 km (3 miles) east of Amed is the quiet coastal village of **Lipah**, where facilities are fast developing, with standards ranging from luxury to budget.

Lontar palms in the coastal region of Tulamben

⑯ Tulamben

Road Map F2. 🚌 from Amlapura & Singaraja. *i* Amlapura, (0363) 21 196. 🖉 🖥 🎎 🛶

Tulamben is a nondescript little village, but it is of interest as the location of the wreck of the American cargo ship *Liberty*, 120 m (396 ft) long and torpedoed southwest of Lombok during World War II. It lies 40 m (44 yards) offshore and, at its deepest point, some 60 m (198 ft) down. The water provides great diving and snorkelling. Day trips off Tulamben can be arranged with dive operations (see p198). Boats can be rented locally

⑰ Gunung Agung

Gunung Agung is a 3,014 m- (9,888 ft-) high, active volcano, the dominant feature of East Bali. It has a profound significance in the life of every Balinese. Communities orientate their houses, temples and even beds in relation to this sacred place, where the spirits of ancestors are believed to dwell. Visitors climbing the mountain should observe rules for temple dress (*see p214*) or risk offending local sensibilities.

Tips for Climbers

Starting point: Either of two base camps: Besakih ①; and Pura Pasar Agung ②, north of Selat.
Getting there: Bus or *bemo* to Besakih from Denpasar, Gianyar and Amlapura. Own transport to Pura Pasar Agung.
When to go: Off-limits during the rainy season (Oct–May), when there are dangerous mudslides and swollen rivers, as well as ceremonies (Mar–Apr).
Guide: Visitors are strongly advised to engage a reliable guide (*see p201*), because the climbs from both base camps are steep and require early-morning starts. The lower slopes are heavily forested. Changes in weather can be dramatic and sudden. Attitudes of local people to climbers may be unfriendly.
Length of climb: Six hours starting from Besakih; three hours from Pura Pasar Agung.

① From Besakih
This climb, the longer of the two routes, goes right to the top of the volcano, where there are spectacular views of Bali and Lombok when the weather is clear.

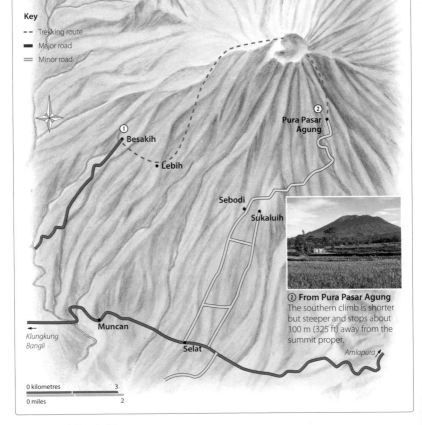

Key

-- Trekking route
━━ Major road
══ Minor road

① Besakih
• Lebih
Pura Pasar Agung ②
Sebodi
Sukaluih
Muncan
Klungkung Bangli
Selat
Amlapura

② From Pura Pasar Agung
The southern climb is shorter but steeper and stops about 100 m (325 ft) away from the summit proper.

0 kilometres — 3
0 miles — 2

The 1963 Eruption of Gunung Agung

Although Gunung Agung had long been thought extinct, in 1963 it erupted dramatically, shooting boulders and ash high into the sky. In all, the event lasted six months. Whole villages were buried; nearly 2,000 people died; and much arable land was laid waste. The rock-filled rivers of East Bali and Agung's bare eastern flank still bear witness to the event. According to local belief the disaster happened because spiritual leaders wrongly timed the performance of Eka Dasa Rudra. This is a Hindu spiritual purification ceremony which takes place every hundred years. Ancient texts suggest that the ceremony should have taken place not in 1963, but in 1979.

Eruption of Gunung Agung (1968) by Ida Bagus Nyoman Rai

⑱ Besakih Temple Complex

See pp120–21.

⑲ Gunung Batur

See pp124–5.

⑳ Kintamani

Road Map D2. 🚌 ℹ️ Penelokan, (0366) 51 370. 🏍️ 🍴 🏨 🛍️

One of the most popular destinations for visitors in Bali is Kintamani, notable above all for its view of a volcano within a caldera. The air here is fresh and the view from Kintamani into the caldera of Gunung Batur (*see pp124–5*) is perhaps the most famous on the island, as the tourist buses testify.

Kintamani is one of three small villages set high on Batur's caldera rim. Penelokan and Batur are the other two. It is hard to distinguish where one ends and the next begins, as they have now merged

together to form a ribbon of development catering for the many visitors who come here. The whole road is transformed into a car park when the tour buses arrive. The hawkers can be particularly persistent.

However, people do not come to look at the village of Kintamani itself – they come to stand in awe of the view. It is worth stopping here just to get a real sense of the scale of the landscape from a high vantage point; here it is easy to see the relative positions of Gunung Batur, the Bali Aga village of Trunyan (*see p125*) down on the shore of the lake, and Gunung Abang on the eastern side of the lake facing Gunung Batur.

There are many places to eat along most of the 10 km (6 miles) of the main road along the crater rim; most have good views. There is also a volcano museum and a market selling fresh local produce.

An ancient shrine in Pura Tegeh Koripan

㉑ Pura Ulun Danu Batur

See pp126–7.

㉒ Pura Tegeh Koripan

Road Map D1. 🚌 from Kintamani. ℹ️ Penelokan, (0366) 51 370. **Open** daily. **Closed** during ceremonies. 🎫 donation. 🎏 temple festival (Oct).

Pura Tegeh Koripan (also known as Pura Sukawana or Pura Penulisan) is one of the oldest temples in Bali, dating from the 11th century or earlier (*see p49*). Set at more than 1,500 m (4,950 ft) on the side of Gunung Penulisan, it is certainly one of the highest (*see p124*). It does not get very much tourist traffic and, therefore, has a peaceful atmosphere.

It is in fact a complex of five temples. Its pyramidal structure, set on eleven levels of terraces along the slope, suggests that it dates from the pre-Hindu-Buddhist era, and is associated with the megalithic culture of Bali.

The main temple, Pura Panarajon, is over 300 steps up and at the highest position in the complex. Inside, there are some stone inscriptions and statues thought to date to the 10th century.

From the slopes of Gunung Penulisan there are good views: on clear days one can see as far as Java to the east, and the Bali Sea to the north.

Scenic environs of Lake Batur in Kintamani

⑱ Besakih Temple Complex

Pura Besakih is a grand complex of 22 temples spread over 3 sq km (1 sq mile) on the slopes of Gunung Agung *(see p118)*, where the Balinese believe the spirits of their ancestors live. Said to have been founded in the late 8th century by the Javanese sage, Rsi Markandya, it later came under the jurisdiction of the Klungkung kingdom. All but two shrines were destroyed in an earthquake of 1917, and it underwent several major renovations in the 20th century, escaping damage in the 1963 eruption of Gunung Agung. Now it is an important focus of modern Indonesian Hinduism.

★ Eleven-tiered Meru
The tall *meru* (pagodas) are shrines for deified kings, ancestral spirits and nature gods.

★ Main Courtyard
This is the main focus of worship at the temple. A *padmasana tiga* (triple lotus shrine) is dedicated to Brahma, Shiva and Vishnu.

Terraced Entrance
The terraces at the entrance to Pura Penataran Agung are an echo of the stepped pyramids of Indonesian prehistory.

Stairs
Only worshippers are allowed to use the entrance stairway.

KEY

① **Footpaths** connect the temples in the complex.

② **In the inner courtyards** of the temple there may have been *meru* towers since the 14th century.

③ **Low walls** surround the temple complex; visitors can view the shrines by walking along the footpaths and looking over the walls.

Pura Ratu Pande
The roofs of this clan temple beside Pura Penataran Agung have been restored with black palm fibre and gilded roof caps.

Pura Penataran Agung

The temple illustrated here is Pura Penataran Agung, the spiritual core of the Besakih complex.

Pura (Temples) in the Besakih Complex

① Peninjoan
② Ratu Madeg
③ Ratu Pande
④ Pengubengan
⑤ Gelap
⑥ Tirta
⑦ Ratu Penyarikan
⑧ Pedharman
⑨ Kiduling Kreteg
⑩ Ratu Pasek
⑪ Penataran Agung
⑫ Dukuh Segening
⑬ Dasukian
⑭ Merajan Kanginan
⑮ Goa
⑯ Bangun Sakti
⑰ Ulun Kulkul
⑱ Manik Mas
⑲ Pesimpangan
⑳ Dalem Puri
㉑ Merajan Selonding
㉒ Jenggala

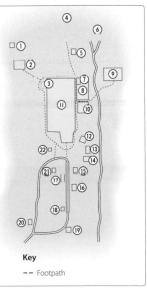

Key
-- Footpath

Gunung Batur, Bali's most active volcano ▶

⑲ Gunung Batur

Although Gunung Batur (Mount Batur) is not the largest volcano in Bali, it is the most active. It is surrounded by a spectacular caldera, which implies that it was once much larger than now, having blown off its top in an eruption. It has erupted on a large scale more than 20 times in the last 200 years. The most devastating occasion was in 1917 when more than 1,000 people died and over 2,000 temples were destroyed. Volcanic activity has made the slopes of Gunung Batur bare and dry, in contrast to the vegetation which covers the slopes of Gunung Abang, on the opposite side of Lake Batur.

Gunung Batur Eruptions
Steam can often be seen puffing from holes on the mountainside from this active volcano.

Tips for Walkers

Walking up to one of the four craters of Gunung Batur takes an hour from **Serongga**, or three hours from **Kedisan**.

A local cartel, the HPPGB, strongly discourages trekking alone, and climbers are advised to take a licensed guide with them. An information centre is located at **Toya Bungkah**, where there is also *losmen* accommodation.

The air can be quite chilly before daybreak, and warm clothing is highly recommended for night treks. Care should be taken to avoid the hot steam issuing from fissures in the rocks.

The slopes of the volcano can be slippery and dangerous, and trekking is not recommended from October to April.

Gunung Penulisan •
Singaraja •
• Pura Tegeh Koripan
(see p119)

• Kintamani

Puwra Ulun Danu Batur •
(see pp126–7)

• Batur

Penelokan

Ubud

Tampuksiring and Ubud

Bangli

0 kilometres   3
0 miles   2

The western slopes of Gunung Batur
The area at the foot of the volcano is covered with lava deposited by old eruptions. The vegetation is sparse here.

Key
━━ Major road
• • Footpath

Lake Batur

This lake is the main Irrigation source for much of the agriculture of Central and East Bali. It is said to be protected by the lake goddess, Ida Betari Dewi Ulun Danu.

VISITORS' CHECKLIST

Practical Information
Road Map D2. 🛈 Jalan Letulila 9, Bangli (0366) 91 537.
🎫 🖉 🖵 📷 📱 Trunyan Bali Aga Village: 🏛 Berutuk (Oct). Batur Volcano Museum, Penelokan. **Tel** (0366) 51 152. **Open** 8am–5pm daily.
🆆 baturmuseum.com

Transport
🚌 from Penelokan & Kintamani.
🚤 from Kedisan.

Shrines on Gunung Abang

In the forest on the peak of Gunung Abang is a temple containing some small, brightly painted shrines.

[Map labels:]
rongga
songan
Pura Ulun Danu
Trunyan
Toya Bungkah
Pura Jati
disan
Gunung Abang
Besakih

Trunyan, on the eastern shore of Lake Batur, reachable most easily by water

Trunyan Bali Aga Village

One of the culturally isolated Bali Aga villages (see p50), Trunyan is accessible by road as well as by boat. Villagers here practise customs found nowhere else in Bali, even in other Bali Aga villages. These include the treatment of their dead bodies, which are placed in pits, and covered by cloth and shabby bamboo canopies. The influence of an ancient tree is said to preserve the corpses from putrefaction. The cemetery is the main feature of interest to visitors. Trunyan is the home of Da Tonta, a 4 m- (13 ft-) high statue of Dewa Ratu Gede Pancering Jagat, patron guardian of the village, which is brought out at the Berutuk festival (usually October). The people here tend to expect "donations" from visitors, whom they now regard as a source of income.

Toya Bungkah

This village near a hot spring has simple restaurants and losmen accommodation.

For keys to symbols see back flap

㉑ Pura Ulun Danu Batur

This temple is one of the most important on Bali because of its association with Lake *(danu)* Batur, which supplies the irrigation system of Gianyar and Bangli through a series of underground springs. From a distance the temple's silhouette can be seen on the rim of the vast Batur caldera. Adjoining this temple are others in the process of enlargement, making up a quite extensive complex.

Temple Flags
Deities and mythical beasts are often depicted in rich colours on temple flags and sculptures.

Third Courtyard
The third courtyard is the most sacred. Three gateways lead from one courtyard to the next.

Garuda
The figure of Garuda, a bird from Hindu mythology, is depicted in this stone relief on the courtyard wall.

★ Central Courtyard
The great quadrangle, shown here occupied by a festive structure of bamboo and straw, is the occasional setting for a *baris gede* dance *(see p34)*.

Offerings to the Lake Goddess

Devotees from all over Bali present elaborate offerings at this temple, which is dedicated to Ida Betari Dewi Ulun Danu, the goddess of Lake Batur. The respect accorded to the goddess is reinforced by events

Offerings of fruits and flowers

in the temple's history. At its former location closer to the lake, the temple was miraculously saved from destruction in the volcanic eruption of 1917, when the lava flow stopped just short of its walls. Another eruption, in 1926, prompted the villagers to move the temple to its present location.

VISITORS' CHECKLIST

Practical Information
Batur. **Road Map** D2.
i Penelokan, (0366) 91 537.
Open 7am–6pm daily.
donation. temple anniversary
(Apr & Oct *purnama*).

Transport

★ **Gold-painted Doors**
The great timber doors of the main temple gateway are reserved for the use of priests on important occasions.

Side Gate
This tall, slender gate, built in a combination of brickwork and *paras* stone decoration, leads to another temple.

Entrance

The *bale gong* is a pavilion housing the temple's set of *gamelan* instruments, including a great gong believed to have a magical history.

NORTH AND WEST BALI

At the heart of North and West Bali is a mountainous, volcanic hinterland. This is ringed by coastal plains where most of the population live. Before the Dutch took over Southern Bali in the early 20th century and a harbour was built at Benoa in the 1920s, much of the contact between the Balinese and the rest of the world took place in this northern and western region of the island.

North and West Bali corresponds to the regencies of Tabanan, Jembrana and Buleleng, of which the administrative capitals are Tabanan, Negara and Singaraja respectively. To the west of Tabanan regency, rice growing gradually gives way to dry fields and forests. The population is increasingly Muslim as one moves west; the older Muslim settlements were established by Bugis sailors in the 17th century. The landscape of Buleleng regency on the north coast consists of steep mountain slopes plunging down to a narrow stretch of dry land which is generally impervious to irrigation – the exceptions are the relatively fertile hinterland of Singaraja town and the plantation area of Munduk and Busungbiu further inland.

The history of this part of Bali has been influenced as much by the sea as by the traditions of the courts: both Singaraja and Negara have the flavour more of Javanese coastal trading towns than of the Balinese centres of aristocratic power. North Bali is more heavily marked by the Dutch colonial presence than the rest of the island, which was colonized later. Following their brutal takeover of Buleleng in 1849, the Dutch set up a Residentie (prefecture) in Singaraja in 1855. Singaraja shows evidence of its Dutch past in its old offices and mansions and the airy, shady atmosphere of the town. Temples evolved an original, even at times humorous, style of bas-reliefs and sculptures where Europeans, cars, boats and other signs of modernity often appear in the places taken by demons and abstract flower motifs in temples further south.

New converts to Christianity were resettled by the Dutch in the hinterland of Negara. Later, several settlements were established along the coast by Madurese migrants.

Ducks being farmed on the coastal plains of western Bali

◄ Statue at Pura Tanah Lot (see p132), a Balinese temple situated on a rocky outcrop by the ocean

Exploring North and West Bali

West Bali has areas of great natural beauty. The mountains, black-sand beaches, coconut plantations and ricefields make up some idyllic landscapes. The eastern part is known for its many impressive temples, and for Gunung Batukau, surrounded by Bali's last remaining primary forest. Near the hill-resort area of Bedugul is a string of mountain lakes in an ancient caldera. On the north coast lies Singaraja, once the Dutch colonial capital. A great expanse of territory is occupied by the Taman Nasional Bali Barat (West Bali National Park), and the adjacent area of protected scrub forest.

Clear waters at Pantai Gondol

Sights at a Glance

For hotels and restaurants in this region see pp176–7 and pp186–7

Ricefield being planted near Tabanan

Getting Around

A car is the ideal means of travelling around North and West Bali, as the distances are relatively great, and public transport is non-existent in remoter places. Along the very busy main road from Denpasar via Mengwi to the port of Gilimanuk, there are branches off to sights including the mountain Gunung Batukau and the coastal temples of Tanah Lot. The main route from Denpasar to Singaraja gives access to sights such as Pura Taman Ayun and Bedugul. Both these major roads are served by *bemo* and public buses, as is the north-coast road from East Bali to Gilimanuk via Singaraja.

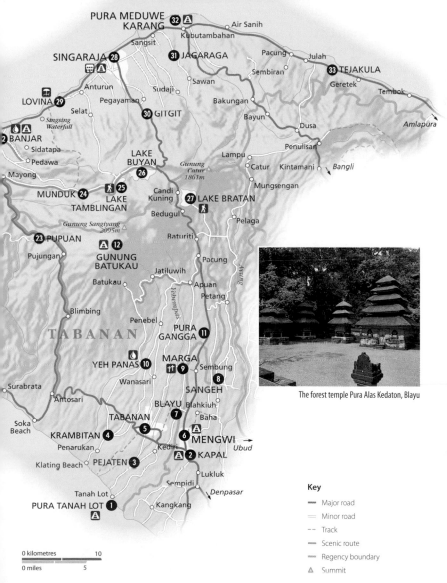

The forest temple Pura Alas Kedaton, Blayu

Key

— Major road

— Minor road

-- Track

— Scenic route

— Regency boundary

△ Summit

For keys to symbols *see back flap*

0 kilometres 10

0 miles 5

Crossing the rocky approach to Pura Tanah Lot at low tide

❶ Pura Tanah Lot

Tanah Lot. **Road Map** B4. 🚌 from Denpasar & Kediri. 🛈 Tabanan, (0361) 811 602. **Open** daily. 🐾 donation. 🎏 temple anniversary. 🚻🛆🏠🛒

One of Bali's most heavily promoted landmarks, Pura Tanah Lot is a temple set dramatically on a small island about 100 m (100 yards) off the coast. It can get very crowded, and it is best to arrive well before sunset, when there are not too many visitors around. As the sun goes down, the shrines make a magnificent silhouette against a glowing horizon – a memorable sight despite the throngs of visitors at this time. The many handicraft, souvenir and refreshment stalls at Tanah Lot are a major source of income for the region's women and children.

The islet – a promontory until the beginning of the 20th century – is accessible on foot at low tide, but only Balinese Hindus may go ashore. It is being eroded by the onslaught of the sea. The cliffs around the island have been carefully reinforced with concrete, and tripods have been sunk into the sea to act as breakwaters.

As its name suggests, the temple is situated at the meeting point of land *(tanah)* and sea *(lot)*. The part that faces the sea is dedicated to the Balinese goddess of the sea, Betara Tengah Segara, while the landward side is thought to be the seat of the gods from Gunung Batukau *(see p137)*. The temple is associated with the saint Dang Hyang Nirartha *(see pp50–51)*. He is said to have advised its construction in order to protect Bali against scourges and epidemics; these destructive forces were thought to originate from the sea.

Environs
Along the nearby coast, numerous temples and shrines have been built to protect Tanah Lot. They include **Pura Pekendungan, Pura Jero Kandang, Pura Galuh** and **Pura Batu Bolong**. The last of these, a short distance north of Pura Tanah Lot and rarely visited by tourists, is at the end of a rocky promontory that leaps seaward to form a natural bridge over the waters of the Indian Ocean.

❷ Kapal

Road Map C4. 🚌 from Kediri and Denpasar. 🛈 Tabanan, (0361) 811 602. 🏠

The most conspicuous feature of Kapal is hundreds of shops selling ready-made temple shrines and somewhat "kitsch" cement

Statuary for sale at Kapal

statues. There is also some attractive earthenware pottery.

In a quiet street leading off the main road is **Pura Sada**, the temple of origin of the royal house of Mengwi *(see p51)*. Damaged during an earthquake in 1917, it was rebuilt in the 1960s by a team of Indonesian archaeologists, based on the 17th-century original. The most interesting part is the 11-tier stone *meru* built in the style of a Javanese *candi*. Such towers are known as *prasada*, and are very rare in Bali. This example is a reminder of the kings' claimed descent from the Majapahit *(see p50)*. The tall, 16 m- (53 ft-) high phallic form emphasizes its dedication to the Hindu god Shiva. Affixed to the sides of the tower are images of the eight lords of the compass directions. Vishnu and Brahma with Shiva, the deities of the Hindu Trimurti (triad), are portrayed on the eastern side. On the lower base of the tower are represented the seven seers of the Hindu-Balinese cosmos. The *candi bentar* (split gate) is decorated with sets of Boma (guardian spirit) heads on the front and back; these are split like the gate itself. The closely packed rows of mini-shrines in the temple yard are said to commemorate the crew of a ship that sank while transporting to Bali the sacred effigy of a Majapahit king.

🅰 Pura Sada
Banjar Pemebetan, near Banjar Celuk, Kapal. **Open** daily. 🐾 donation.

Cluster of small shrines at Pura Sada in Kapal

❸ Pejaten

Road Map B4. 🚌 from Denpasar &
Tanah Lot. 🛈 Tabanan, (0361) 811
602.

The village of Pejaten is home
to a considerable cottage
industry that produces
terracotta roof tiles, earthenware, pots with coloured
glazes, and other decorative
objects often attractively
naive in character. It is a
good place to browse
and bargain.

Environs
About 3 km (2 miles)
northeast of Pejaten
is the village of

**Earthenware pot
produced in Pejaten**

Kediri, where an ornate white
statue marks its centre. Kediri is
important locally for its cattle
market and colourful fabrics.
The road from here south to
Tanah Lot crosses enchanting
rural landscapes.

❹ Krambitan

Road Map B4. 🚌 from Tabanan.
🛈 Tabanan, (0361) 811 602. 🚻

The small town of Krambitan
was an old agrarian kingdom
until the turn of the 20th
century. It still has a village-like
atmosphere and some old
architecture. Krambitan is an
important repository of Balinese
classical culture.
   Two palaces, **Puri Anyar** and
Puri Agung Wisata, operate
as guesthouses. Occasionally,
"royal parties" of Balinese
dances take place, complete
with torches and *tektekan*,
a form of *gamelan* music in
which *cengceng* (cymbals) are
augmented by bamboo sticks
or wooden cowbells.

🏛 **Puri Anyar and Puri
Agung Wisata**
Tel (0361) 812 774/668. **Open** daily.
Closed public hols. 🏃 donation. 🏷

Environs
Klating Beach, on the coast
6 km (4 miles) south of
Krambitan, is an unspoiled
black-sand beach with some
simple *losmen* accommodation
available nearby.

❺ Tabanan

Road Map C4. 🚌 from Denpasar.
🛈 Jalan Gunung Agung, (0361)
811 602. 🚻 🖥 🏠 🚻

This is a bustling commercial
town. The interesting, if somewhat rundown, **Museum Subak**
has mock-ups of the *subak*
irrigation systems of Bali
(see pp24–5), whereby
associations are formed by
owners of land irrigated
by a common water
source. Some traditional
farming implements are
also displayed.

🏛 **Museum Subak**
Jalan Raya Kediri,
Sanggulan. **Tel** (0361) 810 315.
Open daily. **Closed** public holidays.
🏃 donation

Environs
Located in Wanasari, 7 km
(4 miles) north on the road
to Gunung Batukau, **Taman
Kupu Kupu** is a small butterfly
park, home to some rare
species. Black-sand beaches
line the coastal road to Negara
(see p138). **Surabrata**, also
called Balian Beach, 30 km
(19 miles) west of Tabanan,
is charming. It has a fishing
village set by a cliff, and a small

river called "Sacred River" – a
name intended to appeal to
visitors. The surfing is good
and basic accommodation
is available.

🦋 **Taman Kupu Kupu**
Jalan Batukau, Sandan Wanasari.
Tel (0361) 814 282. **Open** daily. 🏃 🏷

❻ Mengwi

Road Map C4. 🚌 from Denpasar
& Bedugul. 🛈 Tabanan, (0361)
811 602. 🚻 🖥

This quiet town was for a long
time the seat of the most
important kingdom in West
Bali. It held sway over the
eastern tip of Java for most
of the 18th century *(see p51)*.
The lanes of the town are a
pleasant setting for a stroll.
At Mengwi is a temple set in
a watergarden, **Pura Taman
Ayun** *(see pp134–5)*.

Environs
The road from Mengwi to
Sangeh offers views of ricefields
and temples. **Baha**, 5 km
(3 miles) north of Mengwi, is a
village restored to its traditional
state, with house compounds
and temples typical of a
Balinese community.

Ricefields in the regency of Tabanan

Mengwi: Pura Taman Ayun

The Taman Ayun ("Vast Garden") temple, in its moated setting, symbolizes the Hindu world set in the cosmic sea. Its *meru* towers represent the mountains, residence of the gods. Located on an axis connecting the mountains with the sea, Pura Taman Ayun is thought to ensure the harmonious circulation of water from the mountains of Bali to the ricefields, then to the sea, and back to the mountains. Originally established in 1740, the temple was restored in 1937. In it there are ancestral shrines of the former ruling Mengwi family and their dependants, as well as shrines dedicated to particular mountains, to the sea and to agricultural deities.

★ **Eleven-tiered Meru**
The tallest *meru* symbolizes the mountain Gunung Batukau *(see p137)*.

Bale
Several *bale* (wooden pavilions) are built on carved stone bases. One contains a lotus throne on which Hindu deities Shiva, Brahma and Vishnu are believed to sit.

KEY

① **Outer moat**

② **Water from the inner moat** is used to cleanse the temple during festivals such as *odalan* (temple anniversaries).

③ **Footpaths** outside the inner moat are accessible to visitors from the outer courtyard and give views of the most sacred part of the temple.

④ The *candi bentar* (split gate) separates the first courtyard from the grassy areas outside. Visitors may pass through here.

Meru
Some of the *meru* towers are shrines to the deities of Bali's mountains, Gunung Batur *(see pp124–5)*, Gunung Agung *(see p118)* and Gunung Batukau *(see p137)*; in the courtyard is a Javanese *candi* (shrine).

Inner Moat
Behind the main gateway, the inner courtyard is surrounded on three sides by a moat, parts of which are filled with lotuses.

VISITORS' CHECKLIST

Practical Information
Mengwi. **Road Map** C4.
Tel (0361) 756 176.
Open 7am –6pm daily.
Closed some sections closed to public except during festivals. 🏛
📷 In the courtyards. 🚫
🎎 *Odalan* (temple festival) on Anggarkasih Medangsia of the Balinese calendar.

Transport
🚌 from Denpasar.

Stone Statues
Guardian figures derived from Balinese mythology stand by the main gate.

Brick Walls
Lavishly decorated walls delineate the main areas of the temple. They are built the traditional way, without mortar.

③

④

★ Kori Agung
On the lintel of the *kori agung* (main gate) is a rare carving of Sai, a guardian figure, with gods and godly seers to each side. The doors are open only during ceremonies.

🕖 Blayu

Road Map C3. 🚌 from Denpasar & Kediri. 🛈 Tabanan, (0361) 811 602.

Blayu, like nearby Mambal, is a scenic village on a road lined with beautiful *kori* house gates typical of the area. Near the village is the monkey forest of Alas Kedaton. In the temple, **Pura Alas Kedaton**, is an ancient statue of Ganesha, the Hindu god of knowledge.

🅰 Pura Alas Kedaton
Open daily. 🐒 💳 📷 Anggarkasih Medangsia.

Meru tower at Pura Alas Kedaton, in the monkey forest near Blayu

🕗 Sangeh

Road Map C3. 🚌 from Denpasar. 🛈 Tabanan, (0361) 811 602. 📷 🏠 ♿

Monkeys are found in many gorges and mountains in Bali, and a good place to see them is the monkey forest of Sangeh, where the palahlar trees (mistakenly thought to be nutmeg trees) are up to 30–40 m (100–130 ft) high. Monkeys can be seen around a small temple, **Pura Bukit Sari**, deep in the woods but signposted on the main road. The monkeys are considered sacred, a tradition deriving from the Hindu *Ramayana* epic, in which Prince Rama allied himself with the monkey kings Subali and Hanoman to attack the evil king Rawana.

The monkeys should be approached with caution. People will be greeted with mischievous grins, but it is not advisable to get too friendly – the monkeys may try to climb

The memorial tower at Margarana

up on visitors' shoulders, and will not get down unless given something to eat. Brusque movements can provoke them to bite. The animals may even take spectacles or money, in which case a *pawang* (monkey tamer) will retrieve the stolen object using a banana as an incentive.

A monkey in Sangeh

🅰 Pura Bukit Sari
Sangeh. **Open** daily. 🐒

🕘 Marga

Road Map C3. 🚌 from Denpasar & Mengwi. 🛈 Tabanan, (0361) 811 602.

The village of Marga is the site of a battle between the Dutch and the Balinese guerrillas in 1946. On the western side of the village is the Margarana

The Battle of Marga

In February 1946, after the Japanese surrendered at the end of World War II, the Dutch strove to re-establish their colonial authority in Bali. Local nationalists led a guerrilla war against them. On 20 November 1946, 94 Balinese fighters under the command of Gusti Ngurah Rai were trapped by Dutch troops west of Marga. Surrounded on the ground and strafed from the air, they fought to the last, in a modern repeat of the ritual *puputan* (*see p55*). After this bloody defeat, resistance waned and Bali was to remain effectively under Dutch control until the end of 1949.

Monument. Besides the graves of the 94 guerrillas fallen at the battle (*rana*) of Marga, the garden contains monuments to 1,372 heroes of the War of Independence in the 1940s. The graves do not resemble Christian, Muslim or even Hindu graves: they are small, *meru*-shaped structures reminiscent of the ancient temples from the Javanese period of Majapahit (*see p50*).

The central monument, not to be mistaken for a Balinese *meru* shrine, is designed as it is to symbolize the day of the proclamation of independence, 17 August 1945. The four steps and five small pillars at its foot represent the year (45); the eight tiers of its roof give the month (August); and the height of 17 m (56 ft) gives the day (17). A statue of Gusti Ngurah Rai (*see p55*) completes the scene.

At Marga, shrines to independence fighters at the Margarana monument

The hot-spring resort and hotel in Yeh Panas

⑩ Yeh Panas

Penatahan, near Penebel.
Road Map C3. 🚌 from Denpasar & Tabanan. **Tel** (0361) 262 356.
Open 6am–8pm daily. 🌊 🛥 🖥 🛶 🏊

It is worthwhile dropping by the Yeh Panas hot springs on the road to Gunung Batukau from Tabanan or Penebel. There are several sulphurous springs in this area. The main hot springs have been turned into a spa, which also has a hotel; those which are open to the public are clearly indicated by signs. There is also a spring temple here.

Hot springs are also to be found in the village of Angsri near Apuan. They are in a pleasant, natural setting, but have no modern facilities.

⑪ Pura Gangga

On a small road leading through Perean to Apuan and Baturiti. **Road Map** C3. 🛈 Tabanan, (0361) 811 602. **Closed** to visitors. 🖥

Pura Gangga is a temple on the main highway to Bedugul. It is named after the holy river Ganges (Gangga) in India, and is set on the lush banks of a small river. The temple has a seven-tier *meru* with a stone base. It is unusual in that the base is open at the front, rather than entirely closed in the usual fashion. Although the temple is not open to visitors, its atmospheric compound and architectural features can easily be viewed from outside the precincts.

⑫ Gunung Batukau

Road Map B2. 🚌 from Denpasar & Tabanan. 🛈 Tabanan, (0361) 811 602. 🖥 🏠 🛥

Gunung Batukau is the second-highest peak in Bali (Gunung Agung being the highest). On its slopes is the last remaining true rainforest on the island. The mountain is much revered by the Balinese as the source of irrigation water for areas to the south and west of it.

The temple of **Pura Luhur Batukau** is located among the lofty trees at its foot. It is seen as very important by the Balinese because of its geographical position at Bali's highest western peak. There is a constant stream of worshippers performing rites or requesting holy water from the temple priests.

The charm of the temple's setting lies in a blend of artifice and nature: the spires of its *meru* shrines and other dark-thatched pavilions appear to be engulfed by the forest. Trees, bushes and grass are all in various shades of green, which contrast with the black and reddish profile of the roofs and walls of the temple. Hence the origin of the name given to the central deity of the temple: Sang Hyang Tumuwuh, "The Ultimate Plant Grower".

In the centre of a nearby artificial pool is a small shrine, dedicated to the Lord of Gunung Batukau and the goddess of nearby Lake Tamblingan (*see pp144–5*).

🅰 **Pura Luhur Batukau**
Open daily. 🌊 donation.
🛥 some areas.

Environs
To the east of Pura Luhur Batukau on the road to Baturiti are the famous rice terraces of **Jatiluwih**, stretching down to the sea in the far distance. Rice granaries line the road in the local villages. Other beautiful rice terraces are to be seen in **Pacung**, at the turn-off to Jatiluwih and Batukau.

Rice-producing lands in Jatiluwih, near Gunung Batukau

Pura Rambut Siwi, a temple on a promontory west of Medewi Beach

⑬ Medewi Beach

🚌 from Denpasar. 🛈 Negara, (0365) 41 060. 🖉 🏖

Medewi is a surfers' haunt on the west coast of Bali. The long, rolling breakers can be 7 m (23 ft) high. The beach is composed of black sand, over which are scattered small black stones. The beach is a memorable sight when the stones glitter under the rays of the setting sun. On the horizon is the shape of the Javanese coast. Visitors will find some basic hotels and restaurants here.

Environs
The **Pura Rambut Siwi** temple complex is built on a promontory, 6 km (4 miles) west of Medewi Beach. The setting offers a fine panorama over the sea. The main temple was established to venerate the priest Dang Hyang Nirartha *(see pp50–51)*, after he cured the local villagers of a deadly illness. There is a single, three-tiered *meru*. A lock of hair *(rambut)*, believed to be the priest's, is kept as a relic in the pavilion shrine, or *gedong*. The temple entrance faces the sea and is guarded by a superbly carved statue of the demonic figure, Rangda *(see p29)*. There are other smaller temples in caves along the nearby cliff.

🅰 **Pura Rambut Siwi**
6 km (4 miles) west of Medewi Beach, then 500 m (1,650 ft) south.
Open daily. 🖼 donation.

⑭ Pengambangan

🛈 Negara, (0365) 41 060.

This Muslim settlement lies on the bank of the Ijo Gading river. Lined up along the shore are brightly painted Bugis boats. Each one has a miniature mosque on top of its mast, a reminder of the Islamic traditions of the Bugis. Not far away is a full-sized mosque, with Islamic arches and a shining dome. Music with a Middle Eastern flavour often blares from the coffee shops here; the place has a particular atmosphere.

Environs
The village of **Perancak**, on the other side of the river, has a mosque with tiered roof in the traditional Indonesian style.

⑮ Negara

🚌 from Denpasar & Gilimanuk. 🛈 Jalan Ngurah Rai, (0365) 41 193. 🖉
🖻 🖼 🖾

The real charm of Negara lies in the Bugis origin of its urban core. On both sides of the Ijo Gading River, south of the central bridge on Jalan Gatot Subroto, is the Bugis community of Loloan. A walk on its streets evokes the atmosphere of Sulawesi, where many early Bugis migrants originated *(see box)*. Wooden houses with elaborately carved balconies line the streets. The most beautiful are at the end of Jalan Gunung Agung and on nearby Jalan Puncak Jaya. Loloan boasts several traditional *pesantren* (Islamic boarding schools); many shipowners' sons were trained as *ulema* (religious scholars) in the holy city of Mecca.

Negara is also known for its *jegog*, *gamelan* orchestras playing huge bamboo instruments *(see p37)*. A sport which was introduced to West Bali by the descendants of the Madurese of East Java is the *mekepung*. This is a race in which jockeys compete in decorated two-wheeled chariots drawn

The *mekepung* buffalo race, a regular event in Negara

by a pair of water buffaloes. The most exciting races can be seen from July to October.

Environs
A small road 4 km (2 miles) west of Negara leads to the quiet

The mosque in Perancak, across the river from Pengambangan

North of Negara, the large Catholic church at Palasari

beach of **Rening**, 8 km (5 miles) away, where bungalows are available. From the nearby Cape Rening there is a beautiful sunset view over the mountains of eastern Java. Another good beach is Candi Kusuma, 13 km (8 miles) west of Negara.

To the north are two Christian villages: **Palasari** (Catholic) and **Blimbingsari** (Protestant). These were established at the end of the 1930s on State land passed by the Dutch to Balinese converts to Christianity, who were excluded from their own community. The architecture in both villages is an interesting mix of Balinese and Dutch-Nordic styles. Near Palasari an irrigation reservoir provides tranquil landscapes.

⑯ Gilimanuk

🚌 from Denpasar & Singaraja.
🚢 from Ketapang, Java. ℹ Negara, (0365) 41 210. 🏧 🏪 🏨 🏤

Gilimanuk is the ferry port to Java. There are many *warung* here catering for travellers who sometimes have to wait hours for a ferry.

The main architectural feature is an enormous arched "gateway to Bali", surmounted by four flaming dragons facing in the cardinal directions, with a throne of heaven in the centre.

Environs

North of Gilimanuk at Cekik, the **Museum Purbakala** (Archaeological Museum), displays some sarcophagi and neolithic tools excavated from a nearby funerary site. Some promising archaeological discoveries have been made here showing signs of pre-Bronze Age human settlement in this area. Also in Cekik is the headquarters of the Taman Nasional Bali Barat (see pp140–41), the nature reserve covering a substantial area of West Bali.

🏛 **Museum Purbakala**
Jalan Raya. No phone. **Open** 9am–4:30pm Tue–Sun. 🏧 🎫

The arched "gateway to Bali" at Gilimanuk

The Bugis in Bali

The Bugis, who are Muslims, are a seafaring people known for their spirit of adventure. They originated in Sulawesi, one of the Greater Sunda islands north of Bali. After Makasar in Sulawesi fell to the Dutch in 1667, thousands fled, many of them sailing to Java and Bali. East Java was in turmoil at the time. In both Java and Bali the Bugis were often hired as mercenaries. The estuary of the Ijo Gading River in the Balinese kingdom of Jembrana was a good anchorage, and in the 1680s a company of Bugis offered their services to the king. In due course they moved up-river, and settled next to the king's palace at Negara. Other Bugis communities settled on Bali's north coast. Bugis mercenaries helped the king of Buleleng, Panji Sakti, occupy Blambangan, Java, in 1697.

As late as the end of the 19th century, a group of Bugis in South Bali were operating as pirates from Pulau Serangan (see p76) near Benoa.

The Bugis controlled Bali's trade with Java until the mid-20th century, when the opening of the ferry link in Gilimanuk destroyed their economic power. Most of them are now impoverished fishermen.

Bugis boats painted in the traditional bright colours

⓲ Taman Nasional Bali Barat

The far west of Bali is occupied by the Taman Nasional Bali Barat ("West Bali National Park"). This is a wildlife preserve established by the Dutch in 1941, bordered by a large area of protected, productive land. The preserve aims to safeguard Bali's remaining wilderness and provides sanctuary for some threatened species. Permits are required for anyone who wants to stay overnight or to penetrate deeply into the park. Only travel on foot is allowed.

★ Mangroves and Wetlands
Mangrove roots protect the coast from erosion; the wetlands are home to fish, mudskippers and crabs.

The Bali Starling Breeding Facility
is a haven for the endangered birds.

Reefs and Marine Life
The park includes the marine environment around Menjangan Island (see p142), a good diving site rich in fish and coral.

Gunung Prapat Agung
332 m (1,100 ft)

Labuhan Lalang

Banyuwedang

Teluk Terima

Pemuteran   Pura Pulaki

Gilimanuk

Makam
⁂ Jayaprana

Cekik

National Park

Gunung Bakungan
△
603 m (1,900 ft)

Gunung Sangiang
△
1,004 m (3,300 ft)

Gunung Kelatakan
△
698 m (2,300 ft)

Gunung Merbuk
△
1,385 m (4,550 ft)

Blimbingsari

Sumbersari

Gunu Mese 1,344 (4,450

Palasari

Malaya

Nature Walk
A short trek, taken with a guide from the park headquarters, passes by rivers and through rainforest. Close to the route are several forest shrines including one with a hilltop view.

Negara

Mende

Perancak

★ Savanna
Along the north slopes of the central mountain range grow deciduous acacia, palm trees and arid shrubs. Plants live for long periods without rain on this dry savanna grassland.

Grasslands
Fertile grasslands stretch out towards the sea near the quiet beach of Pantai Gondol. A fishery research project is located here.

VISITORS' CHECKLIST

Practical Information
Administered by the Indonesian Forestry Service (PHPA). Visitors must apply for permits at these offices. **City Office:** Jalan Suwung 40, Box 329, Denpasar. **Park Headquarters:** Jalan Raya Gilimanuk, Cekik. **Tel** (0365) 61 060. **Open** 8am–4pm daily. **Ranger Station and Branch Office:** Labuhan Lalang. **Open:** 8am–6pm daily.

★ Sambar Deer
The forested mountain slopes are the habitat of these deer, which roam freely in the park.

Key

▬ Major road
═ Minor road
-- Walking trail
▬ Wildlife preserve boundary

Bali Sea

Singaraja
Seririt
Munduk

Gunung Musi
1,244 m
(4,100 ft)

Gunung Patas
1,412 m
(4,650 ft)

Pupuan

Protected Production Land

0 kilometres   10
0 miles   5

The Bali Starling

The Bali starling (*Leucopsar rothschildi*), or Rothschild's mynah, is the only surviving bird endemic to Bali and one of the world's most endangered bird species. Since 2005, when it was estimated that there were fewer than ten Bali starlings in the wild, efforts have been made to raise their numbers.

The conservation project in the West Bali National Park is an internationally supported attempt to save the species, by breeding the birds in captivity before releasing them to the wild. At the breeding facility, Bali starlings are protected from poaching, the principal cause of their declining numbers in the wild.

Medewi Beach
Pekutatan

Denpasar & Tabanan

The endangered Bali starling

Balinese Sapi
These local cattle, descended from the wild *banteng*, now rare, have been domesticated for heavy work in the ricefields.

For keys to symbols *see back flap*

Shrine dedicated to a romantic hero at Makam Jayaprana

⑱ Menjangan Island

🚐 to Labuhan Lalang from Denpasar & Seririt. 🚤 from Labuhan Lalang. ℹ️ Labuhan Lalang, (0365) 61 060. ♿ 🅿️

For diving and snorkelling in a pristine environment, Menjangan Island is not to be missed. Technically part of Taman Nasional Bali Barat *(see pp140–41)*, it owes its name to the Java deer *(menjangan)*, which swim across from the mainland. There are eight main diving points around the island, each with its own marine life. The best is perhaps the Anchor Wreck, named for the encrusted anchor on the reef. **Labuhan Lalang**, on the bay of Teluk Terima, is Bali's nearest point of access to Menjangan Island. Boat tickets may be bought at the office of the Department of Forestry here. The last boats leave for Menjangan Island at 11am and return at dusk. There is basic accommodation at Labuhan Lalang.

A lionfish and coral off Menjangan Island

⑲ Makam Jayaprana

Teluk Terima. 🚐 from Denpasar & Seririt. ℹ️ Singaraja, (0362) 25 141. **Open** daily. ♿ 🅿️

The Makam Jayaprana ("Jayaprana Mausoleum") is also a temple. It has to be reached by a climb from the road *(see p140)*; however, the panoramic view over Gunung Raung in

Java, Menjangan Island and Gilimanuk is ample reward for the effort. The shrine was built on the burial site of Jayaprana, a romantic hero of Balinese folklore. According to legend, Jayaprana had married a woman named Layonsari, of such extreme beauty that the Lord of Kalianget decided to get rid of him and marry her. The king pretended that Bugis pirates had landed in Gilimanuk and sent Jayaprana with a body of soldiers to repel them. When they came to their destination the soldiers killed Jayaprana. However, resisting the advances of the king, Layonsari killed herself to rejoin her beloved Jayaprana in death. Today, suitors ask for favours of love at the grave. It is decorated with statues of Jayaprana and Layonsari.

⑳ Pemuteran

🚐 ℹ️ Singaraja, (0362) 25 141. ♿ 🅿️ 🛏️

Pemuteran is a fast-growing coastal resort and fishing village, with plenty of accommodation options. It has beautiful coral reefs with a profusion of tropical fish. There are good diving and snorkelling spots, and a turtle sanctuary.
It is a convenient place for visitors to Menjangan Island to stay overnight; a boat can be rented here. Some hotels even offer early morning dolphin-spotting excursions.

Environs
A little west of Pemuteran is the small bay of **Banyuwedang**. The name is Balinese for "hot springs". There are many springs along this shore, supposedly with curative powers. They are alternately covered and exposed by the tide. A spa resort, **Mimpi Resort Menjangan** *(see p176)*, has been built over one of them.
Pura Pulaki, about 5 km (3 miles) east of Pemuteran, is a coastal temple near a point where a mountain ridge plunges abruptly into the sea, almost blocking the coastal passage. It is associated with the priest Dang Hyang Nirartha *(see pp50–51)* who is said to have turned the local inhabitants into *gamang* (ghosts). Living around it are mischievous monkeys; they are regarded as holy.

🄰 Pura Pulaki
Banyu Poh. **Open** daily. ♿ donation. 📷 certain areas.

㉑ Pantai Gondol

6 km (4 miles) west of Grogak, across the field next to the Fisheries Research Project (Perikanan). 🚐 ℹ️ Singaraja, (0362) 25 141.

Gondol beach is located at the foot of a small promontory, the Gondol Cape. With beautiful white sand and coral, it is a good, uncrowded spot for snorkelling and diving. However, there are no visitor facilities here.

The beach at Pantai Gondol, still pleasantly undeveloped

Air Panas at Banjar, a natural hot spring popular with visitors

❷ Banjar

Road Map A1. 🚌 to Seririt, then own transport. 🛈 Singaraja (0362) 25 141. 🖉 🖵 📷

Banjar is a town of historic significance, set on the coastal plain with the North Bali uplands as a backdrop. In 1871, when still a semi-independent kingdom run by a brahman family, it put up strong resistance to Dutch encroachment. This confrontation is known as the Banjar War. The ruling family was eliminated in one of Bali's first recorded *puputan*, or "fights to the last" *(see p53)*.

The brahmans from Banjar are famous for their literary talents. In the 19th century they adapted texts from classical Kawi (Old Javanese) into common Balinese.

Brahma Vihara Ashrama *(see p27)* is a Buddhist monastery built in 1970 by a powerful local brahman, Bhikku Giri Rakhita, who converted to Theravada Buddhism, the form of Buddhism prevalent in Thailand. The temple contains many Thai iconographic features. There is an impressive view from the monastery over a nearby valley and the shoreline.

Another highlight of Banjar is the **Air Panas** hot spring, popular with both locals and visitors from nearby Lovina. There are three pools; in the highest one the water is hot. Eight carved

dragon-heads spurt out greenish-yellow, sulphurous water believed to be thera-peutic for complaints of the skin. The hot water is considered sacred by the locals – a temple has been built around the spring, which is set in cool and shady surroundings.

Environs

From Banjar one can visit **Pedawa**, 10 km (6 miles) inland. This remote place is a Bali Aga village *(see p50)*. It was one of the villages which rebelled against the Javanese occupa-tion of 1343, and has retained Hindu cultural features dating from before that time. Indeed, the Hindu triad of Brahma-Vishnu-Shiva was unknown here until recently. While the

Balinese generally build a whole range of shrines for gods and ancestors behind their houses, the people of Pedawa build a single bamboo structure.

There are two routes from Banjar to Pedawa: both run through stunning mountain and plantation landscapes.

In **Sidatapa**, a village on another road running inland from Banjar, some interesting old houses made of bamboo still remain. This is one of the oldest villages in North Bali.

🅰 **Brahma Vihara Ashrama**
Between Banjar and Pedawa.
Tel (0362) 92 954. **Open** 8am–6pm daily. 🦽 donation. 📷

💧 **Air Panas Banjar**
Open 8am–6pm daily. 🦽 donation. 🚻

The Buddhist monastery of Brahma Vihara Ashrama at Banjar

A large bunutan tree spanning the road en route to Pekukatan from Pupuan

㉓ Pupuan

Road Map B2. 🚌 from Denpasar & Singaraja. 🛈 Tabanan, (0361) 811 602. 🖉

Pupuan is Bali's vegetable-growing centre, situated in the rainiest part of the whole island. The area around it is cool and mountainous. The road from Seririt to Antosari travels through some of Bali's most beautiful landscape, with excellent coastal views. It climbs steeply via Busungbiu, Pupuan, and through a forested pass 790 m (2,600 ft) high into lush spice-growing countryside. It then winds down to Blimbing and Bajra before passing rice terraces, with rice barns along the road. The road southwest to Pekukatan passes a coffee plantation area, and at one point is arched by the roots of a huge bunutan tree.

Environs
Blimbing, 12 km (7 miles) to the south, has the nearest accommodation, panoramic views and a restaurant.

㉔ Munduk

Road Map B2. 🚌 from Singaraja & Seririt. 🛈 Singaraja, (0362) 25 141. 🖉 🏠 🖉

Munduk is a highland village amid plantations of coffee and cloves. It is set on a high ridge near the volcanic lakes of Tamblingan, Buyan and Bratan. In the area there are still a few rest-houses from the 1920s, built in a mixed Dutch Colonial-Chinese style. In the village it is possible to visit the workshop of I Made Trip, Bali's most famous maker of bamboo instruments.

Munduk is an ideal base for exploring on rented bicycles, for mountain walks to Pedawa, for ricefield walks to Uma Jero, or for a tour of Lake Tamblingan and Lake Bratan. There are several waterfalls in the area – the most spectacular, 30 m-(100 ft-) high, can be found 1 km (half a mile) along the road eastwards to Bedugul. The path down to the waterfall is dense with clove and coffee trees.

㉕ Lake Tamblingan Tour

This tour of the mountain lakes incorporates a boat trip, a walk and a scenic drive. From Gubug, fishermen take visitors across Lake Tamblingan in a dugout canoe, skirting the north shore where dense forest descends to the edge of the water. The lake is the most unspoiled one on the island and is located in a volcanic caldera. It is surrounded by primary forest with monkeys and many species of birds to discover. The forest resounds with birdsong, especially that of barbets.

③ Pura Ulun Danu Tamblingan
The walk begins with a flight of steps to the temple. From a courtyard the trail leads into the forest.

② Sacred Spring
Inside a cave, marked by parasols and only accessible by water, there is a sacred spring.

① Gubug
A *warung* in the village of Gubug gives information on the area. There is no trail along the north shore and travel by canoe is necessary to see parts of Lake Tamblingan.

Dugout canoe crossing Lake Tamblingan

Parasailing, one of the water activities available at Lake Bratan

㉖ Lake Buyan

Road Map B2 & C2. from Singaraja. Singaraja, (0362) 25 141.

There are great views over the lake from the mountain road – dense forest scrub vanishes at the shoreline into the water. Boats can be hired from fishermen and treks organized to a cave on the slopes of Gunung Lesong, to Gesing or to Munduk.

㉗ Lake Bratan and Bedugul

Road Map C2. from Singaraja & Denpasar. Tabanan, (0361) 811 602.

Lake Bratan offers a variety of water activities such as para-sailing and water-skiing. Visitors can hire boats, and there are guides for treks to peaks such as Gunung Catur and Gunung Puncak Manggu. The lake is the setting for the 17th-century

Pura Ulun Danu Bratan temple, built on a small island and dedicated to the goddess of the lake, Dewi Danu. There is a small stupa-shaped shrine for Buddhist worshippers, with statues of Buddhas occupying niches that mark the four points of the compass. The panorama includes an 11-tiered *meru* located on the shore across a wooden bridge.

The 1.5 sq km (0.6 sq m) **Eka Karya Botanic Gardens** contain 320 species of orchids, a fern garden, a herbarium and a collection of plants used for making *jamu* (traditional medicines). Also here is the Bali Treetop Adventure Park.

To the north of Lake Bratan, the well-manicured Bali Handara Kosaido Country Club *(see p200)* boasts one of the world's best golf courses.

Eka Karya Botanic Gardens
Kebun Raya, west of Candi Kuning.
Tel (0368) 21 273. **Open** daily.
Bali Treetop Adventure Park
Tel (0361) 852 0680. **Open** daily.

④ Pura Pekemitan Kangin
This temple on the ridge, up a long winding flight of steps, overlooks the narrow forested isthmus separating the two lakes.

⑤ Rainforest
Many trails lead into the dense tropical rainforest extending towards Lake Buyan. The vegetation is characterized by vines, creepers and massive trees with huge buttress roots.

⑦ Gubug
From here, the tour continues by car on the ridge-top road.

⑧ Lake Buyan
As you travel along the road, you can enjoy views of the lakes from the caldera rim.

⑥ Pura Dalem Gubug
A short trail leads to this lakeside temple, which has a tall *meru* on a small promontory. A path then leads through open pasture back to Gubug.

Tips for Walkers
Start point: Gubug by canoe.
End point: Return to Gubug on foot and proceed by pre-arranged vehicle on the scenic road along the top of the ridge, heading west to Bedugul.
Getting there: Own transportation via Bedugul or Munduk.
When to go: Mornings. Avoid the rainy season when trails are slippery and infested by leeches.
Tour time: 2–3 hours.

Key
- Boat trip
- Walk route
- Drive route
- Minor road
- Track (some inaccessible)
△ Peak

0 kilometres 2
0 miles 1

㉘ Street-by-Street: Singaraja

With its waterfront mosques, temples, market and well-ordered streets, Singaraja is a pleasant place to stroll around. The harbour has not been dredged for 60 years and its business has mostly shifted to Celukang Bawang, 38 km (24 miles) to the west. However, this area is still one of the most interesting parts of the town, occupied by communities of trading minorities – Chinese, Bugis *(see p139)* and other Muslims. The Balinese community lives further east, while the modern commercial centre is near the market, Pasar Anyar, around Jalan Ahmad Yani and Jalan Diponegoro.

This bustling commercial area is where banks and businesses are concentrated.

To Lake Bratan and Bedugul

JALAN DR SUTOM

JALAN IMAM T

JALAN HASANUDDIN

The banks of the River Buleleng
From the bridge, the old residential houses of Singaraja can be seen along the river banks.

★ Chinese Temple
This temple with its classical red roof tiles, decorated with tablets in gold calligraphy, indicates the strong presence and influence of the Chinese trading community in this part of Singaraja.

To bus terminal

| 0 metres | 50 |
| 0 yards | 50 |

Buleleng River

Key

━ Suggested route

◀ The temple of Komala Tirta at sunrise

Masjid Agung Jamik
The minaret and gleaming dome are prominent features of this mosque set within a large compound.

VISITORS' CHECKLIST

Practical Information
Road Map B1. [i] Jalan Veteran 2, (0361) 25 141.

Transport
[bus] terminal on Jalan Surapati, Jalan Ahmad Yani & at Sangket.

Pasar Anyar is a food and crafts market with a wealth of busy stalls housed in four buildings.

★ **Masjid Nur**
This mosque was built in a style influenced by Indian architecture.

Pabean Harbour
The old harbour attracted settlements of traders from elsewhere in the Indonesian Archipelago; their descendants still live here.

★ **Independence Monument**
The statue commemorates Ketut Merta. During the Independence struggle just after World War II, he was shot from a patrol boat as he raised an Indonesian flag in place of the Dutch colours.

For hotels and restaurants in this region see pp176–7 and pp186–7

Exploring Singaraja

Singaraja, north Bali's main commercial centre, was the administrative capital of Bali in colonial times. Colonial-style architecture remains in streets south of the centre, but buildings erected under the New Order *(see p55)*, such as the Pura Jagat Natha temple, combine monumental scale with traditional style. *Singa* means "lion"; *raja* means "king". The city's identity is expressed in the prominent modern statue of a winged lion where Jalan Veteran meets Jalan Ngurah Rai. The former palace of the kingdom of Buleleng, housing the administrative offices of the regency, was damaged by fire in the brief political disturbances of 1999.

Golden lion standing guard at the entrance of the Chinese temple *(see p148)*

🅐 Pura Jagat Natha

Jalan Pramuka. 🖼 donation.
Pura Jagat Natha, the territorial Hindu temple of the Buleleng regency, is a large complex of buildings covered in fine stone carvings; its towering *padma-sana* shrine *(see p30)* is typical of Balinese temples built from the 1970s on. There are *gamelan* rehearsals in the evenings in one of the courtyards.

🖼 Gedong Kertya

Jalan Veteran 20 & 22. **Tel** (0362) 22 645. **Open** 8am–3:30pm Mon–Thu, 8am–1pm Fri. 🖼 donation.
Gedong Kertya is a library founded by the Dutch in 1928 for the preservation of Balinese lontar manuscripts.

These are specially cut palm leaves inscribed with a stylus and rubbed with blacking to make the script legible. The same technique is used to make *prasi*, illustrations of traditional stories. Gedong Kertya, which contains many thousand such manuscripts, is frequented mainly by Balinese in search of their genealogical origins or potent medicinal recipes.

🖼 Puri Sinar Nadiputra

Jalan Veteran, next to Gedong Kertya. **Open** Mon–Thu & Sat.
Housed in a former palace is the Puri Sinar Nadiputra weaving factory, where you can observe the textile-making process and buy the products. Silk and cotton *ikat* cloth is sold in the adjacent shop.

Environs

In the village of **Nagasepaha**, 8 km (5 miles) south of Singaraja, glass-painting is practised. Its initiator was a local puppet master, Jero Dalang Diah. He used to carve the characters for his stories out of buffalo or cow leather before painting them. In 1950, he was inspired by a Japanese glass-painting and began to paint on glass, using images from Balinese *wayang* stories *(see p34)*. Now, his descendants and several neighbours practise this artform and sell their works.

Singaraja

① Chinese Temple
② Independence Monument and Pabean Harbour
③ Pasar Anyar
④ Pura Jagat Natha
⑤ Winged Lion Statue
⑥ Gedong Kertya
⑦ Puri Sinar Nadiputra

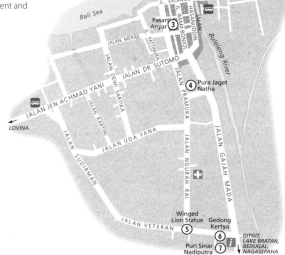

㉙ Lovina

Road Map B1.  Kalibukbuk, (0362) 41 910.

The name Lovina means "I love Indonesia", and is often used for a long stretch of the coast encompassing a series of villages, from Tukadmungga in the east to Kaliasem in the west. The beach resort area has quiet, black-sand coves lined with coconut trees. Outriggers add to the nostalgic charm, and dolphins can often be seen in the sea. For snorkellers, there are still pristine coral reefs.

The tourist facilities of Lovina are on Jalan Binaria, which leads to a modern sculpture of dolphins. To the north are ricefields, coconut groves and hotels; to the south, roads lead to villages with the mountain looming in the background. From the village of Temukus, you can trek to the **Singsing Waterfall**.

㉚ Gitgit

Road Map C1. from Singaraja & Bedugul. Singaraja, (0362) 25 141. to waterfall.

This village is the location of an impressive waterfall, 45 m (149 ft) high, about 400 m (450 yds) from the main road and surrounded by lush vegetation. Another waterfall, 1 km (half a mile) up the hill, is not quite as high, but there are fewer visitors there.

Gitgit, Bali's highest waterfall, is a refreshing stop for sightseers

Pura Beji, a highly decorated temple in Sangsit, near Jagaraga

Environs
Pegayaman, just north of Gitgit, maintains 17th-century Javanese traditions. On the Prophet's birthday (see p47), villagers parade a *tumpeng* (mountain-shaped offering).

㉛ Jagaraga

Road Map C1. from Singaraja. Singaraja, (0362) 25 141.

Jagaraga was the site of a battle in 1849, in which the war hero Patih Jelantik held the Dutch to a long stand-off before he was defeated. The relationship between the Balinese and the Dutch is reflected in the lively reliefs of the local temple of the dead, **Pura Dalem**. These were carved in the early decades of the 20th century. The subjects include aircraft, ships and a European in a car being held up by an armed man.

▣ Pura Dalem
Jagaraga. **Open** daily. donation.

Environs
The central gate of **Pura Beji** in **Sangsit**, 4 km (3 miles) from Jagaraga, is famous for its ornamentation. Garudas (mythical birds) are carved half in the round, half in low relief. The nearby **Pura Dalem** has some grim depictions of the tortures in hell inflicted on those who infringe moral rules.

The country around **Sawan**, 4 km (3 miles) south of Jagaraga, is said to produce some of Bali's best rice. There are impressive river gorges in the area. Sawan is also known for its northern dance and music tradition.

Air Sanih, 12 km (8 miles) from Sangsit, is a small beach resort named after a spring. There is a pleasant beach restaurant and basic accommodation.

▣ Pura Beji
Sangsit. **Open** daily.

Relief in the Pura Dalem, Jagaraga, showing a man driving a car

㉜ Pura Meduwe Karang
See pp152–3.

㉝ Tejakula

Road Map D1. from Singaraja. Singaraja, (0362) 25 141.

The old village of Tejakula is famous for its silver jewellery and its ancient *wayang wong* dance (see p35). This eastern part of the regency of Buleleng is one of the most unspoiled areas of Bali. At Tejakula itself there are some quiet black beaches and idyllic coconut groves.

Environs
Nearby are several Bali Aga villages (see p50). One of them, **Sembiran** (a short way up the mountain road west of Tejakula), has the characteristic stone-paved roads, some megalithic remains, and good views down to the north coast.

㉜ Pura Meduwe Karang

The large temple is notable for its statuary and carved panels which can be examined at close quarters. Although not the most extreme example, the temple shows a flowery style of decoration characteristic of North Bali. There are successive split gates and a set of two symmetrical *gedong*, or pavilions. The highest point is the towering, elaborately decorated Betara Luhur Ing Angkasa shrine.

Split Gates
At each level of the temple the ascent to the main shrine passes through a *candi bentar* (split gate) decorated with relief carvings.

★ **Ramayana Sculptures**
The grand parade of 34 stone figures lined up on the entrance terrace are all characters from the Indian *Ramayana* epic.

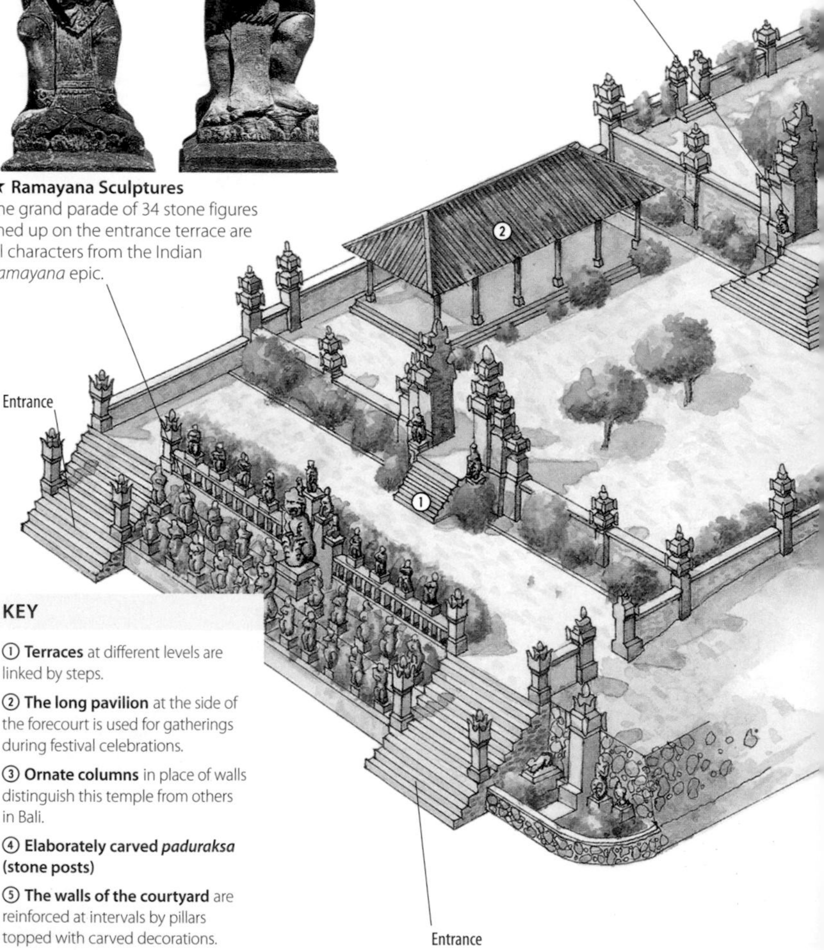

Entrance

KEY

① **Terraces** at different levels are linked by steps.

② **The long pavilion** at the side of the forecourt is used for gatherings during festival celebrations.

③ **Ornate columns** in place of walls distinguish this temple from others in Bali.

④ **Elaborately carved** *paduraksa* (stone posts)

⑤ **The walls of the courtyard** are reinforced at intervals by pillars topped with carved decorations.

Entrance

★ Main Shrine
The impressive Betara Luhur Ing Angkasa shrine honours the "Lord possessing the ground". Offerings are also made at the shrine to the sun-god Surya and to Mother Earth for fertility of the agricultural land.

VISITORS' CHECKLIST

Practical Information
Kubutambahan. **Road Map** C1. from Singaraja. **Open** 8am–5pm daily. Purnama Sasih Kawulu (Feb).

Transport

★ Relief Carvings
This local priest is typical of the subject matter of reliefs adorning the courtyard walls, which show people and scenes from everyday life.

Wall Sculpture
With subjects taken from Balinese legend, these decorate the walls round the central courtyard.

The Cyclist
A westerner on a bicycle is depicted on the side of the main shrine. He is believed to be the Dutch artist W O J Nieuwenkamp, who came here in 1904.

LOMBOK

Glistening paddy fields, verdant hills, rugged mountains and long stretches of white sandy beach make up the landscape of Lombok. A mix of Muslim Sasaks and Hindu Balinese provides a rich diversity of cultures. In terms of both the local economy and facilities for visitors, Lombok is much less developed than Bali, but easily accessible and rewarding to visit.

The Sasaks are the indigenous people of Lombok. Numbering about three million, they are thought to be descended from a hill tribe of North India and Myanmar. The minority Balinese population, about 100,000, live mostly near the west coast.

Lombok's identity has been formed by two major influences. Javanese arrivals in the 14th century brought Islam and Middle-Eastern influences, while the Balinese Hindus, who were the colonial masters of the island from the 16th century until the 1890s, have been an important presence.

The Sasaks and the Balinese provide the island with a rich heritage of dialects and languages, traditional dance, music, rituals and crafts. Beautiful pottery is made and cloth woven, using skills passed down through the generations. The influence of Javanese, Hindu and Islamic cultures can

be seen in architecture and ceremonies. While Muslim Javanese architectural influences can best be seen in the mosques, the Sasaks provided the distinctive shape of the *lumbung* (rice barn), more rarely seen now than in the past.

Lombok appeals to visitors for its natural beauty more than for its architectural heritage. The island's varied geography provides ideal conditions for trekking, wave- and wind-surfing, diving, snorkelling and game fishing. A chain of volcanic mountains in the north is dominated by Gunung Rinjani, which offers good trekking country. Sandy beaches punctuated by extinct volcanic peaks and huge cliffs plunging straight into the Indian Ocean make for a spectacular south coast. The east coast is blessed with calm seas, peaceful beaches, sheltered coves and beautiful coral islands.

A traditional Indonesian village in Lombok

◀ A traditional canoe anchored on the shores of a Lombok beach

Exploring Lombok

Not far from the ferry terminal at Lembar is Mataram, the provincial capital. From here a road runs from west to east taking in the sights of Narmada, Lingsar, and the hill-station area of Tetebatu. A road to the south coast leads to Kuta, a surfing spot and ideal base for exploring the rugged southern coast, which has many beautiful and remote beaches. Lombok's main resort area is Senggigi beach, north of Mataram. Easily accessible from Senggigi are the Gili Isles, an excellent diving and snorkelling location. North central Lombok is dominated by Gunung Rinjani, a huge volcanic peak surrounded by a national park, with opportunities for trekking in remote areas.

A mosque in the town of Selong

Cultivation of *kangkung*, a kind of watercress, near Tanjung

0 kilometres 10

0 miles 5

Getting Around

There are bus and *bemo* services on some main roads in Lombok, particularly the main east–west route from Mataram, and the road to Senggigi. There is little transport elsewhere, even on the road south to Kuta. Independent travellers are strongly recommended to rent their own vehicle, preferably with a driver. Remoter roads can be steep, narrow, or badly surfaced.

The majestic landscape of Taman Nasional Gunung Rinjani

Traditional Sasak dance

Key

— Major road

= Minor road

-- Track

— Scenic route

△ Summit

For keys to symbols *see back flap*

Panoramic view from the hilltop of Gunung Pengsong

❶ Lembar

🚌 🚢 from Padang Bai & Benoa Harbour. ℹ️ ferry terminal. 📷

Lombok's main sea port, in a bay surrounded by hills, is the gateway to the island for passenger car-ferries and a jetfoil from Bali. Crowds of merchants and other travellers mill around Lembar's ferry terminus. Much lively haggling takes place over prices of seats in overloaded buses and vans travelling to other destinations on Lombok. There is a small tourist office, some phones and a few food stalls. At the docks, beautiful Bugis schooners (see p139) and small steamers load and unload cargo.

Environs

The roads around Lembar run through lush, rural scenery. The coast road, skirting the peninsula towards **Sekotong** some 10 km (6 miles) to the south, has good views of the bay and its *bagan*, stationary fishing platforms standing in the sea. Fishermen lower huge nets into which they attract fish with the aid of lanterns. From here skiffs take passengers to the remote coral islands of

Gili Gede and Gili Nanggu. Accommodation on the islands is basic, and visitors mostly provide their own entertainment and food.

❷ Banyumulek

🚌 from Mataram. ℹ️ Mataram, (0370) 632 723 or 634 800. 📷

This village of wooden huts with thatched roofs is a centre for the production of hand-made terracotta pots. Here, visitors can see how they are made and roam among the displays of pots, some decorated with textiles and rattan. Buyers of pots too large to carry can have them shipped abroad if necessary.

Environs

About 3 km (2 miles) west of Banyumulek, an easy climb up **Gunung Pengsong** leads to a good view. From the Hindu shrine at the top, Bali's Gunung Agung and Lombok's Gunung Rinjani are visible in opposite directions. On one side the plain of Mataram stretches to the sea and on the other is an arc of rugged mountains.

❸ Sweta

🚌 ℹ️ Mataram, (0370) 632 723 or 634 800. 🚲 💻 📷

One of Lombok's oldest temples, **Pura Lingsar**, is in Sweta. First built in 1714, the large complex has both Balinese Hindu and Sasak Wetu Telu (Muslim) shrines, as well as a pond containing sacred albino eels. At the **Bertais Market**, fruits, vegetables and spices – onions, garlic, bright red chillies in every size imaginable – are displayed in all their colours. One can also bargain for baskets, textiles, bamboo products, and bridles and stirrups.

The bus terminal serving Mataram is at Sweta.

🅰 Pura Lingsar
North of Sweta. **Open** daily. 🚲
🎭 Perang Topat (Rice Cake War) & Pujawali (Nov–Dec).

❹ Narmada

🚌 ℹ️ Mataram, (0370) 632 723 or 634 800. **Open** daily. 🎭 Duck Catching Festival (17 Aug).

Narmada, built in 1805, was originally a raja's (king's) summer palace. In the gardens is a lake said to represent the crater lake of Gunung Rinjani (see pp162–3). When no longer able to climb the mountain and see the lake, the raja gazed on its likeness. Lotus-filled ponds and terraced gardens recall royal splendours of the past.

Lotus pond in Narmada, a 19th-century royal water palace

Lombok's Pottery Tradition

Pottery is the main product of several villages. Traditionally no potter's wheel is used. Some pots are formed by hand using tools known as "stone and paddle", others are built up by coiling lengths of clay. Water decanters, decorated plates and saucers, vases, huge water containers and lamps are all created by hand. Banyumulek's pots are simple in design and devoid of embellishments; Masbagik specializes in distinctive geometric patterns; and Penujak (see p165) produces pots decorated with animal motifs.

Vase from Penujak

❺ Mataram

Mataram, Ampenan and Cakranegara run together without a break; the whole conurbation is commonly known as Mataram. Mataram proper is the capital of the Indonesian province of West Nusa Tenggara. Its large, whitewashed, high-roofed houses hark back to Dutch colonial days. Ampenan, to the west, was once Lombok's main port and a vital link in the spice trade. Cakranegara, to the east, was the royal capital until a century ago; today, it is a bustling commercial centre.

Exploring Mataram

Mataram is characterized by its parks and wide, tree-lined streets with buildings which echo traditional Sasak styles. There are several monuments, such as the **Kencana Warga Mahardika**, a tribute to outstanding citizenship.

Along the winding streets of Ampenan are homes and businesses of Arab and Chinese merchants. Some of the buildings, now turned into attractive restaurants and cafés, show an Art Deco influence. At sunset, visitors head down to the bustling beach and have a drink in the old colonial bank building.

At the **Lombok Pottery Centre** *(see pp190–91)*, pottery and other handicrafts are sold.

🏛 Museum Negeri

Jalan Panji Tilar Negara 6.
Tel (0370) 637 503. **Open** 8am–2pm Tue–Thu & Sat–Sun, 8–11am Fri.
Closed public hols. 🎫 🎥

The provincial state museum displays local textiles and ceramics, copperwork and woodcarvings, as well as artifacts relating to the islands of West Nusa Tenggara and paintings representing the variety of ethnic cultures.

🏯 Mayura Water Palace

Jalan Selaparang, Cakranegara.
Tel (0370) 624 442. **Open** daily. 🎥
This complex was built in 1844 under the Balinese Karangasem dynasty. The centrepiece is a lake, surrounded by a park dotted with shrines and fountains.

🏛 Pura Meru

Jalan Selaparang, Cakranegara.
Open daily. 🎥
With its three slender, multi-tiered shrines representing the Hindu Trimurti of Vishnu, Shiva and Brahma, this is Lombok's largest Hindu temple complex.

Pura Meru seen from the Mayura Water Palace

Mataram

① Museum Negeri
② Kencana Warga Mahardika Civic Monument
③ Lombok Pottery Centre
④ Mayura Water Palace
⑤ Pura Meru

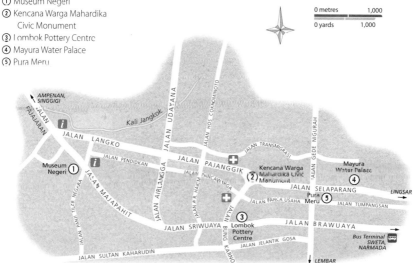

The beach resort area in Senggigi, a major tourist centre of Lombok

❻ Senggigi

🚌 from Lembar & Mataram. **ℹ️**
Mataram, (0370) 632 723 or 634 800.
🎭 Cultural Appreciation Month
(Aug). 🏊 💻 📷 🤿

Senggigi is the most popular
resort in Lombok, attracting
visitors with its white sandy
beaches and small palm-fringed
bays. Although very much less
developed than Kuta in Bali,
Senggigi has a broad range of
accommodation, restaurants
and entertainment facilities.

Although Senggigi Beach is
strictly speaking two glistening
bays, separated by a thrust of
white coral jutting out into the
ocean, the area now known
as Senggigi is a 6 km (4 mile)
strip of road and beachfront.
Restaurants and small cafés line
the colourful main beach road.

The views up and down the
coast, and out across the sea to
Bali, which can be enjoyed from
the coastal road, are majestic.
Swimming off the beach is safe;
and waves suitable for less
experienced wave-riders peel
to the left and right off the reef.
Many people also windsurf here.

Around the reef itself is a
variety of marine life and
beautiful coral. This is a good
spot for relaxed snorkelling.

Environs
An atmospheric temple shrine
stands on a black outcrop of
rock reaching out into the sea
at **Batu Bolong**, 3 km (2 miles)
from central Senggigi. Here,

Hindu devotees make their
offerings at dusk. The crimson
sunsets are beautiful, with the
silhouette of Bali's Gunung
Agung also faintly visible in
the distance.

❼ Gili Isles

🚌 from Senggigi & Mataram
to Bangsal. 🚤 from Bangsal.
ℹ️ Mataram, (0370) 632 723 or 634
800. 🏊 💻 📷 🤿

These three islands, each no
more than 2–3 km (1–2 miles)
across, are visited primarily
because of the diversity and
abundance of colourful marine

life in the coral reefs and crystal-
clear waters around them. They
are all accessible by boat from
Bangsal harbour in Lombok or
from Bali. The best time for diving
here is late April to late August.

Gili Air ("ai-year"), closest
to the mainland and with the
largest resident population,
is quiet around the secluded
hotels, but elsewhere on the
island the local village life is
quite lively. Many restaurants
and bars are mixed in with the
tropical trees and shrubs, and
lodging tends towards the
upper end of the range. This
is a good place for families.

Gili Meno, which offers a real
sense of escape, is the smallest
and least developed of the
islands. It has fewer accommodation options, but the
places to stay are mostly
more up-market than those
on the other two islands.

Gili Trawangan, the largest
and furthest from the mainland,
is the party island. A foreshore
strip of bars and restaurants
tucked in among many simple
losmen (see p170) and hotels
churn out music till the early
hours. The other side of
the island is quieter, with a
variety of restaurants and
accommodation – from backpacker huts, to luxury villas –
drawing a wide range of visitors.

Marine Life in the Gili Isles

Divers *(see pp206–7)* who want to see sharks can generally do so

Brightly coloured coral in the waters off
the Gili Isles

within a day's diving off the Gili
Isles. Reef sharks, which have
no interest in humans, are often
encountered. The coral is fine,
despite damage caused by fish-
bombing in past years. Over
3,500 species of marine life
survive around the Gilis,
compared with 1,500 off the
Great Barrier Reef. In these
waters you can spot the
orange-and-white striped
clownfish, the brightly coloured
parrotfish and the majestic
Moorish idol. There are two
endangered turtle species, the
green turtle and the hawksbill,
living in these waters. Divers at
all levels of ability will find a rich
variety of reef fish and other
underwater life.

A drum known as a *kecimol*, at a Muslim wedding in Tanjung

⑧ Tanjung

🚌 from Mataram. ℹ️ Mataram, (0370) 632 723 or 634 800. 📱 🏠 🗺️

Tanjung's livelihood is based on fishing as well as the agricultural products of the countryside. It is a large village on the road north to the Gunung Rinjani foothills, with a twice-weekly cattle market. It is surrounded by lush country in which coconut groves alternate with ricefields and vegetable gardens. In the river shallows grows *kangkung* (a leafy vegetable rather like watercress), one of Lombok's favourite dishes.

Environs

The road north runs along the black-sand beach and the terrain becomes distinctly arid. Four km (2 miles) from Tanjung on the coast is **Krakas**, famous for fresh, cool spring water. The spring is located underwater 400 m (1,320 ft) offshore at a depth of about 10 m (33 ft). Local fishermen, who will take visitors out in their boats for a small fee, collect the water, which is drinkable. Further north, just past the small town of Gondang, are the **Tiu Pupas** waterfall and seven caves.

⑨ Segenter

🚌 from Mataram ℹ️ Mataram, (0370) 632 723 or 634 800. **Open** 9am–5pm daily. 🐾 donation.

The small settlement of Segenter is a typical, traditional Lombok community, a good place to wander and to see the people going about their daily lives. The inhabitants are less pushy and commercially-minded than those around Senggigi.

In the late morning, many villagers can be seen resting in the "guest huts", open structures with platforms raised above ground level, set between rows of the larger thatched houses which make up the village as a whole.

The people of Segenter lead an almost self-sufficient life; they produce most of the staple food necessary for their daily needs and plant cotton, rice and tobacco to sell at the market.

A house in Segenter, constructed from parts of the coconut palm

⑩ Senaru

🚌 from Sweta & Tanjung. ℹ️ Mataram, (0370) 632 723 or 634 800. 🚿 📱 🏠 🗺️

At a height of over 400 m (1,320 ft) on the lower slopes of Gunung Rinjani, Senaru is braced by cool refreshing air. From here the visitor is rewarded with perfect views of Rinjani to the south and the ocean to the west.

Once a secluded mountain settlement sheltered from the outside world, this village with its traditional-style houses is fast becoming a weekend escape from the heat of the coastal regions.

Senaru has many simple guesthouses and restaurants. It is the most popular departure point for treks and climbs up the mountain (see pp162–3). It is also possible to make arrangements for a trek through the Gunung Rinjani national park and up the volcano. Camping equipment, tent and sleeping-bag rental are available, porters and guides can be engaged and food and other necessities can be bought here.

Environs

An easy 30-minute walk to the west of Senaru leads to the dramatic 40 m- (132 ft-) high **Sendanggile Waterfalls**, where water comes straight off one of the highest peaks in Southeast Asia. Here is the chance to wade in what must be the cleanest and freshest water in Indonesia. A little further uphill is the **Tiu Kelep** waterfall, with a lovely pool perfect for swimming.

Another short 30-minute walk from the village centre is **Payan**, which has thatched huts and a megalithic appearance: this is one of Lombok's few remaining Wetu Telu villages (see p27). Although somewhat commercialized, it is an example of Lombok's aboriginal village traditions. The women wear traditional sarongs and black shirts for weaving and during Muslim ceremonies. The Muslim practices observed here contain both Balinese and Hindu elements.

The Sendanggile Waterfalls near Senaru

⓫ Taman Nasional Gunung Rinjani

This national park is a magnet for experienced trekkers, and for nature lovers. Gunung Rinjani is a volcano 3,726 m (12,224 ft) high, important in the religions and folklore of both the Hindus and the Sasaks of Lombok. Rinjani itself is not active; the smaller Gunung Baru has erupted several times over the last 100 years. In 1995, the skies rained ash, tremors shook the island, and activities in the national park were halted. There have been no such problems since. The tourist information office at Mataram can advise on current conditions. Climbs to the caldera rim and to the summit, which are quite challenging, can be arranged in Mataram, Senggigi or Senaru. Sembalun Lawang is another starting point, but there are fewer facilities here.

The ebony leaf-monkey, frequently seen in Lombok

Trekking from Senaru
Climbs can be arranged with many operators working out of local homestays.

Batu Koq
& Bayan → **Batu Koq**

Senaru

Rinjani Trek Centre

● **Sindang Gila Waterfall**

● **Base Camp**

Camp Site ●

Gunung Senkereang Jaya
2,919 m (9,577 ft)

● **Hot Spr**

Camp Site

● **Tiuteja Waterfall**

Gunung Plawangan
△
2,612 m (8,600 ft)

*Gunung
2,363
(7,752*

Gunung Tanaklayur
2,664 m (8,800 ft)

Gunung Buanmangge
△
1,916 m (6,300 ft)

Bukit Ketimunan
1,602 m (5,200 ft)

0 kilometres — 5
0 miles — 3

★ **Danau Segara Anak**
The blue-green waters of this lake are surrounded by the steep walls of the volcanic crater. Trails lead down to the small, active volcano of Gunung Baru within the caldera.

Mountains near Sembalun
The range of mountains rising on the eastern side of the Sembalun Valley is an impressive sight, particularly seen from the direction of Gunung Kanji.

Bayan & Anyar

Sajang

Sembalun Lawang

Sembalun Bumbung

Gunung Atas Timur

2,238 m (7,400 ft)

Gunung Kanji

2,045 m (6,750 ft)

Gunung Nangi

2,330 m (7,700 ft)

Black-naped Oriole
This bird has bright yellow and black plumage and a rich call note. Other bird species seen in the park include lorikeets, pigeons and thrushes.

p Site

Gunung Propok

2,077 m (6,850 ft)

Gunung Rinjani

3,726 m (12,300 ft)

Sapit

Aikmel & Labuhan Lombok

Key

━━ Major road

═══ Minor road

--- Trekking route

★ **View from Gunung Rinjani**
From the highest point on Lombok, the view stretches beyond the dry volcanic slopes to the coastal plains.

Sembalun Valley
Sweeping views of plantations and small villages nestling in the valley can be seen from the mountain pass, 2,000 m (6,600 ft) high, on the road south to Sapit.

For keys to symbols *see back flap*

Gunung Rinjani towering over plantations near Sapit

⑫ Sembalun

🚌 from Mataram & Tanjung.
ℹ️ Mataram, (0370) 632 723 or
634 800. 🖉 🏊

Lying in a valley surrounded by
mountains is Sembalun, a village
consisting of single-storey
wooden buildings. Visitors are
few here, and there are only a
couple of basic places to stay.
However, there is a pleasant
sense of remoteness. The air is
fresh, and can be quite cold at
night. This is a good place for
walks in the countryside. The
growing of shallots is a major
source of income here, and a
pungent, but not unpleasant,
scent pervades the valley.

From here the view of
Gunung Rinjani is very vivid: the
mountain seems to be almost
within an arm's reach. Sembalun
is the starting point of a Rinjani

climb route more direct than
that from Senaru *(see pp162–3)*,
but the facilities here are not
as good.

Environs
The road east to Sapit runs across
one of the highest mountain
passes in Indonesia. The hairpins
and gradients give good views
over the Sembalun Valley.

⑬ Sapit

🚌 from Sweta. ℹ️ Mataram, (0370)
632 723 or 634 800. 🖉 🏊

Sapit is situated on the eastern
slopes of Gunung Rinjani at
about 800 m (2,640 ft) above
sea level. It is a refreshingly cool
mountain resort commanding
views of eastern Lombok, and of
Sumbawa across the sea
beyond. Blanketing Rinjani's

lower slopes around Sapit are
emerald-green rice terraces
and tobacco plantations.

The village is basic, but
gardens and flowerbeds make
a fresh, orderly impression.
There are some inexpensive
but clean guesthouses here.

Vessels moored in the quiet waters of a
jetty at Labuhan Lombok

⑭ Labuhan Lombok

🚌 from Mataram. 🚌 from Mataram
and Sumbawa. ℹ️ in ferry terminal.
🖉 🏊

The bay around Labuhan
Lombok forms a natural
harbour. A road runs parallel
with the shore, and between it
and the waterside are the
settlements of Bugis fishermen
consisting of houses on stilts.
Colourfully painted trawlers are
moored nearby. The forebears
of this community came from
South Sulawesi *(see p139)*. The
town's Sunday market sells all
manner of produce and daily

House on stilts in the coastal village of Labuhan Lombok

For hotels and restaurants in this region see p177 and p187

needs. At one end of the bay, 2 km (1 mile) from the town, is the ferry jetty for services running east of Lombok to Sumbawa, the next island in the Lesser Sundas group.

🚌 Pringgasela

from Sweta & Labuhan Lombok. *i* Mataram, (0370) 632 723 or 634 800.

The shady village of Pringgasela lies in the cool, quiet foothills of Gunung Rinjani. A mountain stream runs through it beside the road. Many villagers here are weavers, and they are happy for visitors to watch them at work. By tradition, girls in the village learn to weave from around the age of ten. Outside many of the houses textiles are displayed for sale, and the overall impression is colourful. The patterns and colours, with blacks and reds predominant, are characteristic of Lombok.

Basket produced in Loyok

Environs
In the hills south of Pringgasela is another craft centre, **Loyok**, the premier basketware, bamboo and palm-leaf handicraft village in Lombok. The road from Loyok runs parallel to a fast-flowing stream that weaves through a series of beautiful forests and valleys.

🚌 Tetebatu

from Mataram. *i* Mataram, (0370) 632 723 or 634 800.

The hill-station village Tetebatu, with its views of Gunung Rinjani, is a good place for relaxation. The village itself is quite modest, but over an area running 3–4 km (2–3 miles) up the mountain slope there are a number of guesthouses, set among ricefields.
Pleasant walks are to be had in the mountain air, passing large-leaved tobacco plantations. One hike runs to a small river into which flows the Jeruk Manis waterfall – the route is quite strenuous but can be tackled by fit children over ten, as well as adults. Other walks lead to isolated villages and a tropical forest inhabited by monkeys. It is advisable to engage one of the guides who offer their services in the village.

🚌 Sukarara

from Sweta. *i* Mataram, (0370) 632 723 or 634 800.

Many people in Sukarara earn their living by weaving *songket* textiles (see p41). The tourist trade is rather evident here. Large numbers of shops display and sell many varieties of cloth from around the region.

Village women dressed in black will demonstrate their expertise with the loom and are willing to pose for photographs.

🚌 Penujak

from Sweta. *i* Mataram, (0370) 632 723 or 634 800.

Along with Banyumulek (see p158) and Masbagik, Penujak is one of Lombok's main pottery-producing villages, and perhaps the best place to see the process, which the villagers will explain. Traditionally, women made the pots by hand while the men marketed them. Now that export sales have led to increased output, men join in the production process. Each village produces its own distinct pottery decoration and colour, but all the designs are available in all three places.

Traditional earthenware pottery produced in Penujak

A weaver at work on a hand-operated loom in Sukarara

Textiles in Lombok

Hand-woven textiles, of very high quality, are produced in Lombok using traditional backstrap looms. The villages which specialize in textile weaving are Sukarara, Pringgasela, Rembitan and Sade (see p166). There is some larger-scale production around Mataram. In the villages, the entire process of cloth making can be watched by visitors, from the boiling of barks and roots to make dyes, and the soaking of cotton threads, to the weaving of original patterns on the hand-operated loom. The villagers use only natural plants for the dyes. Yellow dye, for example, is made from an extract of turmeric root, while blue comes from the indigo plant. Roots and bark are pounded and boiled; the cotton threads are immersed for 24 hours, and, when dry, are arranged on the loom in the manner demanded by the pattern of the textile.

Typical Lombok sarong

🔞 Rembitan and Sade

ℹ️ Mataram, (0370) 632 723 or 634 800. 🖼️ donation. 🎫 🖥️ 🏛️

The farming villages of Rembitan and Sade, about 3 km (2 miles) apart from one another, are both attractively set against the hillside. Despite the fact that many visitors stop here, and therefore sellers of souvenirs abound, Rembitan and Sade remain good places to catch a glimpse of traditional Sasak life, in which weaving textiles, growing rice and rearing goats and cattle are major occupations. A distinctive feature is the *lumbung*, a bonnet-shaped rice barn. Once a symbol of Lombok, these barns are now rare. The walls of the thatch-roofed barns and houses are made of bamboo or palm-leaf ribs.

🔟 Kuta

🚌 from Sweta. ℹ️ Mataram, (0370) 632 723 or 634 800. 🎫 🖥️ 🏛️ 📷 🎣 Nyale fishing festival (Feb–Mar).

Lombok's Kuta largely retains the character of a sleepy fishing village, and is a complete contrast to its namesake in Bali. Nevertheless, it is developing quite fast. The coastline around it is ruggedly beautiful. Kuta bay has dazzling white sand, and relatively few people. The ocean swells form perfect waves for surfing.

Kuta offers a selection of visitor accommodation, ranging from budget options for backpackers to luxury hotels such as the Novotel Lombok (*see p177*), which has been designed to fit in with the

Kuta's rugged coastline, a paradise for surfers and sun-lovers

building style typical of this part of Lombok.

Environs

There are two other superb beaches not far from Kuta. **Mawun** beach is 8 km (5 miles) west, and attractively isolated. The same distance to the east is **Tanjung Aan**, a wide, sandy bay. Waves crash on rocky outcrops at each end of the bay, but the water on the beach itself is smooth and turquoise.

㉑ Gerupuk

ℹ️ Mataram, (0370) 632 723 or 634 800. 🖥️ 🏛️

The village of Gerupuk is situated on the edge of a long bay. The village's main income, apart from fishing, comes from seaweed cultivation. The seaweed, used as an ingredient in food products for farm animals, grows on semi-submerged bamboo frames in the waters off the beach. After being harvested it can be seen drying in neat bundles along the roadside.

Gerupuk is home to one of south Lombok's most popular surf breaks. In the bay, swells from the Indian Ocean build up and break on coral reefs, creating fine waves. Surfers hire a small skiff for the short trip to the break; the journey gives breathtaking views of the nearby cliffs and rocky crags. The skiffs anchor a short distance from the break and await the surfers' return.

The waves here are considered more user-friendly and forgiving than others on this coast, where the sea can often be rough. They break on coral deep enough not to cause undue worry to board riders, unlike the shallow breaks and steep take-off points of Maui near Selong Blanak to the west. While the waves mostly break right, left breaks also peel off, although less regularly. The surf is best early in the morning before any wind gets up – usually before 9am; but even later in the day when cross-winds blow offshore, the waves are fine. The surfers are mostly Japanese, Australians and locals from Kuta village itself; there is a smattering of Brazilians and French. They generally find accommodation at Kuta Beach.

The waves at Gerupuk, one of the best surfing spots on Lombok's coast

For hotels and restaurants in this region see p177 and p187

㉒ Selong Blanak

ℹ Mataram, (0370) 632 723 or 634 800.

Marked at each end by rocky promontories, Selong Blanak is a tranquil bay with a fishing settlement and tourist accommodation and facilities. On the beach are multicoloured outrigger canoes. Most people come here to surf at a nearby beach known as **Maui**. The waves are exceptionally fast. Because of the steep take-offs and the fact that the waves are ridden over very shallow coral, this is a place for very experienced surfers only.

Coastal landscape near Selong Blanak

㉓ Tanjung Luar

ℹ Mataram, (0370) 632 723 or 634 800. 🚗 💻 📷

The village of Tanjung Luar earns its living from the sea. It is a minor port – travellers from nearby islands land here by means of an inter-island taxi service which uses small outriggers. Many occupations to do with fishing and the sea are represented here and there is a busy fish market. Fishermen return to port after spending several days afloat, and sell their catch beside

Buggy at Tanjung Luar

the water's edge. It is possible to watch huge sharks being brought to shore. Contri-buting to the lively atmosphere are the salt-sellers, the children fishing off the main jetty, and the people giving their boats a new coat of paint.

A short walk from the fish market, lining the beachfront, live some Bugis communities (see p139), their wooden houses raised on stilts. Colourful Bugis schooners, with their distinctive high prows, lie at anchor here. For many people in Tanjung Luar, *cidomo* are the only form of transport. These are small horse-drawn buggies, brightly painted and often decorated with bright red pompoms and tassels.

㉔ Bangko Bangko

🚌 from Lembar. ℹ Mataram, (0370) 632 723 or 634 800.

A popular place for fishing and surfing, Bangko Bangko lies at the end of a peninsula at the southwest extremity of Lombok. A location rather than a village, it can be reached only along a dirt road. The reward for this trip off the beaten track is some spectacular scenery.

Some surfers have named the area Desert Point. The waves that peel to the left off a coral shelf, before slamming into the base of the cliff face, provide great conditions for experienced riders. The un-predictable, often dangerous seas are good for game fishing. A fishing trip can be booked through tour operators in Lembar (see p158).

The harbour at Tanjung Luar, with *Bugis* houses raised on stilts

TRAVELLERS' NEEDS

WHERE TO STAY

Set among tropical gardens and gently swaying palm trees, even the largest of Bali's hotels have a local flavour. This is reinforced by the staff and the island's cultural ambience. Resorts dot the island, and in recent years a number of boutique hotels have sprung up too. For groups, villas can offer a greater sense of privacy than hotels. Lombok is less developed than Bali, but it offers a good variety of accommodation, and new places are opening up all the time. There is little provision specifically for the disabled in the hotels of either island.

Losmen, Homestays, Guesthouses and Cottages

The most common type of low-budget accommodation in Bali and Lombok is the *losmen*. The term is derived from the colonial-era word "*logement*" and once implied little more than a room in a local household. Today it refers to a category of small, inexpensive lodgings, in many areas the only accommodation available. *Losmen* and true homestays are not formally organized and are usually not included in hotel listings.

Losmen generally consist of simple rooms built around a central area. Mosquito nets, a fan and sometimes a bathroom are provided, but you may need to bring your own toilet paper. Large numbers of *losmen* are to be found in Kuta, Central Ubud, the village of Lembongan on Nusa Lembongan and Candidasa; and near the beaches at Lovina and Padang Bai.

Low-cost guesthouses are also common. Rooms in guesthouses – and indeed hotels – are often called "cottages" or "bungalows", and they range from concrete boxes to atmospheric *lumbung* (traditional rice barn-style structures, quite often with thatched roofs).

The outdoor café area at the luxurious Oberoi, in Tanjung *(see p177)*

Hotels and Resorts

Bali's many resorts and hotels tend to be concentrated in the more developed tourist areas of the southern and central regions. There is something for every budget, and good package deals are often available. Lombok has a more limited choice, though the situation is steadily improving: hotels and resorts are concentrated in the west, around Senggigi, on the Gili Isles and in the Kuta area on the south coast.

Bali's larger resorts are particularly suitable for families or visitors looking for an all-inclusive holiday. They generally offer a luxurious experience insulated from the hustle and bustle of daily life, and usually provide baby-sitting services and/or in-house programmes for children. Many of them are part of international chains and offer world-class service and facilities, such as gyms, spas, pools, landscaped gardens, first-class restaurants and cultural shows.

Prices vary according to room, region and season. Most hotel rooms will be equipped with air-conditioning and bathrooms, while cheaper rooms will have fans. The Bali branch of the **PHRI** (Persatuan Hotel dan Restaurant Indonesia, or Indonesian Hotel and Restaurant Association) publishes hotel listings and a star rating, but they tend to be neither complete nor up to date. In theory, the association should help with problems, but it is usually more effective to submit complaints direct to the hotels themselves.

Speciality Hotels and Resorts

Some hotels and resorts cater to visitors interested in certain types of activity, cuisine or cultural experience. For example, those situated on mountains will generally offer trekking, while a number of small homestays in Kintamani, and those close to Gunung Agung, offer trekking to the volcanoes.

For snorkelling and diving, the resorts around Amed and Tulamben on the east coast are excellent choices, as are those on the island of Nusa Lembongan, the North Bali resorts (from where trips can be made to the underwater gardens of Taman Nasional Bali Barat), and the Gili Isles (accessible from Lombok). Balinese cooking courses are also offered by many resorts.

Night falls over the pool and restaurant at Amanusa, in Nusa Dua *(see p174)*

◀ Handmade Balinese jewellery and masks for sale

Clean lines and understated beauty at the Amankila, in Manggis *(see p176)*

For visitors interested in spiritually oriented holidays, Ubud is a popular centre. Some hotels here and elsewhere offer the opportunity to become involved in local village life, and visitors can try their hand at cooking and weaving, among other local crafts.

Bali is also home to several hotels based around – often scenically sited – golf courses.

Private Villas

For people travelling with children, villas can be a good choice, since they are generally fully staffed with housekeepers, baby-sitters, gardeners, security and often a cook. They will typically feature a pool and gardens, satellite television and several bedrooms. For families or groups of friends, villas can offer great savings and give opportunities for private relaxation and entertainment that a hotel cannot match. Pool parties, cocktail parties and barbecues can all be a part of a villa holiday.

Some Bali-based agents offer a selection of villas and will work to find something to suit your budget, personal needs and number of guests. The largest operators are **The Villa Guide** and **Elite Havens**.

Travelling with Children

Bali and Lombok are wonder lands for the young. Locals have a particular fondness for children, and hotel staff will take an interest in them. All the large five-star resorts and many of the smaller ones have good facilities for children, enabling parents to sit back and relax. Some of the facilities on offer are baby-sitting services, organized children's activities, children's clubs and family suites.

Reservations

The Internet is a good means of booking direct or investigating a hotel or resort before making a decision. Bypassing the travel agencies can mean good discounts, but you may find you have no recourse if all is not as promised at your hotel. Most resorts have their own websites, and Bali-based agents have also set up similar services for hotels, private villas and tours. A number of websites are given in the Directory *(see p173)*.

Recommended Hotels

Both Bali and, to a lesser extent, Lombok have an exhaustive range of hotels, resorts and guesthouses. Standards in all price ranges are generally high, but there are also a fair few duds. The recommended options on pp174–7 are some of the best places to stay on the islands. Among the criteria used by our authors to make the selection are: value for money, comfort, quality of service and facilities, character or charm, and location. There is a mix of budget, mid-range and high-end accommodation options, as well as a number of places that are particularly good for certain activities – for example, diving or golf. Although most of the recommended hotels, resorts and guesthouses are located in popular tourist areas, there are several options in off-the-beaten-track or up-and-coming destinations – such as the Menjangan area in the north-west of Bali. A "DK Choice" box is used to highlight an outstanding place to stay.

A balcony with incredible views at the romantic Alila Ubud, in the Ayung River Gorge area *(see p175)*

Spas and Spa Resorts

One of the most prominent facilities offered by Bali hotels to their guests is the spa. Traditional health and beauty treatments derived from local, natural ingredients have been used in Indonesia for many centuries, but it is only in more recent years that they have been made widely available to visitors. Some of Bali's top spas have been rated as among the best in the world. However, visitors on a budget can also indulge – although the smaller salons cannot match the luxury of the most expensive places, some of them offer a range of similar treatments at a fraction of the cost.

Spa and massage room at the Four Seasons Resort, Sayan

Traditional Treatments

Bali's spas aim to provide pleasure and relaxation rather than clinical therapy. They are intended not to treat health problems, but rather to calm the mind and beautify the body. Many of the spas have been designed with couples in mind; with the exception of the local beauty parlours, they offer treatments for both men and women.

A complete treatment will include a full body exfoliation called the *lulur*, an aromatic beauty therapy that has been popular for generations with the Javanese. Other enjoyable experiences include the traditional Balinese massage, a gentle process characterized by long, sweeping hand movements; and the relaxing and therapeutic cream bath, which includes an hour-long head-and-shoulder massage and a natural hair treatment. These are popular with both men and women.

Western influence has made itself felt, particularly through the addition of aromatherapy. Indonesia has an abundance of natural herbs and flowers, and an industry has grown up dedicated to creating high-quality natural oils. Even during a simple massage you will be offered a choice of oils designed to create a variety of moods.

Choosing a Spa

There is an extensive range of spas in Bali. They cater to a wide variety of budgets and preferences. Most spa resorts offer combination packages – these are particularly suitable for first-time visitors, who would like to sample the range of treatments available.

The **Four Seasons Resort** in Jimbaran has a multi-million-dollar spa facility that has won many international awards. A full menu of local and Western treatments is available. One of its specialities is a massage in which water is sprinkled from above, simulating a calming, warm rain shower. Another is a *jamu* (natural remedies) bar where local herbal recipes are prepared.

The **Nusa Dua Spa**, at the Nusa Dua Beach Hotel, was one of the first spas on Bali and it remains one of the biggest. Simple beauty treatments and massages are offered in private rooms, and residents at the hotel who want the full package may enjoy treatments in their villas. Nearby, in Tanjung Benoa, **Jiwa Spa at the Conrad** offers ocean flow massage and smoothing rain body polish, as well as therapies for children.

Thalasso, located at the Grand Mirage Resort, is a French treatment centre. Natural sea water is used in many of its therapies.

Javanese Lulur Treatment

The *lulur* treatment is a traditional beauty ritual which originated in the royal palaces of Central Java. It is the most popular therapy among the many offered by Balinese spas. It usually lasts two and a half hours. A yellow paste is made from a fragrant blend of powdered turmeric, herbs, nuts, grains and other ingredients: this is first spread over the body and then rubbed off to remove dead skin. The skin is then moisturized with splashes of cool yoghurt. This stage is followed by a shower and a scented bath before a long, slow, relaxing massage is performed. There are a number of variations to this treatment, with ingredients ranging from coffee to ginger and spices.

The Javanese *lulur* treatment – a rejuvenating treat for the skin

The spa at the luxurious **Four Seasons Resort** in Sayan is modern and air-conditioned, and features Ayurvedic treatments. Also recommended is the **Spa Uluwatu** at InterContinental Resort Bali in Jimbaran. Treatment pools are among the facilities here. Eastern and Western massage techniques and spa products are offered in beautifully appointed private rooms.

Bodyworks in Seminyak is a small, privately run spa with comfortable rooms and a full range of treatments, ranging from hair colouring to manicures, pedicures and facials. Bodyworks has another salon, larger and more luxurious, in Peti Tenget.

Prana Spa, part of The Villas Bali Hotel & Spa in Seminyak, offers hot and cold plunge pools, reflexology, Ayurvedic treatments and herbal steam rooms. Also in

Seminyak is the **Oberoi** (*see p177*), which specializes in the traditional Javanese *lulur* and body mud wrap treatments, and **Spassion** is one of the few spas offering *ken dedes*, which involves "smoking" the body.

Mandara Spas has taken over the running of some of the best spas; locations include **Padma Resort Bali**, **Nikko Bali** and **Ayodya Resort Bali**.

Nur Salon was one of the first salons to operate in Ubud; it is still traditional in style and very inexpensive. **Bali Hati** boasts pristine massage rooms with a steam room and outdoor Jacuzzi. Prices are quite reasonable. The **Como Shambala** is an up-market wellness retreat, with treatment rooms bordering lush forest. **Bagus Jati Resort**, just north of Ubud, has a Jacuzzi overlooking a stunning gorge. It offers Ayurvedic and

Mandara Spa's signature treatment performed by two therapists

Balinese treatments in a luxurious setting.

Espace is a trendy, white-themed spa offering massage, body treatments and facials. Check out the relaxing, mineral-rich Flores Island Sea Mud exfoliating body scrub.

The Yoga Barn is a rustic, environmentally friendly space dedicated to yoga, movement and healing. In addition to a wide range of yoga classes, it offers holistic retreats.

DIRECTORY

General Information

PHRI (Bali branch)
Villa Rumah Manis, Jalan Nakula, Seminyak.
Tel (0361) 730 606.

Private Villas

Elite Havens
Jl Raya Semer, Kerobokan.
Tel (0361) 731 074.
W elitehavens.com

The Villa Guide
883 Jl Raya Semer, Banjar Semer, Kerobokan.
Tel (0361) 737 498.
W thevillaguide.com

Spas and Spa Resorts

Bagus Jati Resort
Banjar Jati Sebatu, Ubud.
Tel (0361) 978 885.
W bagusjati.com

Bali Hati
Jalan Raya Andong, Ubud.
Tel (0361) 977 578.
W balihati.com

Bodyworks
Jalan Raya Seminyak 63, Seminyak.
Tel (0361) 730 454.
Kayu Jati 2, Peti Tenget.
Tel (0361) 733 317.

Como Shambala
Uma, Ubud.
Tel (0361) 972 448.
W uma.como.biz

Espace
Jalan Raya Seminyar, BR Basangkasa, Seminyak.
Tel (0361) 730 828.
W espacespabali.com

Four Seasons Resort, Jimbaran
Jimbaran Bay.
Tel (0361) 701 010.
W fourseasons.com/jimbaran

Four Seasons Resort, Sayan
Sayan, Ubud.
Tel (0361) 977 577.
W fourseasons.com/sayan

Jiwa Spa at the Conrad
Jl Pratama 168, Tanjung Benoa. **Tel** (0361) 778 788. W conradbali.com

Mandara Spa at Ayodya Resort Bali
Jalan Pantai Mengiat, Nusa Dua. **Tel** (0361) 771 102. W ayodya resortbali.com

Mandara Spa at Nikko Bali
Jl Raya Nusa Dua, Selatan.
Tel (0361) 773 377.
W nikkobali.com

Mandara Spa at Padma Resort Bali
Jalan Padma 1, Kuta.
Tel (0361) 752 111.
W padmaresort bali.com

Nur Salon
Jalan Hanoman 29, Padang Tegal, Ubud.
Tel (0361) 975 352.
Fax (0361) 974 622.

Nusa Dua Spa
Nusa Dua Beach Hotel, Nusa Dua.
Tel (0361) 771 210.

Oberoi
Seminyak, Kuta.
Tel (0361) 730 361.
W oberoihotels.com

Prana Spa
The Villas, Jalan Kunti 118x, Seminyak, Kuta.
Tel (0361) 730 840.
W thevillas.net

Spassion
Jalan Bypass Ngurah Rai (next to Taman Mumbul Real Estate), Nusa Dua.
Tel (0361) 772 434.
W spassion-bali.com

Spa Uluwatu
InterContinental Resort Bali, Jalan Uluwatu 45, Jimbaran. **Tel** (0361) 701 888. W baliinter continental.com

Thalasso
Grand Mirage Resort, Jalan Pratama 74, Tanjung Benoa. **Tel** (0361) 771 888.
Fax (0361) 772 148.

The Yoga Barn
44 Jalan Hanoman, Ubud. **Tel** (0361) 971 236 or 970 992. W theyoga barn.com

Where to Stay

South Bali

CANGGU: Hotel Tugu Bali **$$$**
Boutique   Map C4
Jl Pantai Batu Bolong
Tel (0361) 473 1701
W tuguhotels.com
An antique-filled hotel between
ricefields and a beach. Two suites
contain replica studios of famous
1930s painters, and you can dine
in a 300-year-old temple.

JIMBARAN: Ayana Resort
& Spa   **$$$**
Spa   Map C5
Jl Karang Mas Sejahtera
Tel (0361) 702 222
W ayanaresort.com
This lavish resort boasts a private
beach, two glass wedding pavil-
ions, and a Thalasso spa with one
of the world's largest Aquatonic
seawater pools.

KUTA: Un's Hotel   **$**
Guesthouse   Map C5
Jl Bene Sari 16
Tel (0361) 757 409
W unshotel.com
Rooms here have communal
balconies and terraces and are
set around a pool and gardens.
Centrally located but peaceful.

KUTA: Poppies Cottages   **$$**
Cottages   Map C5
Jl Pantai, Gang Poppies
Tel (0361) 751 059
W poppiesbali.com
This long-standing budget
lodge in the heart of Kuta offers
comfortable, thatched-roofed
cottages and an attractive
pool/garden area.

Amanusa, in Nusa Dua, with its elegant
decor and incredible views

LEGIAN: All Seasons Resort **$**
Resort   Map C5
Jl Padma Utara
Tel (0361) 768 180
W allseasonslegian.com
Located near the beach, this large
modern Accor hotel is aimed
squarely at young backpackers.

NUSA DUA: Amanusa   **$$$**
Luxury   Map C5
Nusa Dua
Tel (0361) 772 333
W amanresorts.com
One of Bali's finest hotels, with
stunning architecture and elegant
decor. Rooms have magnificent
views over the Badung Strait.

NUSA LEMBONGAN: Hai Tide
Beach Resort   **$$**
Cottages   Map E4
Nusa Lembongan
Tel (0361) 720 331
W haitidebeachresort.com
The *lumbung*-style thatched and
bamboo huts here have bed-
rooms accessed by a ladder, plus
stylish ethnic-chic furnishings.

SANUR: Segara Agung Hotel **$**
Resort   Map C4
Jl Duyung 43, Semawang
Tel (0361) 288 446
W segaraagung.com
Situated minutes from the beach,
this hotel features traditional
Balinese architecture, a pretty
garden and four classes of room.

SANUR: Griya Santrian Hotel **$$**
Cottages   Map C5
Jl Danau Tamblingan 47
Tel (0361) 288 181
W santrian.com/griya
This family-run resort's seaside
bungalows are linked by winding
paths in a large garden. The wide
range of facilities include several
aimed at children.

SANUR: Tandjung Sari Hotel **$$**
Cottages   Map D4
Jl Danau Tamblingan 41
Tel (0361) 288 441
W tandjungsarihotel.com
This old, romantic hotel has been
beautifully maintained and is
furnished with local artifacts.
Choose from bungalows and
villas with pavilions and lounges.

SEMINYAK: Amadea Resort
& Villas   **$$**
Villas   Map C4
Jl Laskmana 55
Tel (0361) 847 8155
W amadeabali.com
The two- to four-bed villas with
private pools are the highlights

at this modern hotel, located
on the popular "Eat Street".

DK Choice

SEMINYAK: The Legian **$$$**
Luxury   Map C4
Jl Laksmana
Tel (0361) 473 0622
W ghmhotels.com
This exceptional suite hotel on
Seminyak Beach offers elegant,
contemporary style, a world-
class restaurant, deluxe spa, gym
and a stunning swimming pool
that merges with the ocean.

SOUTH KUTA BEACH:
Bali Dynasty Resort   **$$**
Family   Map C5
Jl Kartika Plaza
Tel (0361) 752 403
W balidynasty.com
Large four-star resort set in beau-
tiful gardens close to the beach.
There is also a children's club,
playground and three pools.

SOUTH KUTA BEACH:
The Sandi Phala   **$$$**
Boutique   Map C5
Jl Wana Segara
Tel (0361) 753 780
W thesandiphala.com
The intimate thatched pavilions
here house elegant suites with
Indonesian decor, local artifacts,
and a veranda or balcony.

TANJUNG BENOA: Grand Aston
Bali Beach Resort   **$$**
Family   Map C5
Jl Pratama 68 X
Tel (0361) 846 8684
W aston-international.com
This lively resort draws guests
back year after year with its great
entertainment, activities and
water sports programme, five
restaurants and a kids' club.

ULUWATU: Banyan Tree
Ungasan   **$$$**
Luxury   Map B5
Jl Melasti, Banjar Kelod, Ungasan
Tel (0361) 300 7000
W banyantree.com
Set amid the rocky splendour of
the Bukit Peninsula, this hotel
offers dramatic Indian Ocean
views and landscaped gardens.

Central Bali

DK Choice

**AYUNG RIVER GORGE:
Alila Ubud**   **$$$**
Luxury   Map C3
*Desa Melinggih Kelod Payangan,
Gianyar*
Tel (0361) 975 963
W alilahotels.com
This romantic retreat comprises
rooms and private villas perched
on the Sayan Ridge with breath-
taking views of the river valley
and distant volcanoes. The pool
has been voted one of the best
50 in the world, and there's also
a Mandara spa and a partially
open-air restaurant.

The perfect spot for a romantic getaway – Alila Ubud, in Ayung River Gorge

**AYUNG RIVER GORGE:
Kayumanis**   **$$$**
Boutique   Map C3
Sayan
Tel (0361) 972 777
W kayumanis.com
Set on the edge of a magnificent
river valley, this intimate sanctuary
consists of luxury villas with pri-
vate pools and bountiful gardens.

**LAPLAPAN: Natura Resort
& Spa**   **$$$**
Villas   Map D3
Banjar Laplapan
Tel (0361) 978 666
W naturaresortbali.com
These luxury villas on the banks of
the Petanu River have secluded
courtyards, open-air bathrooms,
plunge pools and wooden decks.

NAGI: The Viceroy   **$$$**
Villas   Map D3
Jl Lanyahan
Tel (0361) 971 777
W viceroybali.com
Opulent private villas combine
the amenities of an elite hotel
with a setting that is second to
none. There's even a helipad.

**PAYANGAN: Nandini Bali Jungle
Resort & Spa**   **$$**
Villas   Map C3
Banjar Susut
Tel (0361) 982 777
W nandinibali.com
Designed by an acclaimed
Balinese architect, this rainforest
retreat offers affordable luxury
in grass-roofed chalets.

SANGGINGAN: Uma Ubud   **$$$**
Luxury   Map C3
Jl Raya Sanggingan, Banjar Lungsiakan
Tel (0361) 972 448
W theumaubud.com
This beautiful inland retreat is
designed to maximize the views

of the borderless ricefields, jungle,
volcano and Tjampuhan Valley.

TEGALLALANG: Alam Sari Keliki **$**
Family   Map D3
Tromol Pos 03
Tel (0361) 981 420
W alamsari.com
Rooms, suites and family units
here are surrounded by coconut
groves. There is a natural stone
pool and a range of activities,
including craft classes for children.

UBUD: Jati Home Stay   **$**
Guesthouse   Map C3
Jl Hanoman, Padang Tegel
Tel (0361) 977 701
W jatihs.com
Based in the family home of a
well-known local artist, rooms are
basic but comfortable. There is an
on-site gallery, and a range of art
and music classes offered.

UBUD: Siti Bungalows   **$**
Cottages   Map C3
Jl Kajeng 3
Tel (0361) 975 699
W sitibungalow.com
Owned by the family of the late
Dutch painter Han Snel, who lived
in Ubud for many years, these
garden cottages are set in a quiet
compound minutes from town.

UBUD: Alam Jiwa   **$$**
Boutique   Map C3
Nyuhkuning
Tel (0361) 974 629
W alamindahbali.com
Located just south of the Monkey
Forest Sanctuary, Alam Jiwa offers
spacious rooms, friendly service
and free transport into Ubud.

**UBUD: Komaneka at
Monkey Forest**   **$$$**
Boutique   Map C3
Jl Monkey Forest
Tel (0361) 479 2518
W komaneka.com
An oasis in the heart of town,

Komaneka offers deluxe rooms,
suites and villas with private
plunge pools and verandas. The
décor is contemporary and
elegant, using natural materials.

UBUD: Maya Ubud Resort   **$$$**
Spa   Map D3
Jl Gunung Sari Pelitan
Tel (0361) 977 888
W mayaubud.com
Spread across 4 acres of hillside
garden between the river valley
and ricefields, Maya Ubud has
villas and rooms, three restaurants
and an enchanting spa.

**UBUD: Warwick Ibah Luxury
Villas & Spa**   **$$$**
Spa   Map C3
Campuhan
Tel (0361) 974 466
W warwickibah.com
Owned by Ubud's royal family,
this hotel overlooks the Wos
Valley and Pura Gunung Lebah
temple. Suites are spacious,
and there is a Mandara spa.

East Bali

AMED: Good Karma Bungalows **$**
Cottages   Map F2
Selang
Tel (081) 2368 9090
The simple beachside cottages
here each have an open-air
bathroom. The property is owned
by a colourful character called
Baba, who sings to guests and
promotes eco-awareness.

AMED: Santai   **$**
Boutique   Map F2
Bunutan
Tel (0363) 23 487
W santaibali.com
This charming beachfront
hotel offers traditional Balinese
bungalows with four-poster
beds and open-air bathrooms.

For more information on types of hotels *see pages 170–71*

CANDIDASA: Temple Café & Seaside Cottages
Cottages $
Jl Raya Candidasa   Map F3
Tel (0363) 41 629
ⓦ balibeachfront-cottages.com
This immaculate complex has a selection of bungalows – from budget options, to large comfortable ones with kitchenettes.

CANDIDASA: Puri Bagus Candi Dasa
Resort $$
Jl Raya Candidasa   Map F3
Tel (0363) 41 131
ⓦ puribagus.net
Set in a coconut grove beside a white sandy beach, this complex has cottages, two pools, a restaurant and massage pavilions.

CANDIDASA: Watergarden $$$
Boutique   Map F3
Jl Raya Candidasa
Tel (0363) 41 540
ⓦ watergardenhotel.com
Enchanting thatched cottages set among waterfalls and lotus ponds with *koi*. There is a pool, library and bar-restaurant.

GUNUNG BATUR: Lakeview Eco Lodge
Guesthouse $
Penelokan   Map D2
Tel (0366) 52 525
ⓦ lakeviewbali.com
Perched on the rim of an ancient caldera with breathtaking views of Gunung Batur, this hotel has spacious rooms and a decent restaurant.

DK Choice

MANGGIS: Amankila $$$
Luxury   Map E3
Karangasem
Tel (0363) 41 333
ⓦ amankilaresorts.com
This spectacular resort features three tiered pools that cascade down the side of a mountain to the sea. The pavilions, which are nestled in the hillside amongst frangipani and bougainvillea, have king-sized canopy beds and bathrooms with sunken tubs, and are connected to the resort facilities by raised walkways.

PADANG BAI: Hotel Puri Rai $
Family   Map E3
Jl Silayukti
Tel (0363) 41 385
ⓦ puriraihotels.com
Low-key hotel with several accommodation options, including four family rooms plus a pool, restaurant, bar and transport services.

An aerial view of the staggering luxury resort Amankila, in Manggis

TULAMBEN: Tauch Terminal Resort
Diving $$
Tulamben   Map F2
Tel (0361) 774 504
ⓦ tulamben.com
This five-star diving school/resort is built around a deep pool. The *Liberty* wreck is just offshore.

North and West Bali

BEDUGUL: Bali Handara Kosaido Golf & Country Club
Golf $$
Bedugul   Map C2
Tel (0362) 342 2646
ⓦ balihandaracountryclub.com
The 18-hole golf course here has a wonderful backdrop of mountains, forests and Lake Buyan, while the accommodation has the feel of Alpine chalets.

LOVINA: Lovina Beach Hotel $
Cottages   Map B1
Jl Raya Sererit, Kalibukbuk
Tel (0362) 41 005
ⓦ lovinabeachhotel.com
Two-storey, thatched cottages with private terraces sit in lush gardens dotted with fruit trees.

LOVINA: Puri Bagus Lovina $$
Villas   Map B1
Jl Singaraja-Serirt
Tel (0362) 41 386
ⓦ lovina.puribagus.net
Guests can relax here in villas with outdoor showers, a large free-form pool and a café-restaurant.

LOVINA: Damai $$$
Boutique   Map B1
Jl Damai Desa, Kayu Putih
Tel (0362) 41 008
ⓦ thedamai.com
The self-contained bungalows at this Danish-owned retreat perched on a mountainside have four-poster beds and Jacuzzis.

MENJANGAN: Mimpi Resort $$
Diving
Banyuwedang
Tel (0362) 94 497
ⓦ mimpi.com/mimpi-resort-menjangan
Just minutes by boat from Menjangan Island, this is a smart option for divers. Some villas have plunge pools and lagoon views.

MENJANGAN: The Menjangan $$
Resort
Desa Pejarakan
Tel (0362) 94 700
ⓦ themenjangan.com
This eco-village of rooms and clifftop villas overlooks beautiful Bajul Bay and Menjangan Island. Activities include bird-watching, diving, kayaking and horse-riding.

MUNDUK: Puri Lumbung Cottages
Cottages $$
Munduk
Tel (0362) 701 2887
ⓦ purilumbung.com
Surrounded by lily pads and rice-fields, and with views all the way to the coast, this cluster of stilted cottages is a cheerful choice.

PAPUAN: Cempaka Belimbing Guest Villas
Villas $$
Br Suradai, Belimbing   Map B3
Tel (851) 0045 1178
ⓦ cempakabelimbing.com
These award-winning villas are in a spectacular setting of rice terraces and fruit trees against a mountain backdrop.

PEMUTERAN: Taman Sari Bali Resort & Spa
Diving $$
Dusun Pemuteran, Kecamatan Gerokgak, Kabupaten Buleleng
Tel (0362) 93 264
ⓦ tamansaribali.com
Alongside the on-site dive centre, this beachfront hotel has

accommodation ranging from modest rooms to suites.

DK Choice

PEMUTERAN: Matahari Beach Resort & Spa $$$
Spa
Pemuteran
Tel (0362) 92 312
W matahari-beach-resort.com
An impressive beachside resort with four categories of rooms: more expensive options have ocean views. There is also an excellent restaurant, tennis court and spa. Trips to Menjangan Island can be arranged.

PEMUTERAN: Puri Ganesha Villas $$$
Spa
Pemuteran
Tel (0362) 94 766
W puriganesha.com
Each of the four thatched villas here, based on traditional Balinese village meeting places, has a salt-water pool and garden bathroom.

SERIRIT: Zen Resort $$
Spa   **Map** A1
Puri Jati, Desa Ume Anyar
Tel (0362) 93 578
W zenresortbali.com
Set on a hill overlooking the Java Sea, this resort has comfortable rooms, a good restaurant and a yoga and meditation pavilion.

TABANAN: Pan Pacific Nirwana Bali Resort $$
Golf   **Map** B4
Jl Raya Tanah Lot
Tel (0361) 815 900
W panpacific.com
This luxury golf resort blends into the contours of the coastline, with unobstructed views of Tanah Lot.

TABANAN: Waka Gangga $$$
Spa   **Map** B4
Banjar Yeh Gangga, Dusan Sudimara
Tel (0361) 484 085
W wakahotelsandresorts.com/waka-gangga
The concept of this beautiful beachfront resort is "back to nature" and spiritual harmony.

Lombok

GILI ISLES: Hotel Gili Air $
Cottages
Gili Air
Tel (0370) 662 1448
W hotelgiliair.com
Beach-facing cottages here have open-air bathrooms and terraces. There is also a bar-restaurant.

DK Choice

GILI ISLES: Martas $
Guesthouse
Gili Trawangan
Tel (081) 2372 2777
W martasgili.com
Run by a welcoming couple, one of whom is an experienced diving guide, Martas is an economical hideaway, with comfortable split-level rooms, pleasant grounds, a book swap and DVD library, and a wide range of tours on offer.

GILI ISLES: Desa Dunia Beda Beach Resort $$
Boutique
Gili Trawangan
Tel (0370) 614 1575
W desaduniabeda.com
This coconut grove resort is like a small Javanese village, with wooden houses and charming rooms with four-poster beds.

GILI ISLES: Luce d'Alma $$
Boutique
Gili Trawangan
Tel (0370) 612 1717
W lucedalmaresort.com
This Italian-run resort has elegant modern en suites that open on to an 80 m (260 ft) saltwater pool.

GILI ISLES: Villa Bulan Madu $$
Villas
Gili Air
Tel (081) 9073 3044
W bulan-madu.com
On the east coast of the island, these vast, well-equipped villas are set within tropical gardens.

GILI ISLES: Karma Reef Resort $$$
Cottages
Gili Trawangan
Tel (0370) 630 982
W karmaresorts.com
These hip, *lumbung*-style cottages are right on the beach. Popular events are held here on weekends.

KUTA: Yuli's Homestay $
Guesthouse
Jl Pariwisata
Tel (0819) 1710 0983
W yulishomestay.com
Yuli's has cosy rooms with cold-water bathrooms (there's a shared hot shower for guests), two pools and a communal kitchen.

KUTA: Novotel Lombok Resort & Villas $$
Villas
Pantai Putri Nyale, Pujut
Tel (0370) 615 3333
W novotel.com
Decorated in faded desert colours,

the eccentric architecture of this quirky resort is inspired by traditional Sasak villages.

SENGGIGI: Holiday Resort Lombok $$
Family
Jl Raya Mangsit
Tel (0370) 693 444
W holidayresort-lombok.com
Beachside rooms feature contemporary furnishings and offer lovely views of the garden or the sea. A children's pool and ample sports facilities are also available.

SENGGIGI: Puri Mas Boutique Resort $$
Cottages
Pantai Mangsit
Tel (0370) 693 831
W purimas-lombok.com
With its mix of thatched bungalows, rooms and suites, each in a different architectural style, this is one of the prettiest and best-value hotels on Lombok.

SENGGIGI: Sheraton Senggigi Beach Resort $$$
Luxury
Jl Raya Senggigi
Tel (0370) 693 333
W starwoodhotels.com
This is a five-star resort, with all the facilities you would expect from a Sheraton, including classy rooms, a lagoon pool and a spa.

TANJUNG: The Oberoi $$$
Luxury
Medana Beach
Tel (0370) 613 8444
W oberoihotels.com
A multi-award-winning resort set in palm-studded gardens and bordering an exclusive beach. Accomodation is in chic, two-storey villas, and its huge pool merges with the sea.

The award-winning Oberoi Luxury Resort in Tanjung

For more information on types of hotels *see pages 170–71*

WHERE TO EAT AND DRINK

From local dishes to international cuisines, Bali and Lombok cater for all tastes, and good food is available whatever your budget. Travellers are spoilt for choice in the more developed parts of Bali, though options in remoter parts of the island, and in Lombok, are more limited. Credit cards are accepted in smarter restaurants and cafés, and prices on menus are sometimes expressed in US dollars, although payment in rupiah is always accepted. Restaurants will accommodate disabled visitors, although few make any specific provisions.

The open-air restaurant at Alila Ubud in the Ayung River Gorge *(see p184)*

Local Food

The everyday Balinese diet consists of meals based on rice with a little meat, vegetables and the occasional egg. The combination is known as *nasi campur (see p180)*. This and other Balinese dishes are served in most restaurants.

For the "genuine" – and often tastier – article, try the *warung* or *rumah makan* (food stalls or simple restaurants/cafes) where locals eat when away from home. The food here is cheap, fresh and often spicier than in restaurants. Lining the streets and parked at night markets are *kaki lima* (food carts), whose hygiene standards are often questionable.

International Restaurants

Bali offers the world on a plate, with the entire complement of Asian, European and North American cuisines. A large number of foreign chefs have been attracted by the hotel chains, and some have started up their own operations. In turn they have trained many local chefs in foreign food preparation. French, Italian and other Mediterranean cuisines are all part of the enormous range offered in the island's restaurants, and standards are generally high. The prices are also very reasonable by inter-national standards. Some very good Japanese food can be enjoyed in Bali for a fraction of what it would cost in most other places.

Hotel Dining

Many hotels offer excellent meals in surroundings more luxurious than those encoun-tered in most other tourist destinations. The best are often featured in international food and travel magazines. The Alila, Four Seasons and GHM (which includes The Legian) chains have excellent reputations for hiring chefs with signature styles. The major chain hotels all offer the full range of dining styles from coffee shops and cafés to restaurants. It is often possible to eat in the open air. Hotel bars and restaurants are open to the public as well as to guests *(see pp174–7 and pp182–7).*

Cafes and Coffee Shops

Since the 1970s when surfers and independent travellers put Bali on the tourist map, the island has embraced the idea of casual eating. Bars and beach-side eateries serving fairly simple fare are common sights. They serve *nasi goreng* (fried rice), the ubiquitous banana pancake, fresh local fruit juices and grainy Bali coffee. However, growing demand from visitors and increased awareness among locals have fired up the café scene. Particularly in arty Ubud and trendy Seminyak, European-style cafés with espresso machines are common, as are, increasingly, up-market coffee houses serving gourmet blends of freshly roasted Indonesian coffee varieties. Accom-paniments include everything from tiramisu to the delicious *bubur hitam* (black rice pudding).

Alcohol

It would be a pity to visit Bali and Lombok without sampling the local alcohol, especially since imported alcohol attracts very high duties and is extremely expensive. Bintang is a popular, refreshing lager; Indonesian-brewed San Miguel and Heineken are also available. A local wine called Hatten's is light, dry, inexpensive and fairly drinkable. Arak cocktails, made with palm brandy, are a popular choice.

Alcohol is available almost everywhere in Bali, even in small *warung* outside tourist areas. In Muslim Lombok, however, alcohol is available only in tourist areas and up-market hotels, and should be consumed within the premises. Beware bootleg, home-brewed or excessively cheap alcohol on both islands, as it may be tainted with methanol.

Children

The restaurant scenes in Bali and Lombok do not generally cater specifically to children, but it is easy to find something children will eat. Some places will serve a half-portion, and have high chairs available on request; others will not. The larger hotels often offer free buffet breakfasts for children under 12.

Vegetarian Food

There is a wonderful range of tasty and nutritious vegetarian dishes in Bali and Lombok. *Tahu* (tofu) and *tempe* (cakes made of compressed, fermented soya beans) are popular and plentiful, as is *bubur sayur bayam* (rice porridge with spinach leaves, chilli, coconut shavings and coconut milk).

Many restaurants include a variety of vegetarian dishes on their menus. Those with Chinese-style dishes usually offer a wider range. It is possible to get vegetarian versions of non-vegetarian dishes on request. Just make sure your order is stated clearly.

Restaurant Etiquette

Many locals still eat with the right hand and no cutlery (the left hand is never used),

Chefs preparing a meal at Locavore in Ubud *(see p185)*

and well-dressed locals can often be seen eating in this traditional way.

Food will often appear in random order. It is best simply to start rather than wait until everyone is served. Casual clothing is accepted everywhere, but people tend to be more smartly dressed in up-market restaurants. Most restaurants are open-air, so smoking is generally allowed, although an increasing number now have a non-smoking area. Tipping is more common than it once was; expensive places tend to add a service charge anyway. Staff in cheaper local restaurants will be happy with a token tip.

Recommended Restaurants

The tourist hotspots on Bali and Lombok are home to a bewildering array of cafés, restaurants and bars serving everything from Indonesian staples to modern European dishes, super-fresh sushi to zinging Thai curries. Options off the beaten track, however, are more limited. The recommendations on pp182–7 are some of the best places to eat and drink on the islands. Among the criteria used by our authors to make the selection are: quality of food and service, value for money, hygiene and atmosphere. There is a mix of inexpensive, mid-priced and pricier options: food is generally very good value, whatever your budget. Although some restaurants specialize in a particular cuisine, most have international menus that feature dishes from around the world – pasta, pizzas, burgers, steaks and so on – though generally the Indonesian or Balinese options are the most reliable bets. A "DK Choice" symbol signifies an outstanding place to eat or drink.

The buzzing outdoor bar area at beachside hotspot Ku Te Da in Seminyak *(see p183)*

The Flavours of Bali and Lombok

Many of this region's distinctive tastes and cooking styles were influenced by early Chinese, Indian, Arabic and Dutch traders and settlers. Flavoursome curries rely on freshly ground spices, and common seasonings include ginger, lemongrass, kaffir lime leaves and tamarind. Sauces feature coconut milk and the essential trio of fresh coriander, pepper and garlic. A paste of salted and fermented shrimp is also used to enliven and add depth to dishes. Hot fresh chilli appears in fiery accompanying sauces called sambals, and peanuts are typically present as a garnish, or ground into a paste to form a sweet and spicy sauce.

Peanuts

Fresh chillies, a key ingredient in the cuisine of Bali and Lombok

Bali's Harvest

The chain of mountains that divides Bali is responsible for different climatic conditions and soil types, which yield a huge variety of crops. The southern-central plains are dominated by terraced ricefields, while the inland regions support onions, cabbages, papayas, spinach, lettuce, potatoes, carrots, coffee, cloves and peanuts. Fruit, including strawberries, is grown in the cool mountain area of Bedugul. Kintamani is famed for oranges and the Buleleng Regency for its durians. In Tejakula there are acres of mango plantations. The wani, found in the Singaraja area, is a white mango with a distinctive smell, which is cherished by the Balinese. The farmers in the hot and arid northern coastal region cultivate dry-land crops such as maize, cassava, beans and, surprisingly, grapes, a fruit that has been nurtured here since the early 20th century.

Jimbaran Bay Seafood

Every morning at dawn, the Jimbaran fishermen return to shore in their gaily painted

Star fruit   Durian   Mango   Watermelon   Pineapple   Pomelo   Papaya   Passion fruits
Selection of luscious tropical fruit from the islands of Indonesia

Regional Dishes and Specialities

Ginger, lemongrass, kaffir lime and lime leaves

Everyday Indonesian fare comprises rice, vegetables, egg and perhaps a little meat or fish. Known as *nasi campur*, it is usually cooked in the early morning and eaten whenever the need arises. In Bahasa Indonesia the word *lombok* means chilli pepper, and the Lombok people use home-grown hot chillies liberally in their cooking. Traditional white rice is the staple of Sasak food and is served with curries or soup made from vegetables, fish, and a little meat, but no pork. *Taliwang* dishes feature fried or grilled ingredients with a chilli sauce, and anything with *pelecing* in the name is also served with chilli sauce.

Gado gado is a warm salad of blanched mixed vegetables, tofu and egg, with a sweet and spicy peanut sauce.

Selecting the best fruits on offer at an Indonesian market

vessels to trade at the bustling Kedonganan fish market. At sunset the beach becomes the scene of a daily ritual as hundreds of visitors take their seats in the many *warung* – the simple seafood cafés that run virtually the length of the bay and serve up the catch of the day. The fish is displayed on ice at the back of the café, and guests are invited to select the seafood of their choice – mainly whole red and white snapper, barracuda, squid, giant prawns and lobster (the latter two served in their shells). The feast includes a bamboo steamer of rice, along with tasty steamed Balinese water spinach, delicious home-made garlic, tomato and chilli sauces, baked potatoes and a simple dessert of fresh pineapple, watermelon and banana.

Padang Cuisine

Padang food, from the Minangkabau region of West Sumatra, is to be found in the Rumah Makan Padang eating-houses. Glass-fronted cabinets showcase platters and pots filled with cold vegetables,

Fish, straight from the ocean to a Kedonganan market stall

meats and fish. The food is of Indian origin and is typically spicy, featuring plenty of chilli and meat curries. Customers choose a selection of dishes to make up a composite meal. These might include classic dishes such as beef rendang, but also items like *perkedel* (potato cakes), deep-fried corn cakes, the sesame-dipped and deep-fried bean curd known as *tempe*, hard-boiled eggs, liver, brains, lungs, fried chicken, tuna steaks, aubergine (eggplant), cassava leaf and water spinach – all served with rice, curried sauces and chilli sambals.

RIJSTAFEL

The name *Rijstafel*, literally meaning "rice-table", originated with the Dutch plantation owners, who liked to sample selectively from Indonesian cuisine. Steamed white or yellow rice is always the centrepiece, often presented in a cone and capped with a banana leaf. It is accompanied by a range of different meat, poultry, seafood and vegetable dishes, which are often served in handmade coconut pots on a banana-leaf plate. These boiled, grilled, roasted, steamed, wok-fried or deep-fried dishes are complemented by *krupuk* (rice crackers), *acar* (pickled sour vegetables) and a range of chilli and onion sambals and spicy sauces.

Sate lilit may be minced meat or fish, infused with coconut and grilled on a lemongrass skewer.

Bebek bututu is duck stuffed with spices, wrapped in banana leaves and cooked in an earth oven.

Kue dadar are little crêpe parcels, filled with a mixture of palm sugar, vanilla and grated fresh coconut.

Where to Eat and Drink

South Bali

**BUKIT PENINSULA:
The Kitchen & Restaurant
at the Temple Lodge** RpRp
International Map C5
Bingin
Tel (0857) 3901 1572
The wide-ranging menu here
covers everything from Italian to
Indian, Ayurvedic to macrobiotic.
The prawn risotto is particularly
good, as is the fresh baked bread.

**CANGGU: Echo Beach
House** RpRp
Barbecue Map C4
Jl Pura Batu Mejan (Echo Beach)
Tel (812) 3978 466
Tables spilling out on to a
beachside bluff, an extensive
drinks list, friendly staff and great
sunsets. The Sunday evening
seafood barbecue, accompanied
by live music, is a highlight.

**CANGGU: Waroeng
Tugu** RpRpRp
Indonesian Map C4
Jl Pantai Batu Bolong
Tel (0361) 473 1707
This hotel restaurant has success-
fully recreated the ambience of
the Majapahit Hindu Kingdom,
with open sides flanked by a
simple brick kitchen and a clay
oven fuelled by coconut husks.

DENPASAR: Babi Guling Rp
Balinese Map C4
Jl Sutomo
This low-key *warung* serves just
one dish: *babi guling* (roast
suckling pig). There's no sign, so it
can be hard to find. Look for an
open-sided shelter with low
tables and satisfied customers.

**DENPASAR: Pasar Malam
Kereneng** Rp
Market Map C4
Just off Jl Hayam Wuruk
Scores of street-food vendors set
up at this market each evening to
serve inexpensive bowls of soup,
noodles, rice and other traditional
dishes until the early hours.

**JIMBARAN: Jimbaran Seafood
Cafés** Rp
Seafood Map C5
Kedonganan and Jimbaran Beach
A plethora of simple beachfront
cafés with chairs and tables on
the sand lit by flickering candles
serve super-fresh seafood,
including snapper, barracuda,
giant prawns, squid and lobster.

KUTA: Kopi Pot Rp
Café Map C5
Jl Legian 139
Tel (0361) 752 614
Still going strong after 35 years,
this café serves reliably good
coffee (try the iced cappuccino),
cakes and black rice pudding,
as well as main meals (from
Indonesia and further afield).

**KUTA: Kori Restaurant
and Bar** RpRp
Thai Map C5
Gang Poppies II
Tel (0361) 758 605
This open-air pavilion serves
delights such as a Thai-style salad
with fresh blue swimmer crab,
mango, lemongrass and coriander.
Non-Thai desserts are also served.

KUTA: Maccaroni RpRp
Italian Map C5
Jl Legian 52
Tel (0361) 754 662
The distinctive architecture here

features polished grey concrete,
tubular metal and green vines.
The Italian chef produces a mix
of classic pizzas, pasta dishes and
more innovative concoctions.

KUTA: Made's Warung I RpRp
Indonesian Map C5
Jl Pantai
Tel (0361) 755 297
The oldest and most famous
restaurant in Kuta was estab-
lished way back in 1969. Today,
Made's Warung mixes Indonesian
and Western dishes; the former
are generally the better bets.

**KUTA: Mama's German
Restaurant** RpRp
German Map C5
Jl Raya Legian
Tel (0361) 761 151
Mama's opens all day, every day
of the year, and serves up some
hearty Germanic classics. The
sausages are a big hit, as are the
Bavarian meatloaf, goulash, and
the Black Forest gâteau. Good
beer is on offer, too.

KUTA: Poppies Restaurant RpRp
Indonesian Map C5
Gang Poppies I
Tel (0361) 751 059
This romantic garden restaurant
is another stalwart of the Kuta
dining scene, dating back to
1973. The menu features a
combination of Asian and
Western dishes, as well as
seafood and steaks. Book ahead.

KUTA: The Balcony RpRp
Mediterranean Map C5
Jl Benesari 16
Tel (0361) 757 409
This semi open-air hotel
restaurant serves fresh, home-
baked caraway bread, generous
salads, pasta and mains such as
rosemary chicken and seafood
kebabs. There is also a selection
of tapas and classy desserts.

KUTA: TJ's RpRp
Mexican Map C5
Gang Poppies I
Tel (0361) 751 093
A Kuta institution dating back to
1984, this thatched-roof, open-air
pavilion serves authentic

TJ's, in Kuta – the place to go for California-style Mexican food and cocktails

Californian-Mexican cuisine, such as buffalo wings, tacos, enchiladas and fajitas, plus tempting desserts.

LEGIAN: Drops RpRp
Balinese Map C5
Casa Padma Suites, Jl Padma
Tel (0361) 753 073
The concept at this stylish hotel restaurant is one of contemporary international and classic Balinese cuisine. Highlights include the spicy roasted duck salad, the *nasi campur* and the banana spring rolls.

NUSA DUA: Nampu at
Grand Hyatt Bali RpRpRp
Japanese Map C5
Nusa Dua
Tel (0361) 771 234
Swish *izakaya*-style (country inn) restaurant, serving authentic sushi, *sashimi* and *yakitori*. Desserts include black sesame custard with *yuzu* sorbet. There is also a wide selection of sake. Dinner only.

NUSA LEMBONGAN: Café
Pandan at Dream Beach RpRp
Indonesian Map E4
Dream Beach
Tel (0361) 743 2344
Perched on a cliff above the beach, this rustic café enjoys spectacular views. The menu features Indonesian and Nusa Lembongan-style Balinese dishes. The cocktails are superb.

SANUR: Manik Organik Rp
Café Map C4
Jl Danau Tamblingan 85
Tel (0361) 855 3380
Tranquil health-conscious café, with plenty of vegetarian, MSG-free, gluten-free, and raw food options. The smoothies are particularly good. Yoga classes are on offer, and health-food items are sold in the small shop.

SANUR: Gateway of India RpRp
Indian Map C4
Jl Danau Tamblingan 103
Tel (0361) 281 579
This family-run restaurant serves both northern and southern Indian specialities, as well as a good range of more unusual Jain dishes. Try the madras fish curry, tandoori chicken or the prawn korma.

SANUR: Massimo II
Ristorante RpRp
Italian Map C4
Jl Danau Tamblingan 228
Tel (0361) 288 942
There is always a great atmosphere at this popular

Amazing location, stunning views, great food – all at Ku De Ta, in Seminyak

Italian eatery, which serves authentic regional dishes in an attractive space. It also produces some of the best ice cream in Bali.

SANUR: Ryoshi RpRp
Japanese Map C4
Jl Tamblingan 150
Tel (0361) 288 473
Low-key but authentic Japanese restaurant, with indoor and outdoor seating, accessed via a charming little humpbacked bridge. The sushi and *sashimi* are both excellent and good value.

SEMINYAK/KEROBOKAN:
Earth Café Rp
Vegetarian Map C5
Jl Laksmana 99
Tel (0361) 736 645
Most of the vegetarian dishes – burgers, Indonesian staples, curries and stir fries – on the menu here are also organic. There is a great range of smoothies and juices, plus some sweet treats.

SEMINYAK/KEROBOKAN:
Taco Beach Grill Rp
Mexican
Jl Kunti (also at Jl Batu Belig 80)
Tel (878) 6163 2845
This is a simple streetside restaurant with cheerful decor and delicious California-style Mexican food, as well as some Bali fusion dishes, like *babi guling* tacos and burritos.

SEMINYAK/KEROBOKAN:
Zula Rp
Vegetarian Map C5
Jl Abimanyu (Dhyana Pura) 5
Tel (0361) 732 723
Tasty Middle Eastern-style dishes, sharing platters and a range of juices and smoothies are served at this colourful café with a focus on healthy, vegetarian dining.

SEMINYAK/KEROBOKAN:
Motel Mexicola RpRp
Mexican Map C4
Jl Kayu Jati
Tel (0361) 736 688
The glitzy, over-the-top Mexicana decor – think wrestler's masks and Day of the Dead paraphernalia – draws you into this fun joint. Good tacos and potent tequila-based drinks are on offer.

SEMINYAK/KEROBOKAN:
Ryoshi RpRp
Japanese Map C5
Jl Raya Seminyak 17
Tel (0361) 731 152
Ryoshi offers top-notch Japanese cuisine and a range of sake to wash it down with, as well as live jazz performances on Monday, Wednesday and Friday evenings.

SEMINYAK/KEROBOKAN:
Gado Gado RpRpRp
International Map C5
Jl Abimanyu (Dhyana Pura) 99
Tel (0361) 730 955
This is a fine-dining restaurant in a romantic location over looking the sea. The menu darts around the world, but the seafood (and desserts) are particularly strong.

DK Choice

SEMINYAK/KEROBOKAN:
Ku De Ta RpRpRp
International Map C4
Jl Laksmana 9
Tel (0361) 736 969
This famous beachside hotspot remains the place to see and be seen, with wonderful breakfasts, an excellent grazing menu and intimate dining at night. Don't miss the white-chocolate tiramisu and the Australian cheese board.

For more information on types of restaurants *see pages 178–9*

SEMINYAK/KEROBOKAN:
La Lucciola   RpRpRp
Mediterranean   Map C4
Kaya Ayu Beach, Temple
Petitenget, Kerobokan
Tel (0361) 261 047
This classy thatched beach hut
serves great breakfasts, tasty
mains (including swordfish
steaks) and tempting desserts
and cocktails. Enjoy gorgeous
ocean views while eating.

SEMINYAK/KEROBOKAN:
Mama San   RpRpRp
Pan-Asian
Jl Raya Kerobokan 135, Kerobokan
Tel (0361) 730 443
A former industrial warehouse,
this retro restaurant specializes
in Asian street food. Indonesian,
Chinese, Indian, Malaysian,
Singaporean, Thai and Viet-
namese all feature. In addition,
the upstairs lounge is perfect
for a pre-dinner cocktail.

SEMINYAK/KEROBOKAN:
Metis   RpRpRp
Mediterranean   Map C4
Jl Petitenget 6, Kerobokan
Tel (0361) 737 888 **Closed** *Sun lunch*
Slick restaurant with a terrace
overlooking the ricefields. The
menu includes dishes like crispy
pork belly with Swiss chard and
apples poached in white wine.
Reservations are recommended.

SEMINYAK/KEROBOKAN:
Mozaic Restaurant at
Mozaic Beach Club   RpRpRp
International
Jl Pantai Batubelig, Kerobokan
Tel (0361) 473 5796
This is an elegant dining spot
serving gourmet cuisine. Splash
out on the fabulous six-course
tasting menu, which is accom-
panied by an extensive wine list.
For smaller appetites, the king
crab salad is also great.

DK Choice
SEMINYAK/KEROBOKAN:
Sardine   RpRpRp
Seafood   Map C4
Jl Petitenget 21, Kerobokan
Tel (081) 1397 8111
Dishes like crab bisque, smoked
sardines, and miso sea bass
served with soba noodles are
served at this gourmet fish and
seafood restaurant. But there
are also meat options, as well as
a fine cocktail list – try the *arak*
coffee martini. The open-air
dining pavilion is made entirely
from bamboo and has views
over a beautifully lit ricefield.
Reservations recommended.

Array of beautiful dishes in The Restaurant
at Alila Ubud, Ayung River Gorge

SEMINYAK/KEROBOKAN:
Sarong   RpRpRp
Pan-Asian   Map C4
Jl Petitenget 19x
Tel (0361) 473 7809
The menu at this popular eatery
– set in two open-air pavilions –
covers the great cuisines of
South Asia, namely Thai, Chinese,
Malaysian, Indian and Indonesian.

DK Choice
SOUTH KUTA BEACH:
Ma Joly   RpRpRp
French   Map C5
Jl Wana Segara
Tel (0361) 753 780
The coastal views at this enchanting beachfront restaurant
serving classy French cuisine are
eye-popping. Beautiful dishes
include fresh seafood, imported
meat, and tasty vegetarian
options. The bread is home-
baked and there is a selection of
fine wines. Be sure to book.

TANJUNG BENOA:
Bumbu Bali   RpRp
Balinese   Map C5
Jl Pratama Matahari Terbit
Tel (0361) 774 502
This renowned restaurant special-
izes in authentic Balinese cuisine.
It also hosts Balinese cooking
classes and dance performances.

Central Bali
AYUNG RIVER GORGE:
Ayung Terrace at Four
Seasons Sayan   RpRpRp
Pan-Asian   Map C3
Four Seasons Resort at Sayan,
Gianyar
Tel (0361) 977 577
Diners here are treated to a

panoramic vista of the Ayung
River coiling its way through the
chasm below. The pan-Asian
menu features dishes such as
seared scallops with papaya, and
South Indian vegetable curry.

AYUNG RIVER GORGE:
The Restaurant at
Alila Ubud   RpRpRp
International   Map C3
Alila Ubud, Desa Melinggih Kelod
Payangan
Tel (0361) 975 963
The menu offers a harmonious
balance of Balinese, Indonesian,
pan-Asian and Mediterranean
specialities. The multi-course
Balinese *rijsttafel* – a collection of
dishes typical at a ceremonial
meal – is the highlight.

NAGI: CasCades at
The Viceroy   RpRpRp
International   Map D3
The Viceroy, Jl Lanyahan
Tel (0361) 972 111
A breathtaking setting and a well-
executed menu make this one of
the best restaurants in Bali. Feast
on *foie gras*, truffle and morel
velouté, and Beluga caviar and
roasted duck breast on barley
risotto with a liquorice sauce.

SANGGINGAN: Naughty
Nuri's   RpRp
Barbecue   Map C3
Jl Raya Sanggingan
Tel (0361) 977 547
This streetside hangout is reminiscent of a British-style pub and
is well patronized by the expat
community. It is especially
famous for its martinis and daily
barbecues of steaks, lamb chops,
ribs and sausages.

SANGGINGAN: Mozaic   RpRpRp
International   Map C3
Jl Raya Sanggingan
Tel (0361) 975 768
Be prepared for dazzling, eclectic
cuisine at this internationally
renowned restaurant, where the
tables spill out into a romantic,
candlelit garden.

UBUD: Bali Buda   Rp
Café   Map C3
Jl Jembawan 1
Tel (0361) 976 324
A long-standing Ubud institution,
Bali Buda is an organic café that
offers great value juice, smoothies,
teas, sandwiches and main meals.

UBUD: Dirty Duck
(Bebek Bengil)   Rp
Indonesian   Map C3
Padang Tegal
Tel (0361) 975 489
An Ubud stalwart, Dirty Duck is a

sprawling open-air restaurant, full of cosy spots for drinking and dining. There is an extensive menu, including imported steaks and an old-fashioned apple crumble.

UBUD: Ibu Oka   Rp
Balinese   Map C3
Jl Suweta
Delicious *babi guling* is the order of the day at the humble Ibu Oka. There are several branches around town; the original is just north of Ubud Palace. Arrive early for lunch and expect to queue.

UBUD: Seniman Coffee Studio   Rp
Café   Map C3
Jl Sriwedari
Tel (0361) 9/2 085
State-of-the-art equipment, an in-house roastery and expert baristas make this Bali's best coffee shop. There is a range of courses on offer, too, if you want to improve your own skills.

UBUD: Batan Waru   RpRp
Indonesian   Map C3
Jl Dewi Sita
Tel (0361) 977 528
This colonial-style restaurant offers an array of Indonesian dishes, including several that betray Bali's historical Dutch influence, such as *klappertart*, which is a bread pudding with young coconut, raisins and vanilla rum cream.

UBUD: Bollero   RpRp
International   Map C3
Jl Dewi Sita
Tel (0361) 972 872
This breezy restaurant, a fixture on the Ubud dining scene, has something for everyone: well-prepared Indonesian, Asian and Western dishes, inventive cocktails, and divine desserts.

UBUD: Café Havana   RpRp
Cuban   Map C3
Jl Dewi Sita
Tel (0361) 972 973
A lively spot with great Latin music, salsa classes, potent rum-based cocktails, cold beers and lip-tingling Cuban and Caribbean dishes. Don't miss the mojitos.

UBUD: Casa Luna   RpRp
International   Map C3
Jl Raya Ubud
Tel (0361) 977 409
Owned by Janet De Neefe, who is famed for her Balinese cooking classes and is Casa Luna is popular for its weekend brunches, breakfasts and cakes. There is live jazz on Sunday nights.

UBUD: Indus   RpRp
Pan-Asian   Map C3
Jl Raya Sanggingan
Tel (0361) 977 684
With views of the Campuhan River Valley and Mount Agung, Indus offers healthy Asian cuisine, with dishes such as *nasi campur*, smoked duck, vegetarian Indian curries and home-baked desserts on the menu.

UBUD: Melting Wok   RpRp
Pan-Asian   Map C3
Jl Gootama
Tel (0361) 929 9716   **Closed** *Mon*
The French-run Melting Wok offers creative pan-Asian and fusion cuisine, along with Gallic-inspired desserts such as crème caramel. Booking is advised.

UBUD: Nomad   RpRp
International   Map C3
Jl Raya Ubud
Tel (0361) 9/7 169
The long-standing Nomad has been feeding travellers from a wide-ranging menu for decades. The Indonesian-style tapas dishes are ideal for grazing, and there is a tempting cocktail list.

UBUD: Taco Casa   RpRp
Mexican   Map C3
Jl Pengosekan
Tel (0361) 212 3818
South of the centre, this popular Mexican joint has a fantastic array of tacos, burritos, quesadillas, fajitas and enchiladas, as well as a drinks menu featuring jugs of sangria. They also deliver.

UBUD: Terazo   RpRp
Pan-Asian   Map C3
Jl Dewi Sita
Tel (0361) 978 941
The atmosphere is casual and hip at this popular hangout. Signature dishes include double-baked goat's-cheese soufflé and braised Moroccan-style lamb shank on a couscous pilaf.

UBUD: Tutmak   RpRp
International   Map C3
Jl Dewi Sita
Tel (0361) 975 754
Gourmet coffee, hearty break-fasts, great omelettes, sand-wiches, burgers and light meals make Tutmak perfect for lunch or an afternoon snack. There is also a good children's menu.

UBUD: Bridges Bali   RpRpRp
International
Jl Campuhan
Tel (0361) 970 095
This casual fine-dining restaurant, built on seven levels, overlooks the Campuhan River and offers a mix of Asian and Western cuisine, an exceptionally strong wine list, and an excellent cheese-tasting plate.

UBUD: Lamak   RpRpRp
Pan-Asian   Map C3
Monkey Forest Road
Tel (0361) 974 668
Flamboyant local designer Made Wijaya has created a vibrant dining space here - slightly whimsical, but blended with tradition and wit. Dishes include an inventive curried yoghurt-coated smoked butterfish.

DK Choice

UBUD: Locavore   RpRpRp
International   Map C3
Jl Dewi Sita
Tel (0361) 977 733   **Closed** *Sun*
Locally sourced produce is paired with modern techniques to create innovative European dishes like Bloody Mary sorbet, unctuous, slow-cooked oxtail, and passion-fruit madeleines at this exceptional restaurant. There are also five- and seven-course tasting menus (which change every month) and a selection of à la carte options. Book a table in advance.

Cool stylish interior of Locavore, in Ubud, which serves innovative modern European fare

For more information on types of restaurants *see pages 178–9*

East Bali

AMED: Gusto   RpRp
International
Bunutan
Tel (081) 338 981 394
A mix of Indonesian and
European dishes, including hearty
goulash and Wiener schnitzel, is
served at this Hungarian-run
restaurant. Attentive service.
There is also an on-site bakery.

AMED: Sails   RpRp
International
Lean Beach
Tel (0363) 22 006
Situated on a hillside with views
of the Lombok Strait, Sails serves
dishes like fresh fish cooked in
banana leaves. A free hotel drop-
off and pick-up service is offered.

CANDIDASA: Aquaria   RpRp
International   Map F3
Jl Puri Bagus
Tel (0363) 41 127
The creative menu at this tiny
hotel restaurant features dishes
such as mahi-mahi in lime and
tarragon sauce, red chicken curry,
and pineapple crêpes.

**CANDIDASA: The
Watergarden Café**   RpRp
International   Map F3
Jl Raya Candidasa
Tel (0363) 41 540
Enjoy well-priced European and
Asian cuisine on outdoor seating
in a lush water garden. There are
good vegetarians options too.

DK Choice

CANDIDASA: Vincent's RpRp
International   Map F3
Jl Raya Candidasa
Tel (0363) 41 368
This best dining spot in
Candidasa, with an arty vibe,
jazz on the sound system (there
are also live performances
a month) and separate lounge
bar, dining room and candlelit
garden. The menu ranges from
expertly prepared seafood to
healthy salads. Don't miss the
chocolate mousse for dessert.

**GUNUNG BATUR:
Lakeview**   RpRp
Indonesian   Map D2
Lakeview Hotel, Kintamani
Tel (0366) 51 394
This hotel restaurant is perched
on a ridge offering incredible
views of the Gunung Batur
volcano and its crater lake. Banana
fritters for breakfast, a buffet
and à la carte in the evening.

**MANGGIS: The Restaurant
at Alila Manggis**   RpRpRp
Indonesian   Map E3
Alila Manggis, Buitan
Tel (0363) 41 363
A breezy thatched pavilion in
a coconut grove is the venue for
freshly picked produce from the
resort's organic garden. The fresh
fish is particularly good.

PADANG BAI: Martini's   Rp
Indonesian   Map E3
Jl Segara
Tel (0818) 0559 0450
A popular, family-run *warung* that
serves tasty Indonesian fare, such
as *nasi campur*, *nasi goreng* and
pancakes with palm syrup.

**PADANG BAI: Puri Rai
Restaurant & Bar**   Rp
Indonesian   Map E3
Jl Silayukti
Tel (0363) 41 396
The pick of the restaurants lining
the beach and harbour, Puri Rai
has a mix of backpacker favourites,
Indonesian staples, fish and chips,
and vegetarian options, as well
as an innovative drinks list.

**TULAMBEN: Tunjung at
Mimpi Resort**   RpRp
International   Map F2
Mimpi Resort
Tel (0366) 21 642
Tunjung is one of only a handful of
restaurants in this area. Enjoy the
menu of superior international
and Indonesian cuisine in an
open-air bamboo pavilion.

North and West Bali

DK Choice

LOVINA: Akar   Rp
Café   Map B1
Jl Pantai Binaria, Kalibukbuk
Tel (819) 1562 5525
A delightful café with only a
handful of tables and a fine line
in vegetarian food – think meze
dishes, pasta bakes, curries, stir
fries, juices and smoothies, as
well as tea and coffee. The highlight is the range of home-made
ice creams, which are some of
the best you'll find on Bali.

LOVINA: Bakery Lovina   Rp
Deli   Map B1
Jl Raya Singaraja
Tel (0362) 42 225
Come to this great little deli for
European-style home-baked
bread and pastries, sandwiches,
cold meats and cheeses. There is

Dine alongside nature at The Restaurant at
Alila Manggis, in Manggis

also a shop attached selling
imported products – perfect if
you're feeling homesick.

LOVINA: Jasmine Kitchen RpRp
Thai   Map B1
Just off Jl Bina Rai, Kalibukbuk
Tel (0362) 41 565
A sophisticated Thai restaurant
tucked away on a side street,
Jasmine Kitchen is the place to
go for fragrant red, yellow, green
or Penang curries. They have
good ice cream, too.

LOVINA: Khi Khi   RpRp
Pan-Asian/Seafood   Map B1
Jl Raya Singaraja, Kalibukbuk
Tel (0362) 41 548
An old favourite and very
popular with locals, Khi Khi
serves Indonesian classics and a
selection of Japanese and Chinese
dishes, including sweet-and-sour
fish, *mie goreng* and sushi.

**LOVINA: Saraswati Restaurant at
Puri Bagus Hotel**   RpRp
Balinese   Map B1
Puri Bagus Hotel, Jl Singaraja-Seririt
Tel (0362) 21 430
Good, authentic Balinese and
Indonesian cuisine is served here,
including *gado gado*, *nasi goreng*,
roasted duck, and spiced fish in
banana-leaf parcels. It is also a
good spot to enjoy an ice-cold
Bintang beer at sunset.

**LOVINA: The Restaurant
at the Damai**   RpRpRp
Indonesian   Map B1
Damai Villas, Jl Damai, Kayu Putih
Tel (0362) 41 008
One of the top restaurants in the
region, this sits on the side of a
mountain with boundless views
over the ocean. There is a five-
course dinner menu that
changes daily, as well as à la carte
options such as Bloody Mary
soup with a tomato sorbet.

MUNDUK: Ngiring
Ngewedang Restaurant Rp
Café **Map** B2
Munduk Village
Tel (081) 2380 7010
Enchanting, family-run coffee
house and restaurant, with great
volcano views. Robusta and
arabica beans from the neighbouring forests are processed
and sold here, and the banana
fritters are outstanding.

PEMUTERAN: Warung Sehat
at Puri Ganesha RpRpRp
Balinese
*Puri Ganesha Villas, Pantai
Pemuteran, Gerokgak*
Tel (0362) 94 766
Owner Diana Von Cranach
creates healthy gourmet food
inspired by her Balinese mother-
in-law's recipes. The ever-
changing menu makes use of
home-grown organic vegetables
and fresh fish, but no red meat.
There are numerous vegetarian
and vegan dishes on offer.
Reservations are essential.

Lombok

GILI ISLES: Gili Deli Rp
Café
Main strip, Gili Trawangan
This slow-paced café offers a wide
range of coffees and teas, as well
as numerous breakfast and lunch
options (sandwiches, bagels,
baguettes, panini and wraps).

GILI ISLES: Beach House RpRp
Barbecue
Main strip, Gili Trawangan
Tel (0370) 614 2352
A popular venue, especially for
the nightly seafood-and-steak
barbecues, Beach House also
offers tasty dishes such as
Vietnamese calamari salad,
chicken liver pâté, zingy salads
and soups.

DK Choice

GILI ISLES: Scallywags RpRp
Barbecue
Main strip, Gili Trawangan
Tel (0370) 614 5301
Many of the restaurants on the
Gili Isles offer a nightly seafood-
and-steak barbecue, but the
one at Scallywags is the best. In
addition, this outpost of a small
chain of hotels and restaurants
offers inventive snacks, light
meals, sharing plates, mains
and desserts. It is also a good
place to lounge around with
a good book and a coffee,
cocktail or beer.

GILI ISLES: Tir Na Nog RpRp
Irish pub
Main strip, Gili Trawangan
Tel (0370) 613 9463
This lively Irish pub beside the
beach has bottled Guinness and
a menu ranging from nachos
to seafood barbecues, apple
crumble to banoffee pie. There
are also private "DVD pavilions",
with TVs and hundreds of films
to choose from.

KUTA: Ashtari Rp
International
3 km (2 miles) west of Kuta
Tel (0877) 6549 7625
On a hilltop outside of Kuta,
Ashtari is a relaxing spot to while
away an afternoon and enjoy a
gorgeous sunset. Try the veggie
burger or fresh salads. Yoga
classes are on offer, too.

KUTA: Vue at Novotel RpRpRp
Seafood
Novotel Lombok, Mandalika
Tel (0370) 615 3333
A romantic, high-end hotel
restaurant beside a white-sand
beach, Vue has a menu focusing
on seafood, and many dishes
have a French flavour. Splash out
on the succulent lobster.

MANGSIT: Puri Mas
Restaurant RpRp
Seafood
*Puri Mas Boutique Hotel,
Pantai Mangsit*
Tel (0370) 693 831
Sitting right beside Mangsit
Beach, Puri Mas offers delectable
seafood dishes. If you find it
difficult to choose, simply opt
for the seafood platter, which
is laden with lobster, prawns,
snapper and squid.

SENGGIGI: Papaya Rp
International
Jl Raya Senggigi
Tel (0370) 693 616
Located in the heart of Senggigi,
this hip restaurant is decorated
with local artworks and serves
top quality seafood, cooked
in Chinese, Indonesian and
European styles. It regularly
plays host to live music events.

SENGGIGI: Asmara RpRp
International
Jl Raya Senggigi
Tel (0370) 693 619
This large, German-run restaurant
is the best in town. The seafood
and steaks are excellent, but there
are good vegetarian options, too.
There is also a billiards table and a
children's play area.

SENGGIGI: Lotus Bayview RpRp
Italian
Jl Raya Senggigi
Tel (0370) 693 758
A fine spot to enjoy the sunset,
this charming beachside
restaurant is hidden behind
the old art market. The menu
is predominantly Italian, with
wood-fired pizzas and pasta.

SENGGIGI: Taman
Restaurant RpRp
International
Jl Raya Senggigi
Tel (0370) 693 842
A crescent-shaped, two-storey
restaurant surrounded by
flowering shrubs, Taman
offers sandwiches, seafood,
burgers, imported Australian
steaks, Indian curries, and
rotisserie chicken.

TANJUNG. Lumbung at the
Lombok Oberoi RpRpRp
International
The Oberoi Lombok, Medana Beach
Tel (0370) 613 8444
Lombok's finest restaurant is set
in the garden of The Oberoi, with
tables in romantic gazebos. The
inventive menu features dishes
such as king prawn salad and
artichoke soufflé. Reservations
are recommended.

Fine dining in the gazebos of Lumbung at the Lombok Oberoi, Tanjung

For more information on types of restaurants *see pages 178–9*

SHOPPING IN BALI AND LOMBOK

Visitors unused to bargaining may find shopping in Bali and Lombok a frustrating experience, but the temptations can be quite irresistible – in fact, many people travel to the islands just to buy goods for export. Many things easily available in Bali are fashionable elsewhere, and purchasing these direct at the source can be very rewarding. There are many products with "designer" labels on sale. Some are copies, hard to distinguish from the real thing. Others are genuine, produced under licence in Indonesia. Almost everything produced in Bali and Lombok is available in the busier shopping areas of Kuta, Sanur and Ubud. In general, the better presented the shop, the more one pays for the items on offer. Shops selling similar goods, for example basketware, fabrics, furniture, jewellery and paintings, will quite often be grouped together, which is useful for comparing prices.

Kuta Square – a popular shopping destination for visitors

Shopping Hours

Shopping hours vary from area to area, but most shops are open from around 10am until at least 6pm (10pm in Kuta). Markets generally start very early and close before the shops – the stalls usually begin to pack up around 3pm. Shopping in Bali and Lombok can be tiring – it is best to avoid the heat in the middle of the day.

How to Pay

Many shops catering to tourists price their goods in US dollars, but rupiah will be accepted. Major international credit cards, such as American Express, Visa and MasterCard, can be used in most upscale shops and major department stores. Some shops will add a surcharge (usually 3–5 per cent) for credit card payments. Cash is preferred in smaller shops.

Bargaining

Except in shops where prices are clearly marked, bargaining is common practice. Begin by asking the shopkeeper for his price, then make an initial offer, usually a third to two-thirds of the asking price, before then moving towards a sensible compromise.

Hawkers

The hawkers on the streets can be aggressive and aggravating. Many of the goods they sell are of poor quality, and not always cheap. Unless you are interested, avoid eye contact and ignore them completely. In some areas of Bali hawkers are now required to wear coloured shirts with serial numbers. If they are causing trouble, take down their number and report them to the police. Just telling them you will do this is often enough to send them away.

Street hawkers selling goods to a tourist

Entrance to Matahari, the biggest chain store in Bali

Department Stores and Shopping Centres

Department stores and shopping centres are air-conditioned and sell both local and imported goods at excellent prices. Shoes, cosmetics and clothes are popular buys. The biggest chain is **Matahari**, with three stores located in Denpasar and Kuta. **Ramayana** is around the corner from Matahari in Denpasar, and has a variety of speciality shops.

Mal Bali Galeria at Simpang Siur in Kuta has two bookshops, numerous clothing and music shops, and a large duty-free shop. Bali's main shopping centres are: Kuta Square, with sports shops and boutiques; Discovery Mall on Jl Kartika Plaza in South Kuta; Kuta Galleria, with many restaurants and surf shops; Beachwalk on Jl Pantai in Kuta; and Seminyak Square on Jl Kayu Aya.

Bamboo and cane products on display at Pasar Ubud

Markets

Markets are crowded and sometimes airless, but it is worth searching in them for local handicrafts. **Kumbasari Market** in Denpasar is a dense warren of small shops selling goods sourced from around Indonesia. **Pasar Ubud** in Ubud (see p93) sells traditional fabrics, clothes, homewares and all manner of bric-a-brac. **Sukawati Art Market** in Gianyar is loud and claustrophobic, but an excellent source of locally produced crafts. In Lombok, the **Sweta Market**, located at the busy bus station on the eastern side of Sweta (see p158) is packed with colourful stalls selling all kinds of handicrafts made in Lombok, including *ikat* and *songket* fabrics, baskets and pottery.

Supermarkets

The biggest supermarket on the islands is **Carrefour** on Jl Sunset, Banjar, which sells a complete range of Western food and products. **Bintang** in Seminyak has fresh produce and a large range of local and imported food. In Lombok, **Pacific Supermarket** in Mataram has a wide-ranging stock. Bintang is the major supermarket in Ubud and **Hardy's** is the biggest and best in Sanur.

Delis and Bakeries

For visitors in need of a change from local cuisine, there are a number of excellent delis. The following patisseries offer excellent breads, cakes and deli items: **Bali Deli** in Seminyak and **Roti Segar** in Kerobokan; **Le Bake, Bali Bakery** and **Dijon Deli** in Kuta; **The Pantry** in Sanur; and **Casa Luna** and **Kakiang Bakery** in Ubud.

Textiles

There are numerous tailors in Bali, and many visitors rush to have clothes custom-made. For textiles, the main centre is **Jalan Sulawesi** in Denpasar (see p64). Here you will find everything from traditional fabrics to saris, silks, cottons, velvet, lace, wools and rayon in every colour. For fine silks, lace and linens, **Duta Silk**, located beside Matahari in Denpasar, though small, is very popular. **Klungkung textile market** is the best place for traditional textiles. **Threads of Life** in Ubud supports a weaving cooperative.

Clothes

Boutiques in Seminyak are some of the best places for women's fashion, while cheaper clothing may be found at shops in Kuta Square and on the main road in Legian. Recommended shops are **Paul Ropp** and **Body & Soul** in Kuta and Seminyak, and **Biasa** and **Magali Pascal** in Seminyak. Also worth visiting are the boutiques in the five-star hotels of Nusa Dua, Tanjung Benoa, the Bukit Peninsula and Ubud. Balinese garments such as finely embroidered *kebaya* and silk sarongs can be found at **Mama and Leon** in Renon.

Children's Wear

Children's wear in department stores is often very good value.

Threads of Life, which supports sustainable textile art

Kuta Kidz sells printed lycra outfits, surf styles, swimwear, shoes, bags, jewellery, accessories and bedding; **Rascals** has a good range of colourful kids' clothing and batiks. **Kiki's Closet** features trendy Bali-style clothing.

Teenage girls will love the casual and surf clothes at **Surfer Girl**, Kuta, while teenage boys can get authentic surf labels at **Billabong** and **Rip Curl**, also in Kuta.

Casual wear and surfing gear for sale in a shop in Kuta

Jewellery

Silver jewellery comes mainly from the village of Celuk (see p86), in Central Bali. **Suarti**, which offers a large, diverse range and up-to-date styles, has outlets around the island and a large factory in Celuk. In Kuta, **Jonathan Silver** and **Yusuf Silver** offer a good selection. In Ubud, **Treasures** at Ary's Warung has a large range of designer jewellery. **Perlu** is a newer jewellery outlet in Seminyak and worth a visit.

Gold jewellery with intricate designs created from very bright, 24-carat gold is favoured by the Balinese. Gold is generally priced by weight, with a premium added if a lot of work has gone into the piece. The place to go is **Jalan Hasanudin** in Denpasar, where there are many outlets. Prices are good.

Leather Goods

Handmade leather clothing and shoes are popular and inexpensive items to buy in Bali. There are many shops along **Jalan Padma** and **Jalan Werkudara** in Legian which are good places to purchase leather jackets, skirts, shoes and boots.

Puppets

Puppets used in *wayang kulit* (shadow puppet) performances are skilfully fashioned from leather which is painstakingly cut into intricate lacy panels. The best place to purchase puppets is the Babakan neighbourhood near the Pasar Seni markets in Sukawati, or in art and antique shops. Try **Wayan Mardika** and **Wayan Narta** in Sukawati, where it is possible to see puppets being made. Javanese *wayang golek* puppets, which perform in front of the screen and are used in Java to enact old folktales, are popular with visitors. **Wayan Wija** in Peliatan specializes in animal puppets.

A wayang golek puppet

Basketware

Two main types of basketware are available: those from the Balinese village of Tenganan *(see pp114–15)*, and those from Lombok *(see p41)*. Baskets from Tenganan, made of rattan, are intricately and tightly woven. Prices can be high, and visitors should consider buying direct from the village. Rattan baskets made in Lombok are mostly cheaper. A good place to buy them is Sweta Market *(see Markets)*.

Wood and Stone Carvings

The village of Mas is the traditional centre of wood-carving in Bali and here the streets are lined with the carvers' workshops.

The greatest concentration of soft stone carving is in the village of Batubulan and the villages around Singapadu. In South Bali, the shops lining Jalan Bypass Ngurah Rai and Jalan Raya Kerobokan, as well as **Jimbaran Gallery**, are all excellent sources of stone works from all over the island.

Workshop in Seminyak selling furniture made mostly from teak

Pottery

Lombok's pottery is still formed the traditional way and fired in pits in the earth to a strong brick-red *(see p40)*. The use of paints and various other finishes is a quite recent innovation. The **Lombok Pottery Centre** has branches in Kuta (South Bali) and in Mataram (Lombok).

In Jimbaran, South Bali, **Jenggala Keramik** makes an attractive range of stoneware and porcelain. Here, visitors can test their own skills at making and painting pots.

Paintings

There are many highly gifted painters at work in Bali and the standard is high. Paintings in many styles can be bought in the small galleries lining the streets of Ubud. Paintings are also sold at the **Neka Art Museum**, **ARMA** and Pendet Museum in Nyuh Kuning village. Exhibitions at **Ganesha Gallery**, at the Four Seasons, Jimbaran, and the Alila in Kedewatan, are worth visiting. For contemporary art try **Komaneka** in Ubud or **Tony Raka** in Mas.

Balinese painting with a floral theme

Furniture

Indonesian teak furniture is internationally fashionable. There are not many genuine antiques. Sometimes old wood is combined with new pieces to replace those which have been lost or broken. The result can be good, but close inspection is needed. If buying new furniture ensure the wood is sustainably produced and carries a Forest Stewardship Council certificate.

Along the main road north of Seminyak is a busy furniture centre with many shops offering a full range of new and old furniture and home accessories. **Warisan** is one of the best – and most expensive. You can see a wider range at their Sempidi factory. **Lio Collection** on Jalan Raya Kerobokan offers excellent value for money. The other main area for furniture is Jalan Bypass Ngurah Rai, between Sanur and Kuta; the most popular places here are **Nostalgia** and **Victory**.

Changes in moisture, such as exposure to a drier climate or an air-conditioned room, affects wood. Newly manufactured furniture made from wood that has not been properly dried may crack later. Buy from a reputable dealer and be prepared to pay extra for a quality product that will last. Use a good shipping company, such as **MSA Cargo**, **CSA** or **PAL** to ensure furniture arrives in good condition.

DIRECTORY

Department Stores

Mal Bali Galeria
Jalan Bypass I Gusti
Ngurah Rai, Simpang
Dewa Ruci, Kuta.

Matahari
Jalan Dewi Sartika,
Denpasar.
Kuta Square, Kuta.

Ramayana
Mal Bali, Jalan
Diponegoro, Denpasar.
Tel (0361) 246 306.

Markets

Kumbasari Market
Jalan Gajah Mada,
Denpasar.

Pasar Ubud
Jalan Raya Ubud, Ubud.

Sukawati Art Market
Sukawati, Gianyar.

Sweta Market
Jalan Sandubaya,
Sweta, Lombok.

Supermarkets

Bintang
Jalan Raya
Seminyak, Seminyak.
Tel (0361) 730 552.
Jalan Raya Sangginen 45,
Ubud. **Tel** (0361) 972 972.

Carrefour
Jl Sunset Rd, Banjar
Glogor Carik, Pemogan.
Tel (08123) 811 100.

Hardy's
Jalan Danau Tamblingan
193, Sanur.
Tel (0361) 285 807.

Pacific Supermarket
Jalan Langko, Mataram.
Tel (0370) 623 477.

Delis and Bakeries

Le Bake
Jalan Griya Anyari, Kuta.
Tel (0361) 753 979.

Bali Bakery
Jalan Iman Bonjol, Kuta.
Tel (0361) 755 149.

Bali Deli
Jalan Kunti 117x,
Seminyak.
Tel (0361) 733 555.

Casa Luna
Jalan Raya Ubud, Ubud.
Tel (0361) 977 409.

Dijon Deli
Kuta Poleng Art and
Antique Mall, Blok A1–A2,
Jalan Setiabudi, Kuta.
Tel (0361) 759 636.

Kakiang Bakery
Jalan Pengosekan,
Pengosekan.
Tel (0361) 978 984.

The Pantry
Jalan Danau Tamblingan
75a, Sanur.
Tel (0361) 281 008.

Roti Segar
Jalan Bumbak Kerobokan.

Textiles

Duta Silk
Next to Matahari, Den-
pasar. **Tel** (0361) 232 818.

Jalan Sulawesi
Denpasar. Shops on
street

Klungkung Market
Main crossroads
Semarapura, Klungkung.

Threads of Life
Jalan Kajeng 24, Ubud.
Tel (0361) 972 187.

Clothes

Biasa
Jl Raya, Seminyak.
Tel (0361) 730 945.

Body & Soul
Kuta Square and Jalan
Legian 162, Kuta.
Tel (0361) 756 297.

Magali Pascal
Jalan Raya Seminyak 65,
Seminyak.
Tel (0361) 737 907.

Mama and Leon
Renon
Tel (0361) 288 044.

Paul Ropp
Jalan Raya Seminyak
39, Seminyak.
Tel (0361) 731 208.

Children's Wear

Billabong
Kuta Square, Kuta.
Tel (0361) 756 296.

Kiki's Closet
Jalan Raya Seminyak
57, Seminyak.
Tel (0361) 746 4892.

Kuta Kidz
Bemo Corner, Kuta.
Tel (0361) 755 810.

Rascals
Kuta Square, Kuta.
Tel (0361) 754 253.

Rip Curl
Jalan Legian, Kuta.
Tel (0361) 757 404.

Surfer Girl
Jalan Legian, Kuta.
Tel (0361) 757 693.

Jewellery

Jalan Hasanudin
Denpasar. Shops on
street.

Jonathan Silver
Jalan Legian 109, Kuta.
Tel (0361) 754 209.

Perlu
Jalan Laksmana,
Seminyak.
Tel (0361) 780 2553.

Suarti
Jalan Raya Celuk 100 X,
Celuk. **Tel** (0361) 751 660.

Treasures
Ary's Warung, Ubud.
Tel (0361) 976 697.

Yusuf Silver
Jalan Legian, Kuta.
Tel (0361) 758 441.

Leather Goods and Puppets

Jalan Padma & Jalan Werkudara
Legian. Shops on street.

Wayan Mardika
Banjar Babakan, Sukawati.
Tel (0361) 299 646.

Wayan Narta
Jalan Padma, Sukawati.
Tel (0361) 299 080.

Wayan Wija
Banjar Kalah, Peliatan.
Tel (0361) 973 367.

Wood and Stone Carvings

Jimbaran Gallery
Jalan Bypass Ngurah
Rai, Jimbaran.
Tel (0361) 774 957.

Pottery

Jenggala Keramik
Jalan Uluwatu II,
Jimbaran.
Tel (0361) 703 310.

Lombok Pottery Centre
Jalan Kartika Plaza
8 X, Kuta.
Tel (0361) 753 184.
Jalan Sriwijaya 111 A,
Mataram, Lombok.
Tel (0370) 640 351.

Paintings

ARMA
Jl Pengosekan, Peliatan.
Tel (0361) 975 742.

Ganesha Gallery
Four Seasons, Sayan.
Tel (0361) 977 577.

Komaneka Gallery
Jl Monkey Forest, Ubud.
Tel (0361) 977 140.

Neka Art Museum
Jl Raya Campuhan, Ubud.
Tel (0361) 975 074.

Tony Raka Gallery
Jalan Raya Mas, Mas 88.
Tel (0361) 974 538.

Furniture and Shipping

CSA
Jalan Ngurah Rai 109x,
Suwung Kauh, Denpasar.
Tel (0361) 720 525.

Lio Collection
Jalan Raya Kerobokan 2.
Tel (0361) 780 0942.

MSA Cargo
Jalan Hayam Wuruk 238,
Denpasar.

Nostalgia
Jalan Bypass Ngurah
Rai, Sanur.
Tel (0811) 395 082.

PAL
Jalan Sekar Jepun 5,
Gatsu Timor, Tohpati.
Tel (0361) 466 999.

Victory
Jalan Bypass Ngurah
Rai, Sanur.
Tel (0361) 722 319.

Warisan
Jl Kerobokan, Seminyak.
Tel (0361) 731 175.

What to Buy in Bali and Lombok

Decorative art and craft products are probably the best buys in Bali and Lombok. They are sold in all the major tourist centres. More adventurous visitors may choose to buy products in the villages where they are made. Woven textiles, including *songket* and *ikat*, are produced chiefly in East Bali. Jewellery is made in Celuk, south of Ubud. Good basketware, pottery and textiles can be bought in Lombok. Surfwear and other casual clothing is widely available, particularly in the resort areas of South Bali.

Masks
Characters from Balinese mythology are skilfully represented by woodcarvers; the masks are used in theatrical performances.

Carvings
Craftsmen work with a variety of materials including *paras* (a soft, volcanic stone), ceramics, wood and silver. Small figurines include Garudas and Buddhas.

Woodcarving

Paras carving

Puppets from Bali and Java
Many attractive puppets are made or sold in Bali, including the hand-painted puppets made of tanned hide used in Balinese *wayang kulit (see p35)*, and these Javanese-style puppets.

Lombok Pottery
This distinctive, brick-red or black pottery, widely available in Bali and Lombok, is exported all over the world. Most retailers will pack fragile items and arrange shipping.

Lontar Engravings
The village of Tenganan *(see pp114–15)* is known for these engravings on the leaves of lontar palms.

Furniture
Modern and reproduction pieces are made from teak and mahogany. Dutch Colonial-style furniture is popular though there are few antiques. Not all new furniture is made with materials from sustainable harvests, but some shops use recycled timber.

Teak chair

Bamboo table

Carved wood panel

Kites

During kite season in Bali *(see p45)*, local communities collaborate in making kites by hand. Mass-produced kites, made of bamboo and nylon, are also attractive.

Bracelets

Silver pendant

Earrings

Necklace

Jewellery

Celuk is the jewellery centre of Bali. Gold and silver pieces are designed, made and sold here and the level of craftsmanship is high. Designs are contemporary and traditional.

Ikat

Textiles

The most commonly produced cloth is *endek*, for which a single *ikat* dye process is used. Ikat in earthy tones can be found in the markets. Double-*ikat geringsing*, made in Tenganan, is unique to Bali. *Songket* is embellished with gold and silver thread.

Sash

Child's outfit

Fabrics and Custom-made Clothes

Made-to-measure clothes are very affordable – there are many tailors in Bali. Fabrics are mostly rayon but there are imported cottons. The best place to buy fabrics is Jalan Sulawesi in Denpasar.

Batik dress

Lombok Basketware

Rattan baskets can be purchased directly in the villages where they are made or at many local markets.

Luggage

Bali produces finely woven rattan bags and handmade, durable leather goods which are sold in shops and markets. The decoration is usually geometrical.

Leather bag

Woven bag

Star fruit

Nutmeg

Mango

Papaya

Pineapple

Salak

Preserved Fruits and Nuts

Dried fruits and nuts are inexpensive and palatable local snacks that can be bought ready-packaged at supermarkets. The local markets and some *warung* sell strips made up of more than one fruit such as mango, papaya and pineapple. Flavours range from sweet to spicy or tart.

ENTERTAINMENT

Entertainment for the Balinese has traditionally been associated with religious festivals and ceremonies, a major component of which is the performance of dances accompanied by music. Most traditional dances and music are associated with religious ceremonies; however, some have entered the secular arena, and are regularly staged for tourists. Western-style nightlife is concentrated in the tourist areas, especially in South Bali, which is packed with clubs and bars catering to all age groups, musical tastes and budgets. Seminyak's scene is more fashionable than Kuta's. Sanur is more laid-back, as is Nusa Dua, and Ubud has good live music and theatre.

Information Sources

Excellent entertainment listings can be found in *Hello Bali*, *The Beat* and *Bali Advertiser*. *FRV Travel* and *The Yak* magazines, and the English-language daily *Jakarta Post* provide good information, and so do the hotels and notices outside various establishments.

Buying Tickets

It is not difficult to find Balinese dances, as there are performances nearly every night at almost all the tourist centres. Prices start at around Rp50,000. Trips to these performances booked through agents will cost much more, although the price will usually include transport.

The best places to buy tickets for performances on the public stages are the hotel tour desks, and the tour operators and moneychangers to be found throughout Bali's tourist centres. Payment is usually made by cash in rupiah, although US dollars are also accepted.

Dancers with elaborate costumes and masks in Denpasar

Traditional Dance

Most of the Balinese dances staged for tourists are not entirely authentic. Many offer a smorgasbord of extracts and highlights of a variety of traditional dances. Standards, however, are generally very high, and visitors are given an explanatory leaflet which usually comes in a several languages, including English, Japanese, French and German.

There are no seat reservations, so it is a good idea to turn up early.

Ubud, generally regarded as the artistic heartland of Bali, is the place to go for dance, and most visitors to Ubud spend a good part of their evenings at one of the numerous shows staged every night. One of the best venues is **Puri Saren** *(see p94)*, the outer courtyard of the royal palace creating a spectacular backdrop. The main dances performed are the *Ramayana* ballet and the *legong*; the latter is a highly stylized dance performed by two young girls. Tickets at Puri Saren can be purchased through a tour operator or at the door. Nightly performances begin at 7:30pm.

The village of Batubulan *(see p86)* has several stages on which dances are performed. Daily *Barong* and *Keris* performances *(see p29)* by the celebrated Denjalan troupe are staged at 9:30am at the **Pura Puseh**. The Stage Sila Budaya at the **Puri Anom Tegehe Batubulan** is an outdoor theatre that features *Barong* and *Keris* dances daily at 9:30am, and the *kecak (see p34)* and fire dances nightly at 6:30pm. It is generally not necessary to buy tickets in advance.

The **Taman Werdhi Budaya** *(see p65)* in Denpasar has numerous events scheduled throughout the year; its programme can be found in the *Bali Post*. There are often special events on Saturday nights. The Taman Werdhi Budaya is the main venue for the Bali Arts Festival, Bali's premier cultural event, which takes place in June and July.

Legong dancers in gold-painted *prada* costumes

A *gamelan* orchestra accompanying a dance in Ubud

Traditional Music

Every traditional Balinese dance is accompanied by music, but the *gamelan* orchestra *(see pp36–7)* is now heard more widely. Many hotels engage musicians for *gamelan* performances. The music is loud, percussive and intriguing, and it is generally enjoyed by foreigners as much for its showmanship as for the music itself.

A temple is one of the best places to see a *gamelan* orchestra perform; visitors are always welcome to watch and listen. Local tourist offices, hotels and guides can provide details of places and dates.

In Ubud, performances by **Semara Ratih** in Kutuh and **Cudamani** in Pengosekan demonstrate superb musicality. The latter also provide classes for local children and visitors.

Puppet Theatre

The shadow puppet play, or *wayang kulit*, is prominent in Balinese life. Delicately cared for and finely gilded leather figures are one-dimensional representations of the gods and myriad characters in the ancient Hindu epics, the *Ramayana* and the *Mahabharata*. Performed behind a screen by a *dalang* or puppeteer, and illuminated by a flickering candle, the *wayang kulit* is loved by the Balinese. It is rarely staged in its entirety for tourists as these full performances regularly last for hours. Neither is it staged for tourists in traditional authentic form, as this is difficult to follow. However, the *wayang kulit* is sometimes staged at hotels with an emphasis on its

dramatic aspects. A more authentic *wayang kulit* performance can be seen at **Oka Kartini's** in Ubud on Wednesdays and Saturdays at 8pm. *Wayang kulit* is performed at Balinese family and temple celebrations. Special performances by **Wayan Mardika**, **Wayan Wija** and **Nyoman Sumandhi** can be arranged.

A relatively modern innovation is *wayang listrik*, named after its use of lighting and giant shadow images.

Entertainment for Children

The Balinese love children and will pay them a great deal of attention. The larger holiday resorts often have very good in-house children's programmes, and some will accept children of non-guests for a fee. The **Westin Resort Nusa Dua**'s facilities (open to non-guests) are highly recommended. The **Conrad Bali**, **Nikko Bali** and the **InterContinental Resort Bali** also have great kids' clubs.

Children will also love the colour and pageantry of the more dramatic Balinese dances, which are staged at most hotels in Bali.

Two of the more spectacular venues in Bali are the Budaya Cultural Theatre at **Nusa Dua Beach Hotel** and the **Grand**

An elaborately painted puppet

Hyatt's Pasar Senggol, where for an all-in price you choose a meal from the many food stalls and enjoy the show over dinner.

Rafting, trekking and cycling tours are well supervised, safe and fun for older kids. Camel rides beside the Nikko in Nusa Dua are also popular choices for older children. **Bali Adventure Tours** and **Sobek** are excellent operators. The former also organizes white-water rafting and mountain biking trips for kids. At **Kuda P Stables** and **Bali Horse Riding**, horse-riding lessons for children and supervised riding tours are available.

A number of water and nature parks are designed for families. The most popular is the **Waterbom Park & Spa**. The park is well-managed, and safety is a major consideration. To really let the kids run off steam, visit the **Bali Treetop Adventure Park** *(see p145)*, which is fun for all ages and skill levels. South of Ubud, the **Bali Bird Park** *(see pp88–9)*, with over a thousand birds, and the **Bali Reptile Park** *(see p86)* are good family attractions. North of Ubud, the **Elephant Safari Park** *(see p203)* offers a wonderful day out, while south of Gianyar, the **Bali Safari & Marine Park** is home to more than 50 species of animals.

Fun for people of all ages at the Waterbom Park & Spa in Tuban

Nightlife

Bali has been a party island since the first surfers arrived in the early 1970s. All the large resorts here offer in-house entertainment. Outside of the resorts, however, organized nightlife is found only in the major tourist areas.

Each area's character is reflected in its entertainment. Uluwatu, for example, caters to surfers, while Kuta is popular with young revellers and backpackers. Seminyak and Petitenget house more sophisticated and elegant night spots that have emerged to meet the demands of 5-star travellers. There is also a lively and flamboyant gay scene in Seminyak. The dance bars here start getting busy at around 11pm, while Kuta tends to start earlier. Sanur and Ubud are quieter, with many of the bars closing at midnight.

Along Poppies Lanes I and II in Kuta, backpackers congregate in simple bars and hangouts designed for relaxation, and offering beer and videos. **Maccaroni**, **Eikon** and **Vi Ai Pi** are popular places to meet for a drink. Centerstage at the **Hard Rock Hotel** presents live music every night from 8pm, while **Hard Rock Café** offers an excellent line-up of foreign and local bands after 11pm. Along Jl Legian in central Kuta, **Sky Garden**, **M-Bar-Go**, **Apache Reggae Bar**, **Paddy's** and **The Bounty** are the busiest nightclubs. Sanur is not famous for its night-time entertainment but **Arena** is a good pub, attracting an expat crowd with sporting events on the big screen and trivia quiz nights.

The Bounty, one of the many large clubs in South Bali

In Canggu, Echo Beach has a flourishing sunset scene, with live music at **The Beach House** on Sunday nights. In Seminyak, sunset is a great time for volleyball along the beach, coupled with snacks, cocktails and cold beers. **La Lucciola** is a perfect up-market venue for sunset cocktails. Visitors almost invariably head back to the hotel for a shower before moving on to one of Seminyak or Kerobokan's many restaurants for dinner. A popular area for eating out is Jl Petitenget, which runs parallel to the beach, north of Seminyak. In addition to the numerous restaurants, there is a thriving night scene here, especially at **Jenja** nightclub and at the chic beach club venues such as **Ku De Ta**, **WooBar** at W Retreat and **Potato Head**, as well as **Hu'u Bar** and **Mirror**. Much of the action in Jl Abimanyu (also known as Dhyana Pura) in

central Seminyak, takes place at the popular **Frankensteins Laboratory**, as well as **Santa Fe** and the rum and salsa bar **Bahiana**. **Bali Jo**, **Mixwell** and **Facebar** are where the late-night gay scene and drag shows are found. At the end of the street, **SOS Supper Club** at Anantara Resort hosts international guest DJs and singers. **Mannekepis** on the main road offers live music and **Red Carpet Champagne Bar** in Jl Kayu Aya is always busy.

In Ubud, **Laughing Buddha Bar** hosts live bands playing a range of styles. **Jazz Café** has live music most nights of the week.

Lovina has bars with passable reggae and standard cover bands. The two strips leading down to the beach are the setting for happy-hour drinks.

The **Four Seasons Resort** at Sayan, near Ubud, has a spectacularly located bar, as do **Alila Manggis** and **Amankila** near Candidasa.

Rock Bar at Ayana Resort near Jimbaran is an open-top bar perched at a height above the ocean on a rocky outcrop at the base of the cliffs. Nusa Dua's resorts have cocktail bars and beach bars where the sunset can be enjoyed. Uluwatu serves the surfing contingency with a good selection of bars including the star attraction **Single Fin**, which presents live music on Sunday evenings, good pizzas and amazing sunset views.

Ku De Ta, a popular beach bar and restaurant in Seminyak

DIRECTORY

Traditional Dance

Pura Puseh
Jl Raya, Batubulan,
Gianyar.
Tel (0361) 298 038.

**Puri Anom Tegehe
Batubulan**
Jl Raya
Batubulan, Gianyar.
Tel (0361) 298 505/092.

Puri Saren
Jalan Raya Ubud, Ubud.
Tel (0361) 975 057.

**Taman Werdhi
Budaya**
Jl Nusa Indah, Denpasar.
Tel (0361) 222 776.

Traditional Music

Cudamani
Jl Raya Pengosekan,
Ubud. **Tel** (0361) 977 067.
W cudamani.org

Semara Ratih
Banjar Kutuh, Ubud.
Tel (0361) 973 277.

Puppet Theatre

Nyoman Sumandhi
Jalan Katrangan Lane
5D/6, Denpasar.
Tel (0361) 742 3901.

Oka Kartini's
Jalan Raya Ubud, Ubud.
Tel (0361) 975 193.
W okakartini.com

Wayan Mardika
Banjar Babakan, Sukawati.
Tel (0361) 299 646.

Wayan Wija
Banjar Kalah, Peliatan.
Tel (0361) 973 367.

Entertainment for Children

Bali Adventure Tours
Adventure House, Jl
Bypass Ngurah Rai,
Pessanggaran.
Tel (0361) 721 480.
W baliadventure
tours.com

Bali Bird Park
Jalan Serma Cok Ngurah
Gambir, Singapadu,
Batubulan, Gianyar.
Tel (0361) 299 352.

Bali Horse Riding
Tarukan Equestrian
Centre, Jl Nelayan
No. 63, Canggu.
Tel (0361) 738 080.
W balihorseriding.com

Bali Reptile Park
Jalan Serma Cok Ngurah
Gambir, Singapadu,
Batubulan, Gianyar.
Tel (0361) 299 344.

**Bali Safari & Marine
Park**
Jl Bypass Prof Dr Ida
Bagus Mantra, Km 19,8,
Gianyar. **Tel** (0361) 950
000. **W** balisafari
marinepark.com

**Bali Treetop
Adventure Park**
Eka Karyu Botanical
Garden, Candikuning,
Bedugul. **Tel** (0361) 934
0009. **W** balitreetop.com

Conrad Bali
Jalan Pratama Raya 168.
Tel (0361) 778 788.

Elephant Safari Park
Taro. **W** baliadventure
tours.com

Grand Hyatt
Nusa Dua.
Tel (0361) 771 234.

Kuda P Stables
Gang Sabana, Banjar Kang
Kang, Pererenan, Canggu.
Tel (0361) 747 2716.
W kudapstables.com

Sobek
Jalan Tirta Ening 9, Sanur.
Tel (0361) 287 059.
W balisobek.com

Waterbom Park & Spa
Jalan Kartika Plaza, Tuban.
Tel (0361) 755 676.
W waterbom-bali.com

**Westin Resort Nusa
Dua**
Nusa Dua, Bali.
Tel (0361) 771 906.
W westin.com/bali

Nightlife

Alila Manggis
Manggis. **W** alilahotels.
com/manggis

Amankila
Manggis, near Candidasa.
Tel (0363) 41 333.

Apache Reggae Bar
Jalan Legian 146, Kuta.
Tel (0361) 761 213.

Arena
Jalan Bypass, Sanur.
Tel (0361) 287 255.

Bahiana
Jl Abimanyu 4, Seminyak.
Tel (0361) 738 662.
W bahiana-bali.com

Bali Jo
Dhyana Pura Street Arcade
8, Jl Abimanyu, Seminyak.
Tel (0361) 730 931.

The Beach House
Echo Beach, Canggu.
Tel (08123) 978 466.

The Bounty
Jalan Legian, Kuta.
Tel (0361) 754 040.

Eikon
Jalan Legian 178, Kuta.
Tel (0361) 750 701.

Facebar
Dhyana Pura Street Arcade
9, Jl Abimanyu, Seminyak.
Tel (08179) 701 883.

Four Seasons Resort
Sayan, Ubud.
Tel (0361) 977 577.

**Frankensteins
Laboratory**
Jl Abimanyu (Dhyana
Pura) 6, Seminyak.
Tel (0361) 731 622.

**Hard Rock Hotel and
Café**
Jalan Pantai, Kuta.
Tel (0361) 755 661.

Hu'u Bar
Jl Petitenget, Seminyak.
Tel (0361) 736 443.
W huubali.com

Jazz Café
Jl Sukma 2, Tebesaya,
Ubud. **Tel** (0361) 976 594.

Jenja
Jl Nakula 532XX, Kuta.
Tel (081) 1398 8088.

Ku De Ta
Jalan Kayu Aya 9, Semin-
yak. **Tel** (0361) 736 969.

La Lucciola
Jalan Kayu Aya, Kayu Aya
Beach, Seminyak.
Tel (0361) 261 047.

Laughing Buddha Bar
Jl Monkey Forest, Ubud.
Tel (0361) 970 928.

Maccaroni
Jalan Legian 52, Kuta.
Tel (0361) 751 631.

Mannekepis
Jalan Raya Seminyak 2,
Seminyak.
Tel (0361) 847 5784.

M-Bar-Go
Jalan Legian, Kuta.
Tel (0361) 756 280.

Mirror Lounge & Club
Jl Petitenget 106,
Seminyak.
Tel (0361) 849 9799.

Mixwell
Dhyana Pura Street Arcade
6, Jl Abimanyu, Seminyak.
Tel (0361) 736 864.

Paddy's
Jalan Legian 166, Kuta.
Tel (0361) 758 555.

Potato Head
Jl Petitenget, Seminyak.
Tel (0361) 473 7979.
W ptthead.com/potato-
head-beach-club

**Red Carpet
Champagne Bar**
Jl Kayu Aya, Seminyak.
W redcarpet
champagnebar.com

Rock Bar
Ayana Resort & Spa, Jl
Karang Mas Sejahtera,
Jimbaran. **Tel** (0361) 702
222. **W** ayanaresort.
com/rockbarbali/wp

Santa Fe
Jl Dhyana Pura, Seminyak.
Tel (0361) 731 147.

Sky Garden
Jalan Legian, Kuta.
Tel (0361) 755 423.

Single Fin
Blue Point, Uluwatu.
Tel (08155) 868 8995.

SOS Supper Club
Anantara Resort, Jl
Abimanyu, Seminyak.
Tel (0361) 737 773.

Vi Ai Pi
Jl Legian 88, Kuta.
Tel (0361) 750 425.
W viaipi-bali.com

WooBar
W Retreat, Jl Petitenget,
Seminyak. **Tel** (0361) 473
8104. **W** starwood
hotels.com/whotels

OUTDOOR ACTIVITIES

The range and quality of outdoor activities available in Bali and Lombok are exceptional; they are among the best in the world. In addition to the established favourites, such as surfing, fishing, sailing, snorkelling, trekking and diving, there are "adrenalin" sports such as bungy-jumping, skydiving, paragliding, kayaking and ocean and white-water rafting. The energetic visitor can ride surfboards on the waves, horses along the beach, elephants in the jungle and motorbikes into the unknown. Reptiles and birds are there to be observed; there are dolphin cruises, cycling trips into the hills and adventure tours off the beaten track. Tennis and golf are both available in luxurious, 5-star surroundings in Bali's Nusa Dua resort area. In this respect as in others, Lombok is much less developed and more informal than Bali. Its main outdoor attractions are surfing, snorkelling and trekking.

Surfboards available for rent on the beach at Legian

Surfing

Bali is a very popular centre for surfing, offering almost perfect year-round conditions for both beginners and more experienced veterans. Boards and gear can be bought or rented at most beaches. Well-managed surf schools in Sanur and Kuta, such as the popular **Rip Curl School of Surf**, charge by the day or by the hour for private instruction. Also recommended is **Bali Learn to Surf** at the Hard Rock Hotel. The liveliest scenes are around Kuta. For more on the best surfing sites, see pp204–6.

Diving and Snorkelling

Organized tours with experienced guides are a good way to explore the waters off Bali and Lombok. Besides day trips, live-aboard trips that include diving off nearby islands, such as Komodo and Sumbawa, are popular. A valid licence must be produced for dive trips; PADI (Professional Association of Diving Instructors) certification is generally recognized. Most dive operations are professionally run. Good rental equipment is available. **Bali Marine Sports, Dream Divers, Geko Dive, Reef Seen Aquatic, Aquamarine Diving Centre** and **Blue Marlin Dive** all offer a range of trips. For more detailed information on diving sites, see pp206–7.

Windsurfing and Water-Skiing

Sanur is the place in Bali to go for windsurfing; the lagoon (see pp68–9) offers good protection from the ocean swells. Here, as elsewhere in Bali and Lombok, most beachfront hotels will have boards for rent.

The facilities of the **Blue Oasis Beach Club** in Sanur are the best on the island. In addition to windsurfing, it also offers water-skiing. Trick skis and wakeboards are available for rent. All staff are professional and qualified.

A number of windsurfing courses, conducted by Asian windsurfing champions, are available for all ability levels. Courses last 4–6 hours.

Fishing

Several tour operators such as **Bali Fishing** and **Moggy Offshore Cruising Catamaran** specialize in deep-sea fishing trips; they have offices in the Kuta-Legian area (see pp70–71), in the east around Padang Bai and Candidasa (see p112) and in the north at Singaraja (see p150). There are boats from Padang Bai, Candidasa, Amed, Tulamben, Singaraja and Sanur, but most leave from Benoa Harbour (see p76), and trips usually start early and last all day.

Some companies offer yachts and fishing boats with guides for game-fishing charters; the aim is to catch tuna, *mahi-mahi*, mackerel and marlin. Cod, snapper and coral trout can be found on reef-fishing trips.

Depending on your budget, you can choose to go fishing in an outrigger, a small boat or a state-of-the-art Black Watch fishing vessel with experienced crew, full insurance and all electronics and safety gear. Extended charters to the waters off Lombok and islands further east can be arranged.

Outriggers offering game-fishing trips off Lombok

Benoa Harbour, the best-equipped marina in the area

Cruises

There is a range of sailing and yachting options off Bali and Lombok. Cruise options include day trips to offshore islands and remote reefs, or sunset dinners aboard a modern cruise liner, a traditional Bugis schooner or a yacht.

Scheduled sailing cruises ranging from 3 to 14 days depart from Benoa Harbour, the main port of call, and here it is also easy to book daily cruises. Major sailing and yachting companies use this as a home base; it is an interesting place for the boat-lover to explore and a well-stocked bar overlooks the pontoons. From Benoa, it is possible to sail by tall ship to the west coast of Lombok to explore the Gili Isles (see p160) and the waters off Senggigi (see p160), or charter a luxury yacht for a once-in-a-lifetime wedding cruise. Most people, however, prefer to spend a day sailing to the islands of Nusa Lembongan or Nusa Penida (see p79).

Quicksilver Cruises organizes day trips to Nusa Penida on its 37 metre (122 ft) catamaran. It also offers a dinner cruise as well as a voyage in a purpose-built submarine, and fun banana boat rides. **Bali Hai Cruises** offers sailing trips to Nusa Lembongan aboard luxury catamarans fully equipped for snorkelling. On the islands, a full holiday experience is provided, with beach clubs, restaurants, pools and diving and snorkelling equipment (the latter at extra cost). They also have a sailing boat that goes to Lembongan. **Bounty Cruises** has dinner sunset cruises

around Nusa Dua, as well as journeys to Lembongan. On most cruises, children under 14 receive a 50 per cent discount.

If you prefer to be in charge of your own craft, dinghy rentals are available from Sanur, Nusa Dua and Jimbaran. Alternatively, charter a yacht or schooner with 2–16 cabins, an experienced crew and a tour guide.

White-Water Rafting, Ocean Rafting and Kayaking

There is a number of white-water rafting companies offering trips through rapids ranging over Grades 2–4 (from fairly easy to rigorous). Safety standards are generally high, and the environmental impact of these river activities is kept to a minimum.

Sobek, established in 1989 as the first adventure tour company of its kind, is still one of the best. It offers world-class guides and Grade 3 rapids. The Ayung River, northwest of Ubud (see pp100–101), and the Unda River, north of Klungkung (see p109), are the most popular

starting points. Trips organized by **Ayung River Rafting** last from 3 to 4 hours. The Telaga Waja River in East Bali near Muncan and Sidemen (see p109) is also becoming popular. When planning, allow for transfer time from and back to your hotel. **Bali Adventure Tours**' package includes changing rooms, hot showers, towels and food and drinks. Their trip takes you along 8 km (5 miles) of white water against a backdrop of unspoiled rainforest, towering gorges and terraced rice paddies. It includes Grade 2 and 3 rapids.

Always take a change of clothes, a hat and plenty of sunscreen. The price for a rafting trip should include hotel transfers, full instruction, qualified guides, lunch and insurance.

River kayaking, also offered by Ayung River Rafting, is an exciting development. Hurtling through the rapids in a two-person inflatable kayak is a much more intense experience than rafting.

Lake kayaking, a more relaxed option, is offered by Sobek at Lake Tamblingan (see pp144–5).

White-water rafting on the Ayung River

A ride on a banana boat in South Bali

Swimming

The beaches in Bali and Lombok can be superb for swimming, with their secluded bays and crystal-clear seas. However, it is important to take note of any warnings posted or signs indicating bad rips and strong currents as the waters, particularly along the south coasts, can be very dangerous. A safer option for swimming is the hotel pool.

Many of the major international hotels and luxury resorts located in Nusa Dua in Bali *(see p77)* and Senggigi in Lombok *(see p160)* have good swimming facilities.

Club Med in Nusa Dua offers an all-day guest ticket (valid until 5pm) which includes access to the pool plus a range of other sports activities. It also includes an Asian and Western lunch buffet with unlimited wine, beer and soft drinks.

Kuta's **Waterbom Park & Spa** is home to 16 state-of-the-art water slides.

Golf and Tennis

There are five spectacular golf courses in Bali, all open to non-members for a fee, where you can play against a backdrop of ocean views or mountain scenery. Nusa Dua is home to the 18-hole **Bali National Golf Club**, while close by, on the Bukit Peninsula, is the **New Kuta Golf Club**, with ocean views. In Sanur is a 9-hole course at the Grand Bali Beach Hotel. Near the shores of Lake Bratan, high in the hills near Bedugul *(see p145)*, is **Bali Handara Kosaido Country Club**, an award-winning 18-hole golf-resort. The most dramatic golf course in Bali is the 18-hole **Nirwana Bali Golf Club** near Tanah Lot in Tabanan.

Most of the larger hotels provide excellent tennis facilities with floodlit courts, expert coaching, playing partners and racket rental.

Wreathed hornbill

Eco-Tours

Eco-tourism has caught on in Bali and Lombok, and a number of operators are now starting to cater to visitors who prefer ecologically based holidays and activities.

Perhaps the most innovative eco-tours in Bali are led by **JED** (Jaringian Ekowisata Desa or Village Eco Tourism Network). Their packages include a trek to a local village, where a traditional lunch is prepared by, and shared with, the local people. Profits from the tours benefit the whole village.

Dolphin-watching has become popular for a day out, and involves four-hour trips into the waters off South Bali. **Bali Hai Cruises** provides early-morning high-speed cruises along the Nusa Dua and Uluwatu coastline, while **Ena Dive Centre** offers dolphin-watching tours and water sports.

Off the shores of Lovina in the north of Bali *(see p151)*, small, traditional fishing boats, known as outriggers, are used for dolphin-watching. As dolphins are wild animals, the certainty of actually seeing one on a trip can never be guaranteed.

Bird-watching is a little more predictable. The **Bali Bird Park** *(see pp88–9)*, near Singapadu, gives an excellent view of birdlife in Bali and elsewhere in the tropics. Visitors can access

A boat trip at Lake Bratan near the Bali Handara Kosaido Country Club

the **Bali Reptile Park** (see p86) and the Bali Bird Park with a single entrance ticket.

For visitors looking for birds in the wild, bird-watching trips can be arranged to the **Taman Nasional Bali Barat** (see pp140–41). Guided tours to other parts of Bali and Lombok are available by prior arrangement. Morning bird walks around Ubud can be arranged with **Bali Bird Walks**. Bird-watching and trekking around Lake Tamblinga (see pp144–5) and the adjacent high forest can be arranged through **Puri Lumbung**.

For a totally different perspective on Bali, try **Bali Treetop Adventure Park**, where you can walk through the treetops of Eka Karya Botanical Gardens (wearing a safety harness). There are 65 challenges here at all skill levels.

Bottlenose dolphins frolicking in the waters off South Bali

Walking, Trekking and Camping

Sightseeing on foot reveals the unspoiled Bali and Lombok. Trips range from full- and half-day visits to overnight trips to the top of Gunung Rinjani in Lombok (see pp162–3).

Keep Walking Tours offers paddy field and temple treks, and **Bali Herbal Walks** will take you for a leisurely stroll through the hills of Ubud to discover how the Balinese use plants for healing.

Guides are important in remote areas; but well-worn hill paths such as those around Manggis (see p112) and north of Tenganan in East Bali (see p113), Ubud (see pp98–9), and the Ayung River Gorge (see pp100–101) are safe unaccompanied.

Traditional villages such as the Bali Aga villages of Tenganan (see pp114–15), and Trunyan on the

Exploring rural Bali on foot, one of the most rewarding ways

shores of Lake Batur (see p125), can also be interesting.

Try camping in North Bali at Air Sanih (see p151) or the national parks, such as Taman Nasional Bali Barat or Gunung Rinjani (see pp140–41 and 162–3).

Mountain Trekking

Lovers of mountains, and particularly of volcanoes, can undertake treks on Bali's **Gunung Agung** (see p118) and **Gunung Batur** (see pp124–5), as well as on Lombok's **Gunung Rinjani** (see pp162–3). During the wet season from October to April, mountains can be very dangerous places and not suitable for climbing. All trips to volcanoes should be accompanied by professional guides. Reliable tour operators, such as **Mandalika Tours**, organize an interesting variety of trips including walks through the rainforest around Gunung Batukau (see p137). **Bali Sunshine Tours** offers a sunrise trek over the volcanic caldera of Gunung Batur. **Puri Agung Inn Trekking** takes you to the slopes of Bali's highest mountain, Mount Agung.

Car and Bike Tours

Organized four-wheel-drive tours are ideal ways to escape from more developed areas. The price for these day trips should cover lunch, drinks and transfers. **Waka Land Cruise** offers tours by Land Rover to the Waka Louka rainforest camp high in the mountains. If you

prefer, you can rent your own car and explore at your leisure. Check out **SDR Car Rentals** for details. Maps are easy to buy (although not always very detailed or reliable) and roads are generally good. However, driving in Indonesia can be dangerous. People and animals walk into traffic with apparent lack of concern. Always check you are fully insured when driving.

Exploring by motorcycle is enjoyable, although accidents are common. Always inspect the bike and helmet, and insist on insurance. Also watch out for potholes and gravel on the road.

Bali Dirt Bike Tours organizes off-road trail-bike trips. This is an exciting, and safer, alternative to battling with the island's traffic. **Bali Adventure Tours** takes you by car to the rim of Mount Batur, and you can then hop on a bicycle and cycle down.

Touring by bike along the scenic route beside Lake Batur

Cycling

Organized cycling trips on mountain bikes are great for seeing the spectacular scenery in Bali around Ubud, Gunung Batur (see pp124–5) and Sangeh (see p136). **Bali Adventure Tours** offers mountain cycling through Bali's central highlands. Safety equipment is provided as well as drinks, picnic boxes, towels, transfers and insurance. This activity is not suitable for children under ten.

Horse Riding

In Bali you can ride a horse along a deserted beach, through the surf at sunset, or through lush, green paddy fields in the central hills. **Kuda P Stables** and **Bali Horse Riding** (see p197) offer idyllic horse-riding experiences for beginners as well as for experienced riders.

The horses come in various heights – from small ponies to large horses. You can ride with a guide leading your horse, or ride unassisted. Wear long trousers and a pair of shoes (not sandals), and bring lots of sunblock.

Ride on an elephant in the Elephant Safari Park

Elephant Safaris

The ultimate in tropical outdoor activities has to be an elephant safari in the hills and jungles of central Bali. The **Elephant Safari Park** (see p103) is located about 20 minutes north of Ubud in beautifully landscaped gardens at Desa Taro. It offers the opportunity to hand-feed, touch, and interact with these amazing animals. The park's reception centre has a full-size mammoth skeleton, and an extensive graphic display explaining the elephant's natural history.

Elephant rides are available, and there are special rides for children. Prices usually include entrance fees, lunch, hotel transfers and insurance. Bookings can be made through their parent company **Bali Adventure Tours**.

Driving through Balinese countryside on a buggy tour

The Safari Park includes an impressive Elephant Museum, with over 1,000 exhibits, including fossils dating back 5 million years, prehistoric horns, century-old mammoth tusks, and bone carvings. The museum entrance displays the skeleton of a 30-year-old Sumatran Elephant.

The Indonesian elephant is an endangered species so the Safari Park also helps to raise awareness of conservation issues as well as supporting their relocation to special reserves where breeding programmes can take place. Proceeds from the gift shop, which offers an extensive range of elephant paintings, carvings, souvenirs and jewellery, also help to support the park's Elephant Foundation.

The Asian Elephant Art and Conservation Project was set up in 1999 and has been a great success. Its aim has been to teach elephants at the Safari Park to paint artworks using their trunks. The paintings are then sold to raise more funds for elephant conservation.

Canyon Tubing and Buggy Tours

Get close to nature with Bali's canyon tubing experience. Hidden between Bali's mountains is the fast-flowing Siap River, which was previously inaccessible. **Bali Quad Discovery Tours** organizes canyon tubing

and buggy adventure trips. The tour enables you to explore the river by sailing down it on an inflatable tube, as well as driving a buggy or quad bike through ricefields, jungle and a Balinese village. All tours include hotel transfers, refreshments and personal insurance.

Seawalking

Seawalking is a safe and unique diving system that makes walking on the bottom of the ocean possible. A large diving helmet filled with air is worn while walking underwater, at a depth of 15 ft (5 m). Participants undergo a short safety and instruction lesson beforehand. **Seawalker** arranges such tours in Bali.

Paragliding and Parasailing

Paragliding off the windy cliffs at Uluwatu in the south of Bali (see p80) is an experience possible only in the afternoons, subject to weather conditions. Trained and experienced instructors accompany novice fliers on a 20-minute tandem ride. **Exofly** is a professional paragliding club. This is not suitable for children under ten.

Tanjung Benoa (see p76) is the best place for parasailing. **Bali Hai Cruises** offers 10-minute parasailing trips.

Parasailing over the scenic Lake Bratan in the central mountains

DIRECTORY

Surfing

Bali Learn to Surf
Hard Rock Hotel, Kuta.
Tel (0361) 761 869
ext 8116.

**Rip Curl School
of Surf**
Jl Arjuna, Seminyak, Kuta.
Tel (0361) 735 858.

Diving and
Snorkelling

**Aquamarine Diving
Centre**
Jalan Raya Seminyak
2A, Seminyak.
Tel (0361) 730 107.
W aquamarine.com

Bali Marine Sports
Jalan Bypass Ngurah Rai,
Blanjong Sanur.
Tel (0361) 270 386.
W bmsdivebali.com

Blue Marlin Dive
Gili Trawangan, Lombok.
Tel (0370) 613 2424.

Dream Divers
PT Samudra Indah
Diving, Lombok.
Tel (0370) 692 047.
W dreamdivers.com

Geko Dive
Jalan Silayukti, Padang
Bai, Klungkung.
Tel (0363) 41 516.
W gekodive.com

Reef Seen Aquatic
Jalan Raya Pemuteran,
North Bali.
Tel (0362) 92 339.
W reefseen.com

Windsurfing &
Water-Skiing

**Blue Oasis
Beach Club**
Sanur Beach Hotel, Sanur.
Tel (0361) 288 104.
W blueoasisbeach
club.com

Fishing

Bali Fishing
Jalan Candidasa
007, Candidasa,
Karangasem.
Tel (0361) 774 504.
W bali-fishing.com

**Moggy Offshore
Cruising Catamaran**
Bali International Marina,
Jalan Pelabuhan, Benoa
Harbour, Denpasar.
Tel (0361) 723 601.

Cruises

Bali Hai Cruises
Benoa Harbour.
Tel (0361) 720 831.
W balihaicruises.com

Bounty Cruises
Benoa Harbour. **Tel** (0361)
726 666. **W** balibounty
cruises.com

Quicksilver Cruises
Jalan Kerta Dalem 96,
Sidhakarya, Denpasar.
Tel (0361) 727 946.
W quicksilver-bali.com

White-Water
Rafting, Ocean
Rafting and
Kayaking

Ayung River Rafting
Jalan Diponegoro T508-
29, Denpasar. **Tel** (0361)
238 759. **W** ayungriver
rafting.com

Bali Adventure Tours
Adventure House, Jl Bypass
Ngurah Rai, Pesanggaran.
Tel (0361) 721 480.
W baliadventure
tours.com

Sobek
Jalan Tirta Ening 9, Sanur.
Tel (0361) 287 059.
W balisobek.com

Swimming

Club Med
Lot N-6, Nusa Dua.
Tel (0361) 771 521.

Waterbom Park & Spa
Jalan Kartika Plaza, Tuban.
Tel (0361) 755 676.
W waterbom-bali.com

Golf

**Bali Handara Kosaido
Country Club**
Pancasari Village, Bedugul.
Tel (0362) 221 182.

Bali National Golf Club
Nusa Dua. **Tel** (0361) 771
791. **W** balinational
golf.com

New Kuta Golf Club
Pecatu, Jimbaran.
Tel (0361) 848 1333.
W newkutagolf.com

Nirwana Bali Golf Club
Jalan Raya Tanah Lot,
Kediri, Tabanan.
Tel (0361) 815 970.

Eco-Tours

Bali Bird Park
See p197.

Bali Bird Walks
Tel (0361) 975 009.
W balibirdwalk.com

Bali Hai Cruises
See Cruises.

Bali Reptile Park
See p197.

**Bali Treetop
Adventure Park**
See p197.

Ena Dive Centre
Jalan Tirta Ening 1, Sanur.
Tel (0361) 288 829.
W enadive.co.id

JED
Jalan Pengubengan Kauh
St 94, Kerobokan-Kuta.
Tel (0361) 366 9951.
W jed.or.id

Puri Lumbung
Munduk Village, Banjar
District, Buleng Regency.
Tel (085) 100 210 675.
W purilumbung.com

**Taman Nasional
Bali Barat**
Jalan Raya Gilimanuk,
Cekik. **Tel** (0365) 61 060.

Walking, Trekking
and Camping

Bali Herbal Walks
Jalan Jembawan, Ubud.
Tel (081) 2381 6020/4.
W baliherbalwalk.com

Bali Sunshine Tours
Jl Himalaya Utara, Pondok
Indah Raya III/1, Gatot
Subroto Barat, Denpasar.
Tel (0361) 414 057.
W bsmtours.com

Keep Walking Tours
Jalan Hanoman 44, Ubud.
Tel (0361) 970 581.

Mandalika Tours
Jalan Hang Tuah Raya 11,
Sanur. **Tel** (0361) 287 450.
W balimandalikatour.
com

**Puri Agung Inn
Trekking**
Tirta Gangga.
Tel (0366) 23 037

Car, Cycling and
Bike Tours

Bali Adventure Tours
See White-Water Rafting.

Bali Dirt Bike Tours
Tabanan.
Tel (081) 755 8032.
W baliwilderness.com

SDR Car Rentals
Jalan Merta Ayu 9,
Kerobokan.
Tel (0361) 735 258.

Waka Land Cruise
Jl Imam Bonjol 9, Denpasar.
Tel (0361) 484 085.
W wakahotelsand
resorts.com

Elephant Safaris

Bali Adventure Tours
See White-Water Rafting.

Elephant Safari Park
Taro, Tegallalang, Gianyar.
Tel (0361) 721 480.

Canyon Tubing
and Buggy Tours

**Bali Quad
Discovery Tours**
Jalan Wirasatya VI 7 X,
Suwung Kangin, Denpasar.
Tel (0361) 720 766.
W baliquad.com

Seawalking

Seawalker
Club Aqua Bali, Padang
Galak, Sanur.
Tel (0361) 281 408.
W clubaquabali.com

Paragliding and
Parasailing

Bali Hai Cruises
See Cruises.

Exofly
Tel (081)
W exo'

Surfing and Beach Culture

Bali and, to a lesser extent, Lombok, have a vibrant beach culture. Surfers made Bali a popular destination from the 1960s onwards, and for many visitors the beaches are still the most alluring features of both islands. The whole range of beach activities is available – from surfing, windsurfing and water-skiing to less energetic options such as sunbathing and a beach massage. Conditions for beach life, including surfing, are best during the months from May to September. For those who cannot take their own gear, water sports equipment can be rented on all the more popular beaches, particularly those of South Bali.

Surfboards for rent on Kuta Beach

Canggu beach offers high-performance surfing popular with locals and visitors. Best before midday, the swells roll in over the rock-bottom forming peaks that split left and right.

Windsurfing

Bali offers good surf on many of its beaches, with Sanur and Tanjung Benoa considered the best places for windsurfing, with their world-class waves and fast, good-sized breaks.

The sail enables the wind to lift the board over waves, as well as move forward.

The windsurfing board, made of fibreglass, has a mast and a sail.

Top Surfing Areas

Surfers off Bali and Lombok make most use of the south-facing beaches. These catch the ocean swells arriving from the directions of southern and western Australia. Tide are available at surf shops al magazine, *Surf Time*, nformation on surfing s and other events.

Bali Sea

Bali

Canggu ● ● Sanur
Kuta ● ● Pulau Serangan
● Padang-padang
Uluwatu

Lombok

● Desert Point

Maui ● ● Gerupuk

Indian Ocean

| 0 kilometres | 75 |
| 0 miles | 50 |

Beach massage services are common to most of Bali's popular beaches. Prices are generally low and negotiated by the hour.

Parasailing, seen here at Tanjung Benoa, has become a very popular activity. Other options include jet-skiing, banana boating, the fly fish (a flying mattress), water-skiing and windsurfing.

Kuta beach is the birthplace of Bali's surfing tradition. The sand-bottom beach wave breaks with thin lips attract surfers of all levels of skill – this is a good place for beginners. Watch out for rip tides.

Bali's wave breaks give opportunities for acrobatics.

Safety Precautions

- Not all beaches have visitor or medical facilities.
- Remember that lifeguards are found only on popular beaches such as Kuta and Nusa Dua.
- Keep between the safety flags, if there are any.
- Use high-protection sunscreen.
- Wear sunglasses and a hat.
- Pack a first-aid kit.

On Sanur beach, sailing boats can be rented. Shown here is a hobie cat, a small catamaran notable for its speed. Boats of this kind flip easily, so caution needs to be exercised in high winds or lively seas, conditions sometimes encountered here.

Diving in Bali and Lombok

Bali's dive sites are rich in marine life, lush coral gardens and reef walls. There are several shipwrecks. Top sites include Menjangan Island *(see p142)* for its variety of soft and hard coral; Tulamben, site of the *Liberty* wreck; and Nusa Penida and Nusa Lembongan *(see pp78–9)* for sightings of the ocean sunfish. Lombok offers good diving and snorkelling off the Gili Isles. The PADI (Professional Association of Dive Instructors) system of certification is generally recognized. The greatest concentration of diving-trip operators is in the South Bali resort areas *(see pp62–3)*.

Diving instruction off Pemuteran, where the current is minimal, and visibility is good. There are many such diving schools on Bali where PADI certification can be obtained.

The reef wall is a haven for many forms of marine life.

The blackspotted puffer fish can be found in the coral gardens off Menjangan Island, where walls dominate the reef structure.

Dive Site Ratings There is a good variety of sites around these islands. Divers should know the level of experience required in any dive site before braving the waters.	Snorkelling	Novice Diving	Advanced Diving	Expert Diving
① Menjangan Island	●	■	●	■
② Pemuteran	●	■	●	■
③ Tulamben	●	■	●	■
④ Candidasa	●		●	■
⑤ Nusa Penida			●	■
⑥ Sanur	●	■	●	■
⑦ Nusa Dua	●	■	●	■
⑧ Gili Isles	●	■	●	■

Apparatus can be rented from the many PADI-certified organizers of diving trips.

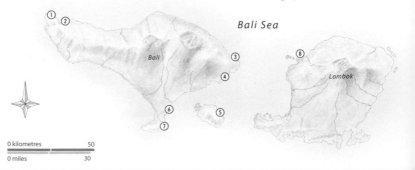

Bali Sea

Bali

Lombok

0 kilometres   50
0 miles   30

A diver's platform is attached to the rear of a boat. It is often used to facilitate the training of novice divers, who can explore shallow depths of around 15 m (50 ft) at the most.

The coral hawkfish can sometimes be seen in the waters off Nusa Penida, where marine life includes jacks, tuna, manta rays, reef sharks and, on rare occasions, whale sharks.

A correctly equipped diver can explore marine and coral life in safety provided due regard is given to strong currents in some areas

Marine Life

The rare ocean sunfish, known in Bali as the "mola mola", migrates through Balinese waters in great numbers from November to February. It is a memorable sight. The absence of a distinct tail fin gives the fish a "chopped off" appearance.

Fish of the Gobiidae family dwell in the crevices and branches of coral. There are many hundreds of species of these fish living in the Indo-Pacific region and they are easily observed by divers in the waters of Bali and Lombok.

SURVIVAL GUIDE

PRACTICAL INFORMATION

Bali and Lombok, like the rest of Indonesia, have been undergoing profound and rapid changes since the end of the Suharto regime in 1998. The furious pace of development exerts continuous pressure on the social and physical landscape. Visitors should be prepared for unexpected changes in prices, regulations, facilities, phone numbers, office hours, street names, and even attitudes. Check websites *(see p213)* for the latest information.

Bali is generally more developed than Lombok. There is an international airport at Denpasar. The tourism infrastructure is most developed in the beach resorts of South Bali, in Ubud, the "cultural heartland" of Bali, and increasingly in the north and east. Tourism in Lombok is concentrated on the northwest coast around Senggigi; outside this area, tourism services are scarce. Most visitors go to Bali first, to savour its busy nightlife, absorb its charming culture and get accustomed to the warm climate. They then move on by sea or air to Lombok, to enjoy its quieter pace and unspoiled natural beauty.

When to Go

High seasons in Bali and Lombok, with attendant crowds and higher prices, are from mid-December to mid-January (Christmas–New Year period), and in July and August. The weather is most pleasant from May to September *(see pp44–7)*.

Visas and Passports

To enter Indonesia, your passport must be valid for at least six months after the date of departure. Airport immigration officials may ask to see a ticket out of Indonesia, or proof of funds for the duration of your stay and for onward travel, without which you may be refused entry.

Tourist visas are only valid for 30 days, and they are non-extendable. Visitors coming from 15 countries, mainly in the Far East, do not need a visa, and those from 63 other countries (including the USA, the UK, Australia and Japan) may purchase a visa on arrival. Check with your local Indonesian consulate because citizens of some countries need to apply for a visa in their home country prior to travelling.

There are plans (but no date as yet) to double the list of countries not requiring a visa, including several European nations, the USA and Canada. Check for the latest information before travelling.

Surfboards available for rent on the beach at Sanur

Driving Permits

If you plan on driving in Indonesia, you must have an International Driving Permit, which can best be obtained in your own country if you already have a valid driver's licence.

If you plan to drive a motorcycle, ensure that your International Driving Permit includes a motorcycle permit – this is better than going through the laborious process of obtaining a motorcycle permit in Bali.

Immunization and Health Precautions

While there are no legal medical requirements for visitors from most countries, cholera, hepatitis A, typhoid and polio inoculations are recommended, and tetanus shots should be up to date. Dengue fever has been reported in Bali and Lombok, and malaria is a real risk in Lombok, so consult your physician about preventive and emergency medication before you begin your trip.

What to Take

Casual clothes in lightweight natural materials are recommended, with at least one set of smarter conservative clothes *(see pp214–15)*, should you need to visit a government office. A wide range of sports equipment for diving, golf, surfing, snorkelling and tennis can easily be rented or bought at most sports locations.

Most medicines are available in the major towns, but if you require special medication, it is wise to bring a full supply in the original packaging. You may also wish to bring some first-aid items such as antiseptic cream, aspirin, sticking plaster, diarrhoea medication and insect repellent. If you wear prescription spectacles, bring a spare set.

Casual clothes are acceptable in resorts and tourist areas

◀ A stunning blue lagoon in Bali

It is possible to exchange rupiah in and outside Indonesia. Visitors are advised to purchase some rupiah before entering the country, at least enough for taxi fare from the airport and spending for the first day.

Two-pin plug of the type used in Bali and Lombok

Electricity and Electrical Appliances

Electricity generally runs at 220V–240V AC. In some rural areas, the system still runs on 110V, and some remote areas do not have electricity at all. Power supplies may be unstable.

You may need a plug adaptor with two-pronged, parallel pins. You should buy an adaptor if necessary before you travel.

Customs and Duty-Free

Indonesian customs regulations allow foreign nationals to import 200 cigarettes (or 50 cigars or 100 grams of tobacco) and 1 litre of alcohol. Visitors may be asked to declare photographic and electronic equipment. There are restrictions on the import and export of products such as ivory and turtle shell, on things made from endangered species, and on the export of antiquities and certain cultural objects. Check with an Indonesian embassy or consulate for details. There are duty-free shops in Bali and in the departure area of the airport. Import or export of rupiah is limited to Rp100 million per person.

Duty-free shop logo

Facilities for Disabled Travellers

Provisions for disabled people are, as in much of Asia, inadequate. Facilities for the disabled that are available are not as sophisticated as they are in the United States and in Europe.

The terrain is often hilly, and there are stairs and steps everywhere. Wheelchair access is very rare. Pavements rarely have slopes to aid getting on or off them; most are high and uneven. Many public places are accessed by steps; very few have ramps, and wheelchair users will find public transport inaccessible.

The more up-market hotels, however, are slowly becoming increasingly aware of the needs of disabled travellers. Some of the more modern 5-star hotels have wheelchair access, and villas usually have spacious bathrooms and extensive grounds, suitable for wheelchair users.

Steps to temple hindering wheelchair access

Facilities for Children

In Bali and Lombok, children are treated with great respect and appreciation. In fact, small children are likely to be greeted (in some places) with far more enthusiasm by hotel staff than by fellow guests. Some hotels have special rates, facilities and activities for children of various ages, so ask your hotel. Because Indonesian children are constantly attended and included in general society, no special safety measures are taken for them, and there are

Child enjoying herself in a pool with a rubber ring

few facilities outside of resorts specifically for children. Parents of small children need therefore to be especially alert to environmental hazards such as stairs, unguarded edges and traffic.

Paraphernalia for infant care is available in department stores and most pharmacies.

Children will find much to keep themselves happily occupied in Bali and Lombok. There is an enormous range of activities available: water-based activities in beaches, pools and water parks; jungle rides, trekking, rafting and mountain biking; and music and dance performances. For more information on activities suitable for children, see p195 and pp198–203.

The Law

For drivers, motor insurance is both obligatory and highly recommended. You must tell the police (see p216) if you intend to spend more than 24 hours in a private home. Notify your consulate if you are arrested for a crime. Inform the police and your consulate if you are in an accident where someone is injured or there is property damage; if your passport is lost or stolen; if you are the victim of any other crime; if you give birth; or if someone in your party dies.

Warning

Indonesian law prescribes the death penalty for trafficking in illegal drugs, and heavy penalties for possession of weapons.

Tourist Information and Service Centres

There are government-run tourist information offices (Dinas Pariwisata Pemerintah Propinsi Daerah Tingkat I Bali) in each regional capital; in some towns there may be several branches. These offices offer a range of brochures on major tourist sites. Some of the offices in outlying areas away from the main tourist hubs are not as efficient as you would expect, especially when dealing with telephone enquiries.

Tourist areas also have information centres. Opening hours are normally 7:30am–3pm from Mondays to Thursdays and 7:30am–2pm on Fridays. Offices in major tourist sites, such as those in Kuta, Sanur and Ubud, have longer opening hours.

Another good source of local information is the many small businesses in tourist areas, which also offer some or all

Locals starting their day early at the morning market at Sidemen

A tourist information centre offering a variety of services

of the following services: telephone, fax, email, tours, car and bicycle rentals, airline bookings, cargo packing and shipping, currency exchange, video rental, film processing, postal service and post restante, and sale of tickets for cultural performances.

Time

Bali and Lombok are eight hours ahead of Greenwich Mean Time (GMT), in the same time zone as Perth; Jakarta is seven hours ahead. Because of the proximity to the equator, days and nights are of almost equal length and vary little throughout the year. Night falls very quickly, at around 6–7pm.

Open (buka) and closed (tutup) signs

Opening Hours

For farmers and market vendors, the day begins before dawn – in Muslim Lombok, with prayers amplified from the mosques. By two in the afternoon, it is time to rest. Banks, government offices and many small businesses mostly follow this pattern. Businesses catering to tourists keep hours more like their guests, opening mid-morning and closing mid-evening, every day except major public holidays (see p47).

Tourist sites, such as temples, are open during daylight hours every day. Museum hours and opening days vary. Government office hours are 8am–4pm, although some places may close earlier, especially on Fridays. Banks are generally open from 8:30am to 3pm from Mondays to Fridays, although some are open on Saturday mornings.

Christian Worship for Visitors

The dominant religion in Bali is Hinduism, while that in Lombok is Islam. However, there are several Christian churches offering services in English, such as **Kuta International Christian Church**. Some hotels, such as the **Nusa Dua Beach Hotel** and the **Grand Bali Beach Hotel** in Sanur also offer services on demand on Sundays at which both hotel guests and non-residents are welcome.

Cagar Budaya Nasional (National Heritage Site)

Keep an eye out for small white signs with black lettering marked "Cagar Budaya Nasional"; they indicate a national heritage site. In Bali, some of these are historic sites, but many are temples. Until the 1990s, most temples were open to anyone as long as you wore a temple sash. That is no longer the case. Except for very important temples, those not designated as "Cagar Budaya Nasional" are likely to be closed, except during their anniversary festivals, when anyone who is correctly dressed and not in a taboo condition (see p215) may visit. Cagar Budaya Nasional sites generally have a visitors' kiosk with a guest book and donation box – a few thousand rupiah is enough – and there are sarongs and sashes which you may borrow to fulfil temple dress requirements. Some sites may charge an admission fee.

A Cagar Budaya Nasional sign marking a national heritage site

Balinese-style toilet signs, typical of those found in restaurants

Public Toilets

Public toilets are scarce in Bali and Lombok, except at major tourist stops. Hygiene is poor and toilet paper rare. Toilets (kamar kecil) consist of a "squat" toilet and a large bin of water (bak mandi), with which you flush the toilet and cleanse yourself. Toilet signs – "wanita" (female) or "pria" (male) – are often elaborate woodcarvings at tourist areas.

Conversion Chart

Imperial to Metric
1 inch = 2.54 centimetres
1 foot = 30 centimetres
1 yard = 0.9 metres
1 mile = 1.6 kilometres
1 ounce = 28 grams
1 pound = 454 grams

Metric to Imperial
1 centimetre = 0.4 inches
1 metre = 3 feet 3 inches
1 metre = 1.11 yards
1 kilometre = 0.6 miles
1 gram = 0.04 ounces
1 kilogram = 2.2 pounds
1 litre = 0.22 gallons
1 litre = 1.8 pints

Fabric sold by length in a textile shop

DIRECTORY

Useful Phone Numbers

Ngurah Rai International Airport Information
Tel (0361) 751 011.

Useful Websites

[W] expat.or.id
[W] bali-paradise.com
[W] bali-portal.com
[W] balibagus.com
[W] balitourismboard.org
[W] baliupdate.com
[W] lombok-network.com
[W] thevillaguide.com

Tourist Information Services

Badung
Badung Tourism Authority (South Bali, Java, West Nusantara and Lombok), Jalan RayaKuta 2, Kuta.
Tel & Fax (0361) 756 176.
[W] lbadung.go.id

Denpasar
Regional Office of Tourism, Art and Culture, Jalan Raya Puputan Niti Mandala, Denpasar.
Tel (0361) 225 649.
Fax (0361) 233 474.
[W] bali.go.id/tourism

Denpasar
Bali Toursim Authority (DIPARDA), Jalan S Parman Niti Mandala, Denpasar.
Tel (0361) 222 387.
Fax (0361) 226 313.
[W] balitourism authority.net

West Nusa Tenggara
Provincial Tourist Service, Jalam Langko 70, Ampenan, Lombok.
Tel (0364) 21 730.
Regional Office of Tourism, Art and Culture, West Nusa Tenggara, Jalan Singosari 2, Mataram, Lombok.
Tel (0370) 632 723 or (0370) 634 800.
Fax (0370) 637 233.

Foreign Consulates

Australia
(also represents Canada, New Zealand, and other Commonwealth countries in emergencies.) Jalan Hayam Wuruk 886, Denpasar.
Tel (0361) 241 118.
Fax (0361) 221 195.
[W] dfat.gov.au/bali

Great Britain
Jalan Tirtanadi 20, Sanur.
Tel (0361) 270 601.
Fax (0361) 287 804.

United States
Jalan Hayam Wuruk 188, Renon, Denpasar.
Tel (0361) 233 605.
Fax (0361) 222 426.

Immigration Offices

Airport
Kantor Imigrasi Ngurah Rai Tuban, Jalan Raya I Gusti Ngurah Rai, Tuban.
Tel (0361) 751 038.

Denpasar
Kantor Imigrasi Denpasar, Jalan Di Panjaitan, Niti Mandala, Renon.
Tel (0361) 265 030.

Lombok
Kantor Imigrasi Lombok, Jalan Udayana 2, Mataram, Lombok.
Tel (0370) 632 520.

Christian Worship

English-language services:

Christian City Church
Jalan Diponegoro 148, Denpasar. Tel (0818) 567 802.

Eastern Orthodox Church Service
(Divine liturgy.) Mykonos Restaurant, Jalan Kayu Aya (Laksmana) 52.
Tel (0361) 733 253.

Kuta International Christian Church
(Interdenominational.) Jalan Patimura, Legian.
Tel (081) 7976 5673.

Sanur
(Interdenominational.) Grand Bali Beach Hotel, Sanur (6:30pm Sun).
Tel (0361) 286 022.

St Joseph Church
(Catholic holy mass.) Jalan Kepundung, Denpasar.
Tel (0361) 233 729.
St Franciscus Xaverlus, Jalan Kartika Plaza, Kuta (6pm Sat & 8am Sun).

Etiquette

Visitors behaving with due courtesy will generally be made welcome in Bali and Lombok. Indeed the greatest pleasure of travelling in Indonesia is getting to know its very hospitable and gracious people. The Balinese are an extroverted, cheerfully self-confident people; the Sasaks of Lombok are more reserved. The inhabitants of both islands will treat tourists well, especially those with a little knowledge of local manners.

Balinese dressed up in formal attire for a ceremony

What to Wear

The dress code at resorts is very relaxed, and shorts and bare arms and shoulders are generally accepted. Upper-end hotels may require "smart casual" dress in the evenings. However, most Indonesians may be offended by immodest attire and visitors should be sensitive to this when entering towns and villages.

Within tourist enclaves, dress is very casual. A hat or cap and comfortable shoes that slip off easily are best for touring – Indonesians generally remove their shoes before entering a home.

When visiting a government office, conservative dress is obligatory: for men, long trousers and long-sleeved shirt, shoes and socks; and for women, a knee-length dress or skirt, a blouse that covers the upper arms, and shoes rather than rubber flip-flops.

Outside tourist areas, especially in Lombok, conservative dress is a sign of courtesy. Ubud's dress code is more conservative than that of beach resort areas. Some Ubud visitors adopt the sarong.

Languages

Most locals who deal with tourists speak some English, and there are guides trained in Japanese and major European languages.

Bahasa Indonesia is the national language of Indonesia. It is based largely on Malay, for centuries the trading language of the archipelago, and uses the Latin alphabet. Verbs take suffixes and prefixes, making it difficult to look up a word in a phrasebook without knowing its root form. It is easy to master a simplified form of Bahasa Indonesia that is widely used with visitors.

The Balinese and the Sasaks of Lombok maintain their indigenous languages which share a common base with Javanese, and are written with a Sanskrit-based alphabet. There is a complex system of parallel vocabularies to reflect status rankings, and mistakes can cause offence.

The lotus, a symbol of grace in Bali

Tourists at a temple wearing the required sarong and waist sash

Social Behaviour

In Bali and Lombok, certain social rules are observed, which, if followed by visitors, will open up a warm exchange; and if ignored, may cause embarrassment or even seriously offend.

Always give and receive things with the right hand, never the left. Avoid pointing with the index finger, especially at a person: this gesture may be taken as a physical challenge. If you must point at something, only use the thumb of your right hand. To be very polite, do so while cupping your right elbow. Never point to anyone or anything with your foot.

Avoid touching anyone's head, even a child's – a person's head is considered the most sacred part of the body – and do not stand next to someone who is sitting down. If you need to walk past someone who is sitting on the ground, it is best to bend from the waist and murmur something apologetic ("Maaf" or "Sorry, sorry").

In a social situation with Indonesians where refreshments are served, wait until you are invited before you begin drinking or eating. (Indonesians wait until they are bidden several times before they do so.) Similarly, do not sit down until you are directed to a place; spatial placement holds a significant social code for Indonesians.

As far as possible, do not express anger or behave in a confrontational manner. Any extravagant displays of emotion will make you look foolish. As in much of Asia, it is considered coarse to call attention to oneself unnecessarily, especially while in public. Gracious behaviour is much appreciated by Indonesians and will get better results than an angry outburst.

Indonesians frown on public displays of private affection – these are considered embarrassing to others and therefore rude.

Social Encounters

It is usual to greet people whether you know them or not, and to acknowledge those nearby with a smile and a nod when you arrive or leave a place. Polite conversation often takes the form of an exchange of questions. Westerners may find these intrusive – the best solution
is to ask questions in return.

Visitor taking off his shoes before entering a Balinese home

Places of Worship

Hindus in Bali and Lombok observe strict rules in regard to their temples, which they believe must be observed by everyone, including visitors, for safeguarding the spiritual hygiene of sacred places. These rules mainly concern dress requirements and conditions of *sebel* (taboo).

A waist sash, and in many places a sarong, is the dress required of anyone entering a temple or other holy ground, whether or not there is a ceremony in progress. These may be borrowed at temples that regularly accept tourists, but it is easy to buy your own almost anywhere.

There is no moral censure attached to being in a state of *sebel*; on the contrary, to acknowledge this state is a mark of self-awareness. These rules should be observed, even if they conflict with your religious beliefs.

Conditions of *sebel* are: menstruation or having an open wound – this relates to a prohibition on shedding blood in a temple; bringing food into a temple as it clashes with offerings; being physically or mentally ill, or in a state of

psychic disturbance; being in a state of bereavement (for the Balinese, up to 42 days from the date of the death of a close relative); and having given birth within the past 42 days (thought to attract attention from spirits).

There are other rules that should be observed when entering temples, especially during festivals.

Ask permission before entering a courtyard, as some gates are reserved for priests and holy objects. It is best to stay quietly at the back of a courtyard until invited. Do not walk in front of anyone who is praying, or a priest performing a ritual.

Photography is restricted in some temples, so check with temple attendants before using a camera.

Temple offerings should also not be touched, and temple walls and shrines must never be climbed. It is considered sacrilegious to do so unless one is a priest.

There are rules that should be observed when entering mosques: visitors should take off their shoes before going into a mosque, and cover up shoulders, arms and legs; women should cover their heads with a scarf, and must not enter when menstruating.

Bargaining

Except for shops and department stores with fixed

Bargaining for a straw bag at a market

prices, many vendors and shopkeepers expect customers to bargain before finalizing a sale. Indonesians consider it fair that tourists pay higher prices than the (usually much poorer) locals. Be realistic. To get a good price, learn the prices of goods elsewhere before making a purchase, then disarm the vendor by being polite.

Unwelcome Attention

If you do not wish to buy something from a street or beach peddler, or accept the offer of "transport", it is usually enough to say quietly "No, thank you".

Avoid giving money to children. If you have a small gift for them, give it to their parents instead.

Women are regarded with respect in Indonesia, and it is rare for foreigners to be bothered by sexual harassment. However, dressing modestly helps.

Hawkers peddling their wares to a potential buyer

Personal Security and Health

Visitors to Bali and Lombok generally face no greater personal danger than sunburn and perhaps a day or two of digestive upset. It is important, however, to bear in mind that visitors are operating in a "parallel economy" which is conspicuously richer than that of the largely poor, local population; that it takes some time for visitors from temperate areas to adjust to the tropical climate; and that the sanitation and medical infrastructure is not yet as complete as in developed countries. In general, tourists should follow the same precautions they take when visiting their own local cities.

Cycling down a one-way street in Kuta, a convenient way to travel

Looking After Your Property

Violent crime in Bali and Lombok is rare; but tourist areas attract delinquents, and you should treat your belongings with care.

Most hotels offer some form of lock-up storage. Use it. To leave valuables lying around un-attended is to invite theft. Put valuables and important docu-ments in your hotel safe. Lock the doors and windows of your hotel room when you are not there. Be on guard against pick-pockets and bag-snatchers, who usually operate on the street or in crowded places such as public transport vehicles and airport terminals. At banks and espe-cially at moneychangers, count cash carefully at the counter and put it immediately in your wallet before leaving the premises. Do not let the moneychanger handle the money after you have counted it.

Make a note of the serial numbers of your camera, computer or other equipment, and keep photocopies of documents such as your passport data and visa pages, credit cards and driving licence – these will come in useful in the event of a police report or an insurance claim.

Personal Safety

Tourists in Bali and Lombok are generally treated as valued guests. If you travel alone late at night off the beaten track, you will certainly attract attention from local people, but probably in the form of concern for your welfare. Women travelling alone should exercise the usual precautions.

A police patrol car

An ambulance

In places such as Kuta where there is a developed nightlife, be alert, as you would in any other country.

Some cases of armed robbery have been reported in the remoter parts of Lombok, especially around Gunung Rinjani. You should seek local advice before travelling in this area alone.

If you are pestered by someone, immediately seek out a crowded place. Be aware that if you are robbed and you call out for help, this may arouse an entire village, who could well enact "street justice" on the spot, with tragic consequences for any person accused, so be cautious about accusing anyone.

The 2002 terrorist attacks in Indonesia resulted in travel warnings from some countries. Check your government's travel advice for most recent infor-mation. It is also advised not to get involved in political demonstrations while in Bali.

Medical Facilities

There are 24-hour clinics in the major tourist areas for minor illnesses and first aid. The fact that they cater mainly to tourists is reflected in their prices. The clinics include the **Bali International Medical Centre (BIMC)**, in both Kuta and Nusa Dua, the **SOS Clinic**, the **General Hospital Lombok** and the **Ubud Clinic**. There is an extra charge for house calls.

The local equivalents to these clinics are the Puskesmas, not always staffed round the clock, and not as well equipped. Major hotels have doctors on call. There are public hospitals (*rumah sakit umum*) in every regional capital – the best is in Sanglah, Denpasar. There are a few private hospitals. Visitors are strongly advised to take out medical evacuation insurance before travelling.

Common Ailments

The most common health problems for visitors are over-exposure to the sun, digestive troubles, infections arising from untreated surface cuts and motorcycle mishaps.

Use a sunblock and renew it after you swim; avoid the beach (sunny or not) between 11am and 2pm; and wear a hat. Resist the temptation to make a motorcycle tour in your bathing suit – not only will you look silly (crash helmets are obligatory), your skin will be scorched by both sun and wind. Wear protective clothing, and beware of the exhaust pipe, which can give your leg a deep, slow-to-heal burn.

Bottled water

Tropical ulcers are infections that can arise when surface wounds such as cuts, blisters or scratched mosquito bites go unattended. Even very minor wounds should be washed with soap and water and treated with antiseptic powder or cream.

Treat stomach upsets with a mild diet (boiled rice and black tea is an effective remedy). Severe diarrhoea must be followed with a rehydration treatment; neglect of this can be fatal for infants. The water of a

Hats and shades for sun protection

young coconut is also effective. If you suspect cholera, see a doctor.

To minimize digestive problems, avoid fresh fruit that you do not peel yourself. Drink only bottled water, checking first that the seal is intact. Food at local food stalls is always fresh, but it is highly spiced and hygiene is questionable. In some tourist places, on the other hand, excessive faith in refrigeration can result in food being stored too long. In cases of serious doubt, plain rice with a little salt is generally safe.

APOTIK ANGKASA
(NO. SIA : PO. OO. O2. SIA : RA VII. 98. 2915)
JL. KEMAYORAN. BANDARA NGURAH RAI
TELP. 763102

A street sign indicating a local pharmacy (apotik)

Pharmacies

Pharmacies are known as *"apotik"* and are generally abundant in towns. There is usually a qualified pharmacist on hand who speaks some English and can advise on medications. Imported, branded medications are relatively expensive; cheaper, generic equivalents are often easily found.

Snakes and Insects

Snakes (*ular* in Bahasa Indonesia, *lelipi* in Balinese) can sometimes be seen – Bali still has field and water snakes. Most are harmless. The brilliantly coloured green tree viper has a poisonous bite which can be fatal to small children and the physically weak. It inhabits ricefields and trees. Do not go into thick vegetation without adequate protection, and make warning noises. Cobras have been sighted in gardens in South Bali.

Scorpions and centipedes sometimes lurk in quiet corners; their bite is not generally dangerous, but can be very painful. Mosquitoes are prevalent in coastal areas. Use repellents and protective clothing, and burn mosquito coils (*obat nyamuk*), available in most hotels and restaurants.

DIRECTORY

Emergency Services

Ambulance Tel 118.
Fire Tel 113.
Police Tel 110.
Red Cross Tel (0361) 226 465.
Rescue Tel 115, 111 or 151.
Worldwide Emergency Assistance Tel (0361) 228 996.

Clinics

Bali International Medical Centre (BIMC) Kuta
Jalan Bypass Ngurah Rai 100 X, Kuta. **Tel** (0361) 761 263.
Fax (0361) 764 345. email: info@bimcbali.com w **bimcbali.com**
Open 24 hours.

Bali International Medical Centre (BIMC) Nusa Dua
Kawasan BTDC Blok D, Nusa Dua.
Tel (0361) 300 0911. **Fax** (0361) 300 1150. email: nusadwua@bimcbali.com **Open** 24 hours.

General Hospital Lombok
Jalan Pejanggik, Mataram, Lombok. **Tel** (0370) 622 254.
Open 24 hours.

Siloam Hospital
Jalan Sunset Road 818, Kuta, **Tel** (0361) 779 900
w **siloamhospitals.com/hospitals/siloam-hospitals-bali**

SOS Clinic
Jalan Bypass Ngurah rai 505x, Kuta. **Tel** (0361) 710 505. **Open** 24 hours. w **internationalsos.com**

Ubud Clinic
Jalan Raya Campuhan 36, Ubud.
Tel (0361) 974 911. **Open** 24 hours. w **ubudclinic.com**
Emergency dental care is available at the 24-hour clinics.

Environmental Hazards

The tropical sun is deceptively strong; so too are the currents of the Indian Ocean on the south coasts of Bali and Lombok. Not all beaches have lifeguards or markers. Drownings are common. Rivers which cross beaches and empty into the sea have traversed towns where sanitation can be poor or even non-existent. For this reason, and because of mudslides, avoid even upstream rivers for bathing.

Banking and Local Currency

Since the 1997 financial crisis, exchange rates between Indonesian and other currencies have fluctuated wildly, as have prices encountered by visitors. Modern banking and exchange facilities are available in the bigger towns and tourist centres. Major international credit cards are widely accepted. Although cash and traveller's cheques in other major currencies can be exchanged, US dollars are most widely welcomed. Many tourist services are priced in US dollars. Local currency will often be used for giving change.

An automatic teller machine, or ATM, at a bank

A branch of BCA, an Indonesian bank, in Kuta

Banking Services

The only foreign banks in Bali are **ABN Amro** and **Citibank**. In Bali, the main offices of the major Indonesian banks are in Denpasar, with branch offices in the regional capitals, as well as in Kuta, Sanur and Ubud, and in major hotels. Major banks in Lombok are in Mataram. Most banks in tourism areas have facilities for exchanging foreign currency. It is possible to wire money directly to a bank in Indonesia.

Traveller's Cheques and Moneychangers

Traveller's cheques, not normally accepted in place of cash in Bali and Lombok, may be cashed at most banks and moneychangers, usually for less favourable rates than currency. Bring your passport for identification. Exchange facilities are widely available in Bali and in major tourist areas in Lombok. Elsewhere, visitors should carry cash. Authorized moneychangers are found in abundance in tourist centres. Elsewhere, rates may be disadvantageous. Abuses have been reported, so exercise normal precautions.

Automatic Teller Machines (ATMs)

Electronic banking has grown rapidly, and ATMs can be found at banks all over the island, as well as at the airport's international and domestic arrival halls. Major international credit cards are also widely accepted.

A moneychanger in Seminyak

DIRECTORY

Credit Cards

American Express
c/o Pacto Ltd, Grand Bali Beach Hotel, Sanur.
Tel (0361) 288 449 or (0361) 288 511, ext. 1111 (for traveller's cheques).

BCA Card Centre
(for BCA, Visa, MasterCard and JCB Cards) Jalan Raya Kuta 55 XX, Kuta.
Tel (0361) 759 010 or (0361) 759 011 (for lost or stolen Visa cards).
Tel (001) 803 65 6576 (toll-free).

Banking Services

The major banks in Indonesia are used to dealing with foreign exchange, credit card advances and telegraphic transfers. Normal weekday banking hours are 8am–3pm and on Saturdays 8–11am.

ABN Amro
Jalan Teuku Umar 10, Denpasar.
Tel (0361) 224 225.

Bank Danamon
Jalan Raya Legian 87, Kuta. **Tel** (0361) 761 620.

Bank Lippo
Jalan Thamrin 77, Denpasar.
Tel (0361) 236 046.

Bank Mandiri
Jalan Danau Tamblingan 27, Sanur.
Tel (0361) 282 663.

Bank Negara Indonesia
Grand Bali Beach Hotel, Sanur. **Tel** (0361) 288 511.
Jalan Gajah Mada 30, Denpasar.
Tel (0361) 227 321.

Jalan Langko 64, Mataram, Lombok.
Tel (0370) 622 788.
Jalan Legian 359, Kuta.
Tel (0361) 751 914.
Jalan Monkey Forest 2, Ubud. **Tel** (0361) 975 986.
Jalan Surapati 52 A, Singaraja.
Tel (0362) 22 648.
Nusa Dua Beach Hotel, Nusa Dua.
Tel (0361) 771 906.

Citibank
Jalan Teuku Umar 208, Denpasar.
Tel (0361) 269 999.

Credit Cards

Major international credit cards (such as American Express, Visa and MasterCard) are accepted at most establishments that cater for visitors (in tourist areas) in Bali and Lombok, and they are becoming more widely used by Indonesians. Cash advances on credit cards are available at most banks, but this is usually subject to a commission fee and a maximum withdrawal. Inform your bank before travelling to avoid problems using your card.

Local Currency

The Indonesian currency unit is the rupiah. The currency fluctuates, so be sure to check the latest rates. Carry an adequate amount of currency in small denominations: people may often not be able to give change for large notes. Some old notes are still in circulation. Be cautious when receiving soiled or damaged notes. The current import and export limit is Rp100 million per person.

Bank Notes

Notes come in the following denominations: Rp1,000, Rp2,000, Rp5,000, Rp10,000, Rp20,000, Rp50,000 and Rp100,000.

1,000 rupiah

2,000 rupiah

5,000 rupiah

10,000 rupiah

20,000 rupiah

50,000 rupiah

100,000 rupiah

Coins

Coins come in denominations of Rp25 and Rp50 (rare and virtually worthless), Rp100, Rp200, Rp500 and Rp1,000. Some coins from earlier designs are still in circulation.

100 rupiah

200 rupiah

500 rupiah

1,000 rupiah

Communications and Media

Communications with the rest of the world are good in the major tourism centres, and steadily improving throughout Bali and Lombok. Telkom is the government-owned telephone utility, and offers Internet service; Indosat is a major telecom service provider. *Wartel* (from "*warung telkom*", or "telecom shops") are public telecom service outlets run by local businesses. International phone rates are among the highest in the world, especially if you make calls chargeable to your hotel bill.

Wartel office providing phone services

Reaching the Right Number

Indonesian telephone numbers are composed of the country code (62), an area code, and a 5- or 6-digit number. When making an *interlokal* call to other places within Indonesia, a zero is added before the area code.

Area Codes

South Bali
Badung regency: **361**
Central Bali
Gianyar regency: **361**
East Bali
Bangli regency: **366**
Klungkung regency: **366**
Karangasem regency: **363**
North Bali
Buleleng regency: **362**
West Bali
Tabanan regency: **361**
Jembrana regency: **365**
Lombok: 370

Telecommunications in Bali and Lombok

Telephone offices known as *wartel* and branded *Wartel Telkom* or *Wartel Aifa* may be used for local and international calls, although long-distance and international calls are expensive. There are very few public telephones on the street.

If you have easy access to the Internet, Skype, Facebook Messenger, WhatsApp and Viber are the most popular and cost-efficient means of communication, both for local and international calls.

Prepaid "Hello" cards, for use on landlines, are available at many Internet shops and offer a cheaper rate if you plan on making a lot of calls. Some local phonecard services also accept "Hello" cards; check details with the vendor before buying. Prices for "Hello" cards start at around $20.

Mobile phones are common among most Indonesians. Mobile phones in Indonesia use GSM or CDMA phone systems.

Check whether your mobile phone operator has an agreement with one of the GSM or CDMA operators in Indonesia, such as Simpati, or Pro-XL. If so, you will be able to buy phonecards for topping up your mobile phone. There are shops and kiosks on nearly every street selling these, and they offer good value for money as well as convenience. The card may cover a limited area, all of Indonesia or international coverage, so check the details before buying.

If you do not own a mobile phone, or if you forget to bring one with you, another option is to rent one for the duration of your stay. This can easily be done in Bali, where some companies helpfully arrange to deliver the phone to, and collect it from, your hotel. Visit www.balidiscovery.com/phones for more information on this service.

Fax services are available at *wartel* offices, business centres and Internet cafés. Charges are made for sending and receiving faxes, and they are based on phone rates, plus the number of pages sent. Be aware that the rates vary widely.

Postal Services

The Indonesian post office provides all the services you would normally expect. International delivery normally takes 8–10 days but can be unreliable. There are many informal postal-service outlets at tourist shops where you may buy stamps and post letters. The central post office is on the main road in Renon in Denpasar. Post offices in Ubud, Kuta and Singaraja have *poste restante* services. For mailing packages, it is more secure to go through an established courier service such as **DHL**, **FedEx** or **UPS**.

Typical Indonesian phonecard, available at local shops

Courier

Major international courier services have offices in Bali and Lombok. Most are based in Denpasar, although FedEx, DHL and UPS have branches in Ubud. You may have to take your package to one of their offices. **Elteha** also delivers packages within Indonesia.

Internet

Indonesia has more than 50 Internet Service Providers (ISPs). Users should check with their services for international access numbers. The simplest way to get online is through **Telkom**'s dial-up number, which offers free access with no registration.

Wi-Fi is readily available in numerous cafés, restaurants, hotels and holiday villas in Bali and Lombok. Internet cafés can also be found. Most offer broadband connections, but some are still quite slow. Recommended Internet cafés include **Global Xtreme**, **Roda Internet Café**, **Nominasi International Business Centre**, **Millennium Internet**, **Highway** and **Wi Fi Connection**.

Television

Satellite television is widespread in urban Indonesia and is found in all major hotels. Indonesia has more than ten private TV channels and the government-run TVRI. Bali TV has numerous cultural programmes with lots of music and traditional dancing. All the local channels are in the Indonesian languages, although they offer some American programmes and foreign films.

Newspapers and Magazines

English-language daily newspapers – primarily the American *International Herald Tribune* and the *Jakarta Post* – are available in tourist outlets and (at higher prices) many street vendors.

English-language magazines include *Hello Bali*, a free monthly magazine for tourists available at hotels and dining outlets, and the monthly *Bali and Beyond*, a tourism, art and culture magazine that covers events in Bali and Lombok. The quarterly *Yak* focuses on the Seminyak area.

The free biweekly newspaper *Bali Advertiser* is aimed at the expatriate community, but has good information about restaurants, tours and activities that may be of interest to short-term visitors.

The Beat is a free entertainment and gig guide. It is published every two weeks and is widely available.

Hello Bali magazine

DIRECTORY

Useful Dialling Codes

Local Directory Enquiries
Tel 108.

National Directory Enquiries
Tel 0809 108 108.

International Directory Enquiries
Tel 102.

Operator-Assisted International Calls
Tel 101.

International Direct Dialling
Tel 001, 017 or 008.

Postal Services and Couriers

DHL
Jalan Bypass Ngurah Rai, Tuban. **Tel** (0361) 768 282.
Jalan Bypass Ngurah Rai 155, Sanur.
Tel (0361) 283 818.

Jalan Legian Kaja 451, Kuta.
Tel (0361) 762 138.
Jalan Raya Ubud 16, Ubud.
Tel (0361) 972 195.

Elteha
Jalan Pengosekan, Ubud.
Tel (0361) 977 773.

Elteha Lombok
Jalan Koperasi 81 Ampenan, Mataram, Lombok.
Tel (0370) 631 820.

FedEx
Jalan Bypass Ngurah Rai 72, Jimbaran.
Tel (0361) 701 727.
Jalan Raya Ubud 44, Ubud. **Tel** (0361) 977 575.

UPS (United Parcel Service)
Jalan Bypass Ngurah Rai 2005. **Tel** (0361) 764 439 or (0361) 766 676.
Jalan Hanuman 17, Ubud.
Tel (0361) 977 161.

Internet

Highway
Jalan Raya Ubud.
Tel (0361) 972 107.
🌐 highwaybali.com

Global Xtreme
Jalan Kerobokan 388x, Kuta. **Tel** (0361) 736 833.

Millennium Internet
Jalan Senggigi, Senggigi, Lombok.
Tel (0370) 693 860.

Nominasi International Business Centre
Jalan Monkey Forest, Ubud.
Tel (0361) 975 067.

Roda Internet Café
Jalan Bisma 3, Ubud.
Tel (0361) 973 325.

Telkom
Free Internet access with no registration
Tel 0809 89 999.
In dialogue box, key in username "telkomnet@instan" and password "telkom". **Tel** 162 (Information).

Wi Fi Connection
Bali Deli, Jalan Kunti 117x, Seminyak.
Tel (0361) 738 686.

Computer Sales and Rental

Adi Computer
Jalan Tukad Yeh Penet 2, Renon, Denpasar.
Tel (0361) 236 531 or (0361) 238 430.

Harry's Computer
Jalan Teuku Umar 173, Denpasar. **Tel** (0361) 232 470 or (0361) 266 773.

Rimo Complex
Jalan Diponegoro, Denpasar.
Tel (0361) 233 206.

TRAVEL INFORMATION

Bali is one of the main gateways into Indonesia. The international Ngurah Rai Airport serves many airlines from around the world, and its harbour is equipped with customs and immigration officers. Lombok's airport handles international arrivals from Singapore on Silk-Air, from Malaysia on Air Asia, and from Port Headland on Virgin Australia. Arkefly, iFly and Nordwind come in from Amsterdam, Moscow and Krasnoyarsk respectively. It is possible to reach Bali and Lombok from within Indonesia by bus and ferry. Transport from the airport is handled by airport taxis and hotel shuttle buses. An airport tax is levied upon departure.

Aircraft arriving at Ngurah Rai Airport in Bali

Flying to Bali

The Ngurah Rai International Airport in Bali is in Tuban, south of Kuta, but the destination is referred to as Denpasar.

Major international airlines currently serving Denpasar include **Garuda Indonesia**, Indonesia's national carrier, Hong Kong Airlines, KLM, Philippine Airlines, Air New Zealand (seasonal), **Air Asia Indonesia**, Asiana Airlines, **Cathay Pacific**, **China Airlines**, **EVA Air**, Hainan Airlines, Japan Airlines, Korean Air, **Malaysia Airlines**, **Jetstar Airways**, Qatar Airways, **Singapore Airlines**, **Thai Airways International**, Transaero and Virgin Australia.

There are frequent direct flights from Australia and some countries in East Asia, such as Singapore, Thailand and Japan. Other carriers go no further than Jakarta, but they may make onward connections to Denpasar via Garuda Indonesia.

There are many daily flights between Jakarta and Denpasar. Many travellers from Europe fly to Singapore, from where there are direct flights every day to Denpasar on Garuda and Singapore Airlines.

Carriers from Taiwan (China Airlines) and Hong Kong (Cathay Pacific Airways) stop in their own capital cities.

Airfares and Taxes

Fares are highest during the high season, but this varies according to the airline. For instance, "high season" for Jetstar includes the southern hemisphere summer holidays in December.

The airport levies a nominal departure tax on domestic flights. Taxes on international flights are higher.

Getting to and from the Airport

The Ngurah Rai Airport is about a 45-minute drive from Kuta, Nusa Dua and Sanur, and about 90 minutes from Ubud.

Transport from the airport is restricted to special airport taxis, hotel shuttle buses and private vehicles. Several car-rental companies (see p225) have facilities at the airport.

To get a taxi, go to the taxi kiosk just outside the airport arrivals building exit (turn right). Fares are posted and range from about Rp55,000 (for South Kuta Beach) to about Rp250,000 (for Ubud). A levy of 30 per cent extra is placed on out-of-town services. Obtain a voucher at the kiosk, and you will be guided to your assigned taxi. This system eliminates touting and gives all drivers a fair chance to obtain fares. When you arrive at your destination, give your voucher and the fare to the driver.

Fares are in rupiah. There are moneychangers just inside the exit door, and exchange rates are usually quite favourable at the airport. ATMs in the international and domestic terminal buildings accept major credit cards.

For transport to the airport, there are, apart from taxis, cheap tourist shuttle buses from the most popular tourist centres (see pp224–5).

A tourist information outlet offering tickets and reservations

Travelling to Islands off Bali

The island of Nusa Penida is not usually considered a tourist destination, except for the most rugged and intrepid of travellers. It can be reached by small boats from Sanur Beach, from Kusamba Beach or Padang Bai. Nusa Lembongan, off the northwest coast of Nusa Penida, is a popular destination for day trips and overnight trips. Companies such as **Bali Hai Cruises**, **Bounty**

An airport taxi

Cruises and **Island Explorer Cruises** offer day trips to the island. **SeaTrek** goes to the eastern islands in traditional Indonesian-style schooners.

Flying to Lombok

Bali's airport is a major terminal for Indonesian domestic flights, and it is served by a number of domestic airlines. Air travel between Bali and Lombok's airport at Praya is handled by **Merpati Nusantara Airlines**, Wings Air Indonesia, TransNusa, **Garuda Indonesia** and **Lion Air**. Schedules are subject to change depending on demand, but currently there are about ten daily flights. Flight time is about 25 minutes, and there is a departure tax for each leg of the trip. International airlines serving Lombok with scheduled flights are Silk Air from Singapore, Air Asia from Kuala Lumpur and Johor Bahru, and Virgin Australia from Port Headland.

Travelling to Lombok by Sea

The cheapest way to cross the Lombok Straits is by ferry, although the voyage takes nearly a whole day. Ferries travel from Padang Bai in East Bali to Pelabuhan Lembar (Lembar Harbour) in Lombok at 60- to 90-minute intervals. The crossing takes four hours (or longer, depending on conditions). Seasoned travellers get to Padang Bai well in advance in order to choose one of the newer and safer ferries. Seating is available in an air-conditioned saloon; however, this is not as pleasant as being

Ferries at Pelabuhan Lembar (Lembar Harbour)

on the deck. Note that there is an extra charge for bicycles, motorcycles and cars. Tickets are purchased at the harbour.

There are alternatives to the ferry. The **BlueWater Express**, operated by BlueWater Safaris, offers daily fast boat facilities, as do **Scoot Fast Cruises** and various other companies. Perama Shuttle offers a bus and boat ride to Senggigi daily at 6am for about Rp450,000. The bus leaves from several points in Bali for Padang Bai, and the passage is on a fast boat.

An alternative is to take their bus from either Kuta or Ubud at 9am to catch the regular ferry to Lembar.

Travelling to Islands off Lombok

The most convenient way to get to the Gili Isles from Senggigi is by shuttle boat. This can be arranged in advance from Bali. You can charter an outrigger boat from Senggigi or Bangsal. Cruise options are also available.

The BlueWater Express fast boat, travelling to Lombok

Travelling by Road

The only means of land travel within Bali or Lombok is by road. Getting around Bali, especially in the south and in Ubud, is becoming increasingly hectic as cars and motorcycles become more numerous. Inexpensive public transport, such as *bemo* and buses, is available throughout Bali and Lombok. However, many people prefer to rent a car with a driver. Tourist shuttles are also good alternatives.

Public Transport

Public transport in Bali and Lombok is cheap, but not always convenient for visitors, since it becomes scarce after dark, and the routes are designed to serve the needs of the local population rather than tourists.

Buses, used mainly by locals, operate long-distance inter-city and inter-island routes. Main routes are from Denpasar to Singaraja, Denpasar to Amlapura and Sweta to Labuhan Lombok. Fares (non-negotiable) are paid to the driver or the conductor. Tickets cannot be bought in advance except for inter-island trips. The main terminals in South Bali are around Denpasar: at Batubulan in the north; at Kereneng in central Denpasar; and at Ubung in the west.

Bemo are minivans that drive along pre-determined routes. Small *bemo* service a town while large *bemo* travel between towns, such as from Denpasar to Ubud or Kuta. Fares are low (less than Rp5,000 within a town and less than Rp10,000 between towns), but it may take several hours to cover a distance of 15 km (10 miles), and tourists are sometimes overcharged. *Bemo* are often very hot and crowded, and do not tend to adhere to set routes and times. They are not favoured by tourists or those on a tight itinerary.

Taxis

In South Bali, metered taxis with air conditioning can be flagged down or called by phone. Sometimes drivers will try to negotiate a flat fee; it is usually better to use the meter. Some drivers are reluctant to go to Ubud at night because it is hard for them to find a fare for the return trip. Usually a 30 per cent surcharge is added to the fare.

Bahasa Indonesia and Balinese road signs

Tourist Shuttles

Tourist shuttles – minivans or minibuses that travel between tourist destinations at regular intervals – are very convenient. They are popular with backpackers and a good way to meet other travellers. Several companies run services between the major tourist destinations on a regular schedule for reasonable, posted fares (Rp50,000– 300,000). It may be necessary to book in advance.

Car and Motorcycle Rental

Car rental is popular in Bali and Lombok, and many international agencies are represented. Good self-drive rates can be negotiated with local agencies. As road conditions become more crowded, it is well worth paying a little extra to have the services of a driver, who will act as a guide as well.

Rental options range from the charter of a minivan to the rental of a luxury car, complete with a chauffeur and multilingual guide.

The major tourism centres are lined with local agencies that rent cars and motorcycles. Vehicles for rent range from a Volkswagen Safari to a BMW. The most popular are the Toyota Avanza and the Toyota Kijang (good for up to eight people).

You may negotiate directly yourself, or ask your hotel to arrange a rental for you. Be sure to clarify whether the price includes fuel and insurance. Insurance is obligatory, and helmets are compulsory for motorcyclists. Check that the vehicle's lights, brakes, signals and horn are in good working order before you drive off.

You should obtain your International Driving Permit in your home country before your arrival in Bali or Lombok (see p210).

Motorcycle was once the most popular way of getting around and motorcycle hire is still widely available in tourist centres, but traffic conditions make biking increasingly hazardous. It is not recommended in crowded South or Central Bali or in towns.

A taxi

A bemo

A tourist shuttle

Driving in Bali and Lombok

Indonesians drive on the left-hand side of the road. In the event of an accident, the foreigner will very likely be deemed liable even if he or she is not at fault. Traffic regulations and driving conventions in practice do not always coincide: motorbikes overtake on either side; drivers pull out into traffic without looking – they expect you to avoid them. Right of way belongs to whoever is bigger or flashes his lights first. As the pavements (sidewalks) are scarce and narrow, pedestrian traffic flows onto the roads, and includes livestock, pushcarts, religious processions and cyclists going the wrong way. In Lombok, traffic is much lighter, but you must watch out for pony carts.

Motorcycles in Singaraja – the most popular form of transport for locals

Rice drying on the road – an obstacle to watch out for

It is normal practice to sound the horn briefly before over-taking. Traffic lights are scarce; at intersections where you are going straight ahead rather than turning, hazard lights should be used. In towns, one-way systems are increasingly common.

Parking in towns and at markets is supervised by a parking attendant who collects a small fee (generally Rp2,000–5,000 depending on the vehicle) and helps you get back on to the road

Driving just after dark is generally inadvisable because of poor visibility and, in particular, the inadequate lighting on bicycles and motor-cycles. Drivers should watch out for piles of black sand on the road (dumped there for the next day's building activities).

Motorcyclists in particular should avoid driving at dusk because of the number of flying insects.

Indonesians are generally glad to help anyone in trouble on the road. It is customary in such situations to offer some small compensation in return.

Pony carts, a hazard for drivers in rural areas

DIRECTORY

Terminals

Batubulan Terminal
Batubulan.
Tel (0361) 298 526.

Kereneng Terminal
Jalan Hayam
Wuruk, Denpasar.
Tel (0361) 226 906.

Mandalika Terminal
Sweta, Lombok.

Tegal Terminal
Jalan Imam
Bonjol, Denpasar.
Tel (0361) 980 899.

Ubung Terminal
Jalan Cokroaminoto,
Denpasar.
Tel (0361) 427 172.

Taxi Service

Bali Taxi (Bluebird)
Tel (0361) 701 111.

Komotra Taxi
Tel (0361) 744 2929.

Ngurah Rai Taxi
Tel (0361) 724 724.

Wahana Taxi
Tel (0361) 244 555.

Tourist Shuttles and Services

Danasari
Poppies Lane 1, Kuta.
Tel (0361) 755 125.

Perama
Jalan Legian 39, Kuta
Tel (0361) 750 808.

Jalan Hanoman, Ubud.
Tel (0361) 974 722.

Vehicle Rental

Avis Rent-a-Car
Danan Tam Blingan 27,
Sanur. **Tel** (0361) 282 635.
w avis.com

Hertz
Grand Bali Beach Hotel,
Area Cottage 50, Sanur.
Tel (0361) 266 962.
w hertz.com

SDR Car Rental
Jl Merta Ayu 9,
Kerobokan.
Tel (0361) 735 258.

Wira Rental Car Bali
Kori Nuansa Utama
Selatan III/16, Jimbaran.
Tel (081) 236 158 243.
w rentalcarbali.net

General Index

Acknowledgments

Dorling Kindersley would like to thank the following people whose contributions and assistance have made the preparation of this book possible.

Main Contributors

Andy Barski is a motorcycle enthusiast and writer who has written extensively on travelling around the Indonesian archipelago, where he has been based since 1987.

Bruce Carpenter first visited Bali in 1974. He has written numerous books and articles on Balinese art and culture.

John Cooke taught zoology at Oxford University before becoming a wildlife film-maker, photographer and writer.

Jean Couteau settled in Bali in 1979. He writes short stories and art criticism in French, English and Indonesian.

Diana Darling is a freelance writer and editor who has lived in Bali since 1981. She is the author of *The Painted Alphabet: a Novel* (1992), based on a Balinese tale.

Sarah Dougherty arrived in Bali in 1993 to become editor of *Bali Echo* magazine. She contributes to many international publications and is working on a cookbook.

Tim Stuart is a travel writer, photographer and teacher of business communication. With his wife Rosa, he publishes Lombok's only English-language travel magazine, *Inilah!*.

Tony Tilford is a wildlife photographer and writer with wide experience of Indonesian flora and fauna. An avid traveller, he is in search of common and exotic subjects.

Additional Contributors
Rachel Lovelock, Shafik Menghji

For Dorling Kindersley
Managing Editor Anna Streiffert
Publishing Manager Kate Poole
Senior Publishing Manager Louise Lang
Director of Publishing Gillian Allan
Publisher Douglas Amrine
Production Marie Ingledew, Michelle Thomas
DTP Vinod Harish, Vincent Kurien, Azeem Siddiqui,
Map Co-ordinators Uma Battacharya, Mohammed Hassan, Jasneet Kaur, Casper Morris, Dave Pugh,

Revisions Team
Helle Amin, Emma Anacootee, Claire Baranowski, Shruti Bahl, Tessa Bindloss, Christine Chua, Emer FitzGerald, Lydia Halliday, Victoria Heyworth-Dunne, Sumita Khatwani, Hoo Khuen Hin, Kok Kum Fai, Shikha Kulkarni, Rachel Lovelock, Helen Partington, Pollyanna Poulter, Rada Radojicic, Marisa Renzullo, Patricia Rozario, Preeti Singh, Alice Saggers, Sands Publishing Solutions, Dora Whitaker, Karen Villabona.

Additional Photography
Luis Ascui, Rucina Ballinger, Koes Karnadi, Rachel Lovelock, Ian O'Leary, Rough Guides/Martin Richardson.

Fact Checking
Rucina Ballinger, Anak Agung Gede Putra Rangki, Anak Agung Oka Dwiputra, Rachel Lovelock.

Proofreading and Indexing
Hilary Bird, Susanne Hillen, Kay Lyons

Special Assistance
Edi Swoboda of Bali Bird Park; Ketty Barski; Steve Bolton; Georges Breguet; Georjina Chia and Kal Muller; Lalu Ruspanudin of DIPARDA, Mataram; Justin Eeles; Peter Hoe of evolution; Ganesha Bookshop; David Harnish; Chris Hill; Jean Howe and William Ingram; Rio Helmi of Image Network Indonesia; I Wayan Kicen; Lagun Sari Indonesia Seafood Pte Ltd; Peter and Made of Made's Warung; M Y Narima of

Marintur; Rosemarie F Oei of Museum Puri Lukisan; Jim Parks; David Stone; The Vines Restaurant; Bayu Wirayudha, Made Widana and Luh Nyoman Diah Prihartini.

Photography Permissions
The publisher would like to thank all the parks, temples, museums, hotels, restaurants, shops, galleries and sights for their kind permission to photograph at their premises.

Picture Credits
Key: a-above; b-below/bottom; c-centre; f-far; l-left; r-right; t-top.

The publisher would like to thank the following individuals, companies and picture libraries for permission to reproduce their photographs and drawings:
Aifa Wartel: 220tl. **Alamy Images**: Ace Stock Limited 181c; Sabena Jane Blackbird 8-9; cbstockfoto 89tl; Charles O. Cecil 104; Roger Cracknell 27/ Indonesia 23, 68cr; Philip Game 182bl; imagebroker/Manfred Bali 68br; Ivoha 155b; John Kershaw 150tr; redbrickstock.com/Patria jannides 92tr; Jochen Tack 180cl; travelib 71cra; travelstock-48 179b, 183tr, 196bl. **Alila Hotels and Resorts**: 171b, 175tr, 178cl, 184tc. **Aman Resorts**: 170bl, 171tl, 174bl, 176tr. **A.A. Gede Ariawan**: 92cb.
Bes Stock: 204cla, 204–5c, 206–7c, 207bl; © Alain Evrard 47cla, 205tl; © Globe Press 28cr; **Bali Quad Discovery Tours**: 202tc; **Blue Marlin Dive Center, Lombok**: © Clive Riddington 160bc.
Corbis: Remi Benali 18.
Dreamstime.com: Bjulien03 12bl, 128, Florian Blümm 83b, Youssouf Cader 208-209, Olga Khoroshunova 146-147, Alexander Kosachev 12tc, Edmund Lowe 56-57, Pzaxe 15tr, Iryna Rasko 82, Maura Reap 13t, Sihasakprachum 2-3, Skyrial-bali 14b, Punnawit Suwattananun 69tl, Thungsarnphoto 168-169, Vivianng 11cr, Whitcomberd 13br.
Editions Didier Millet: 3c, 24br, 26cl, 29tl, 32tr, 36tr, 49bc, 49bcl, 50bl, 51clb, 52cl, 55tl, 87tr, 92bl, 190tl, 195tr, 198cla, 199t; © Gil Marais 27bl; © Tara Sosrowardoyo 50bc, 50br.
Four Seasons Resort: 172cl,
Getty Images: AFP/Sonny Tumbelaka 71cr; Education Images 15bc; Flickr/ William Cho 119bl; Rio Helmi 186tr; Photographer's Choice/Steve Satushek 181tl.
Photo And Print Collection Of The Koninklijk Instituut Voor Taal-, Land- En Volkenkunde (KITLV),
Leiden: Woodbury & Page, Batavia 52br, Neeb 53tl, 54tc. **Restaurant Locavore**: 179tr, 185br; **Lonely Planet Images**: Tom Cockrem 70tr.
Made's Warung: 71tl; **Mandara Spa**: 173tr; **Kal Muller**: 23crb, 23br, 206tr, 206cla, 207tl, 207cra, 207crb; **Museum Puri Lukisan**: 20c, 28br, 38cla, 38bcl, 38br, 38–9c, 39cr, 39bl, 39br, 91br, *Bubuk Sah and Gagak Aking* I Cokot (1935) 92cla, 96tr, 96cla, 96bl, 96bc, 97tc, 97cr, 97bl, 101tr.
Neka Art Museum: 38tr, 39tr, 48, 100cr, 119tl; **The Nieuwenkamp Foundation, Vleuten**: 9c, 53br, 217c; **Novotel Benoa Bali**: 172bc.
Oberoi Hotels & Resorts: 170c, 177br, 187bl.
© **Photobank/Tettoni, Cassio And Associates Pte Ltd**: 22cla, 22cra, 22bl, 22crb, 26tr, 26c, 31br, 34tr, 34cl, 34bcl, 34br, 35tr, 35cla, 35cra, 35clb, 35crb, 35bl, 36–7c, 37tl, 37cr, 37bl, 37br, 40tr, 41cra, 41clb, 41br, 42cl, 42bl, 42–3c, 52tc, 53crb, 61b, 74–5, 93tl, 95tr, 110cl, 129b, 157tr, 157cr, 163bl, 194c, 194bl, 195tl, 196tr, 198br, 205tr, 205br; **Prima Foto**: 34cra, 201cl.
Reefseekers Dive Centre: 140cla; **Robert Harding Picture Library**: Gavin Hellier 122-123; Kay Maeritz 60. **Morten Strange/Flying Colours**: 140br; **SuperStock**: Vidler / Mauritius 154.
Tc Nature: 22tr, 23bl, 85br, 88tr, 88cl, 88c, 88cr, 88bl, 89tr, 89bc, 89br, 98tr, 98clb, 98bc, 99tr, 99crb, 113cla, 113crb, 113bc, 114bl, 140tr, 140clb, 141ca, 141bl, 142tl, 144crb, 144bl, 145br, 200c, 201tc; © John Cooke 23cra, 58tl, 125tl; © Tony Tilford 23clb, 58tl, 89bl, 141br; **Threads of life**: 189bc.
Adrian Vickers: 54bl. ZFL PRCo: 78tl.

Front Endpaper: Left: Dreamstime.com: Bjulien03 tl, Iryna Rasko tr; Robert Harding Picture Library: Kay Maeritz br. **Right**: Alamy Images: Charles O. Cecil tc; SuperStock: Vidler / Mauritius tr;.

Jacket Front – AWL Images: Michele Falzone Main; DK Images: Rough Guides / Martin Richardson bl.

Further Reading

History

Bali in the 19th Century Ide Anak Agung Gde Agung (Jakarta: Yayasan Obor Indonesia, 1991)

Bali Profile: People, Events, Circumstances (1001–1976) Willard A Hanna (American Universities Field Staff, 1976)

Bali at War. a History of the Dutch-Balinese Conflict of 1846–49 Alfons van der Kraan (Monash Asia Institute, 1995)

In Praise of Kuta: From Slave Port to Fishing Village to the Most Popular Resort in Bali Hugh Mabbett (January Books, 1987)

Lombok: Conquest, Colonization, and Underdevelopment, 1870–1940 Alfons van der Kraan (Heinemann Educational Books, 1980)

Negara: the Theater State in 19th Century Bali Clifford Geertz (Princeton University Press, 1981)

Society and Culture

Adat and Dinas: Balinese Communities in the Indonesian State Carol Warren (Oxford University Press, 1993)

The Changing World of Bali: Religions, Society and Tourism Leo Howe (Routledge, 2005)

Bali: A Paradise Created Adrian Vickers (Tuttle, 1997; first published 1989)

Bali: Cultural Tourism and Touristic Culture Michel Picard (Archipelago Press, 1998)

Bali, Morning of the World Luca Invernizzi Tettoni and Nigel Simmonds (Periplus, 1997)

Bali: Rangda and Barong Jane Belo (University of Washington Press, 1949)

Bali: Sekala and Niskala F B Eiseman (Periplus, 1989)

Bali: Studies in Life, Thought, and Ritual (Foris Publications, 1984)

Bali Today: Real Balinese Stories Jean Couteau with Usadi Wiratnaya et al (Spektra Communications, 2005)

The Balinese Hugh Mabbett (January Books, 1985)

Being Modern in Bali: Image and Change ed Adrian Vickers (Yale University Southeast Asia Studies, 1996)

The Food of Bali ed Wendy Hutton (Periplus World Food Series, 1999)

Island of Bali Miguel Covarrubias (Periplus, 1999; first published 1937)

The Peoples of Bali Angela Hobart, Urs Ramseyer and Albert Leeman (Blackwell, 1997)

Perfect Order: Recognizing Complexity in Bali J Stephen Lansing (Princeton University Press, 2006)

A Sacred Cloth Religion: Ceremonies of the Big Feast Among Wetu Telu Sasak Sven Cederroth (Nordic Institute of Asian Studies, 1991)

Arts and Architecture

The Art And Culture of Bali Urs Ramseyer (Oxford University Press, 1977/1987)

At Home in Bali Made Wijaya, photography Isabella Ginannesch (Abbeville Press, 1999)

Bali: the Imaginary Museum Michael Hitchcock and Lucy Norris (Oxford University Press, 1996)

Bali Modern: The Art of Tropical Living Gianni Francione, photography Luca Invernizzi Tettoni (Tuttle, 1999)

Bali Sketchbook watercolours Graham Byfield, text Diana Darling (Archipelago Press, 1998)

Bali Style Rio Helmi and Barbara Walker (Times Editions, 1995; Thames & Hudson, 1995; Vendome Press, 1996)

Balinese Dance in Transition: Kaja and Kelod I Made Bandem, Frederik Eugene Deboer (Oxford University Press, 1995)

Balinese Dance, Music and Drama I Wayan Dibia, Rucina Ballinger (Periplus Editions, 2005)

Balinese Gardens photography Luca Invernizzi Tettoni, text William Warren et al (Periplus/Thames and Hudson, 1996/2000)

Balinese Music Michael Tenzer (Periplus, 1991/1994)

Balinese Textiles Brigitta Hauser-Schublin, Marie-Louise Nabholz-Kartaschoff and Urs Ramseyer (Periplus, 1991/1997)

Dancing Out of Bali John Coast (Periplus Editions, 2005)

The Epic Of Life: A Balinese Journey Of The Soul Idanna Pucci (Alfred van der Marck Editions, 1985)

The Folk Art of Bali Joseph Fischer and Thomas Cooper (Oxford University Press, 1998)

Kecak: The Vocal Chant Of Bali I Wayan Dibia (Hartanto Art Books, 1996)

The Language of Balinese Shadow Theater Mary Sabine Zurbuchen (Princeton University Press, 1987)

Masks of Bali: Spirits of An Ancient Drama Judy Slattum, photography Paul Schraub (Chronicle, 1992)

Monumental Bali A J Bernet Kempers (Periplus, 1991/1997; first published 1977)

Music in Bali Colin McPhee (Da Capo Press, 1976; first published 1966)

W O J Nieuwenkamp: First European Artist in Bali Bruce W Carpenter (Archipelago Press, 1998)

Perceptions of Paradise: Images of Bali in the Arts Garrett Kam (Dharma Seni Museum Neka, 1993)

Pre-War Balinese Modernists 1928–1942 Dr F Haks et al (Ars et Animatio, Haarlem, the Netherlands)

Ulat-ulatan, Traditional Basketry in Bali Fred B Eiseman Jr (White Lotus, 1999)

Vessels Of Life: Lombok Earthenware Jean McKinnon (Saritaksu, 1996)

Nature

Bali – Periplus Action Guide Wally Singian, David Pickel (Periplus, 2000)

The Birds of Java and Bali Derek Holmes, illustrations Stephen Nash (Oxford University Press, 1989)

Butterflies of Bali Victor Mason (Saritaksu Publications, 2005)

Diving and Snorkeling Guide to Bali and the Komodo Region Tim Rock (Pisces, 1996)

The Ecology of Java and Bali Tony Whitten et al (Oxford University Press, 1997)

Flowers of Bali Fred Eiseman (Periplus, 1994)

Fruits of Bali Fred Eiseman and Margaret Eiseman (Periplus, 1994)

Travelogues and Memoirs

Bali: the Last Paradise Hickman Powell, photography André Roosevelt (Oxford University Press, 1930/1989; Dodd, Mead, 1936)

Bali: People and Art Gregor Krause (White Lotus, 2000; first published in German 1926)

The Birthmark: Memoirs of a Balinese Prince A A M Djelantik (Periplus, 1998)

A House in Bali Colin McPhee (Tuttle/Periplus, 2000; first published 1946)

A Little Bit One O'Clock William Ingram (Ersania Books, 1998)

The Night of Purnama Anna Matthews (Jonathan Cape, 1965)

Our Hotel In Bali: ... A Story Of The 1930s Louise G Koke (January Books, 1987)

Stranger In Paradise: the Diary of an Expatriate in Bali 1979–80 Made Wijaya (Wijaya Words, 1984)

Travelling to Bali: Four Hundred Years of Journeys Adrian Vickers (Oxford University Press, 1995)

Fiction

Bali Behind the Seen: Recent Fiction From Bali trans and ed Vern Cork (Darma Printing, 1996)

The Edge of Bali Inez Baranay (Angus & Robertson, 1992)

The Painted Alphabet: a Novel Based on a Balinese Tale Diana Darling (Tuttle, 2001; Graywolf, 1994; Houghton Mifflin, 1992)

The Sweat of Pearls: Short Stories About Women of Bali Putu Oka Sukanta, trans Vern Cork (Darma Printing, 1999)

A Tale from Bali Vicki Baum (Tuttle/Periplus, 2000; first published 1937)

Books for Children

Bye, Bye, Bali Kai Harriett Luger (Browndeer, 1996)

The Dancing Pig Judy Sierra (Gulliver, 1999)

The Haughty Toad, And Other Tales From Bali Victor Mason, illustrations by artists of Pengosekan (Bali Art Print/Hamlyn, 1975)

Rice Is Life Rita Golden Gelman (Henry Holt, 2000)

Glossary

Architecture
atap: palm-leaf thatched roof
bale: pavilion
candi bentar: split gate
gedong: enclosed pavilion
kori: roofed gate
kori agung: grand gate
kulkul: drum tower
meru: multitiered shrine
padmasana: tall shrine to the Supreme Deity
pelinggih: shrine, spirit house
pura: temple
puri: palace, house of nobility
rumah: house
wantilan: public pavilion with double roof
warung: coffee stall, small shop

Arts and Crafts
geringsing: warp- and weft-dyed textile, "double ikat"
ikat: warp resist-dyed textile
kayu: wood
lontar: type of palm; palm-leaf book
lukisan: painting
mas: gold
pande: metalsmith
paras: volcanic stone used for building and statuary
patung: statue
perak: silver
prada: gilt-painted cloth
songket: textile with supplementary weft thread, often gold or silver
tapel: mask
tenunan: weaving

Music and Dance
arja: Balinese opera
baris: classical solo male dance
baris gede: a sacred dance for rows of male dancers
Barong: large sacred effigy danced by two men
belaganjur: processional percussion orchestra
gambuh: ancient court dance
gamelan: percussion orchestra
gangsa: bronze-keyed instrument
kebyar: vigorous style of *gamelan* music; vigorous solo dance
kendang: drum
keris: sacred wavy-bladed dagger
legong: classical dance for three females
prembon: mixed programme
Rangda: sacred demonic effigy, consort of the Barong
rejang: sacred dance for rows of female dancers
suling: bamboo flute
tari: dance

topeng: masked dance based on geneological tales
trompong: bronze instrument with 8 to 12 kettle gongs
wayang kulit: shadow puppet theatre
wayang wong: masked dance based on Hindu epics

Dress
baju: shirt, dress
baju kaus: T-shirt
destar: head cloth for Balinese males
gelungan: ornate headdress
jilbab: head cloth for Muslim females
kain: cloth; long hip cloth, unsewn
kebaya: traditional jacket for females
peci: hat for Muslim males
sarong: sewn long hip cloth
selendang: ceremonial temple sash
sepatu: shoes

Religions and Community
banjar: village association
hari raya: any religious holiday
karya: work, especially collective ritual work
mesjid: mosque
odalan: temple festival
pedanda: high priest
pemangku: temple priest
penjor: festooned bamboo pole
pura dalem: temple of the netherworld
pura desa: village temple
pura puseh: temple of origins
sebel: taboo
sunat: Islamic ritual circumcision
tirta: holy water
yadnya: Hindu ritual (generic)

Food
air minum: drinking water
ayam: chicken
babi guling: roast pig
babi: pork
bakar: grilled
bebek tutu: smoked spicy duck
buah-buahan: fruit
cumi-cumi: squid
daging: meat
gado gado: vegetarian dish with peanut sauce
garam: salt
goreng: fried
gula: sugar
ikan laut: fish
jeruk nyepis: lime
jeruk: orange; citrus
kelapa: coconut
kopi: coffee
makan: eat

mie: noodles
minum: drink
nasi: food; rice; rice meal
pedas: hot (spicy)
pisang: banana
roti: bread
sambal: spicy condiment
sapi: beef
sate, sate lilit: small skewers of barbecued meat
susu: milk
teh: tea
telur: egg
udang: prawn, shrimp

Nature and Landscape
bukit: hill
burung: bird
danau: lake
gunung: mountain
hujan: rain
jalan: road
laut: sea
mata hari: sun
pantai: beach
pohon: tree
sawah: ricefield
subak: irrigation cooperative
sungai: river, stream
taman: garden, park
tanah: ground, earth, soil

Travel and Transport
bemo: public minibus
cidomo: rubber-tyred pony cart (in Lombok)
dokar: pony cart
jukung: outrigger sailing canoe
mobil: car
sepeda motor: motorcycle

Miscellaneous
adat: customary law
bagus: good, handsome
baik: good
Bapak: polite term of address for a man
bayar: pay
cantik: pretty
dingin: cold
Ibu: polite term of address for a woman
mahal: expensive
murah: inexpensive
panas: hot, warm
pariwisata: tourism
puputan: suicidal fight-to-the-end
roko: cigarette
sakit: hurt; sick
selamat jalan: farewell ("on your journey")
terima kasih: thank you
tidak: no, not
tidur: sleep
uang: money

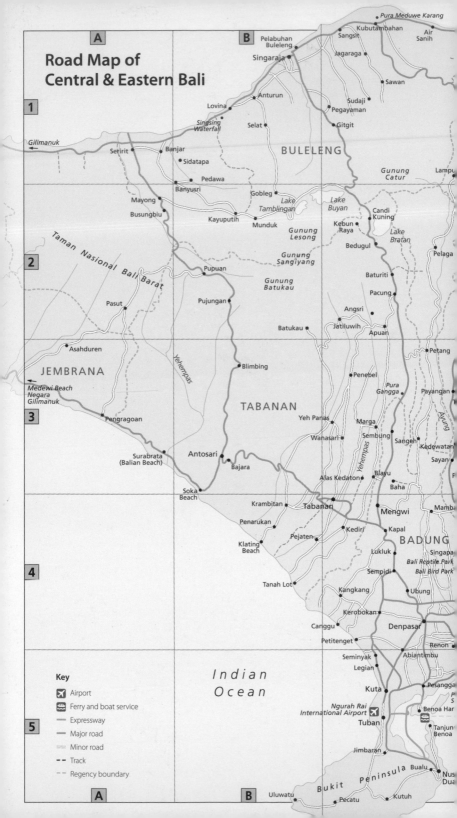